I0816617

The Curious Mind of Elon Musk

The Curious Mind of Elon Musk

9 Ways He Thinks Differently

Charles Steel

Published by Greenleaf Book Group Press
Austin, Texas
www.gbgpress.com

Distributed by Greenleaf Book Group

For ordering information or special discounts for bulk purchases, please contact Greenleaf Book Group at PO Box 91869, Austin, TX 78709, 512.891.6100.

Design and composition by Greenleaf Book Group and Carlos Esparza
Cover design by Greenleaf Book Group and Carlos Esparza

Publisher's Cataloging-in-Publication data is available.

Print ISBN: 979-8-88645-431-4

eBook ISBN: 979-8-88645-432-1

To offset the number of trees consumed in the printing of our books, Greenleaf donates a portion of the proceeds from each printing to the Arbor Day Foundation. Greenleaf Book Group has replaced over 50,000 trees since 2007.

Printed in the United States of America on acid-free paper

26 27 28 29 30 31 32 33 10 9 8 7 6 5 4 3 2 1

First Edition

For my mother,

Jane Howe (1945–2010)

"My religion, for the lack of a better word, is one of curiosity."

—Elon Musk

Curious *(adjective)*

1. Inquisitive; eager to question and comprehend.

   Drawn to the unknown and the unusual in order to learn.

2. Strange; beyond comprehension as out of the ordinary.

   Demanding attention as difficult to define and categorize.

3. *Archaic.*

   Careful; diligent in making something with attention to detail.

   Made with unusual care and intricacy.

Contents

Introduction

In July 2023, Elon Musk hosted a live broadcast with eleven young recruits to announce his ninth and newest company, xAI. Musk's men wanted to build artificial intelligence (AI) that could reason and make discoveries that might help us understand the universe.

Led by Igor Babuschkin, they spoke of their passion for math, physics, and logic and their mission to create a general-purpose problem-solving machine. Greg Yang spoke of his fascination with free will, Gödel, and quantum mechanics. Kyle Kosic mentioned the need to give other companies some competition and not to be distracted by the political and social issues of the day. Ross Nordeen was the last to speak and highlighted the importance of creating tools to ask the right questions.

A slick, corporate presentation this was not. These engineers were clones of Musk—quirky, intense, and formidably bright—although he noted they were "reluctant to be self-promotional" and so encouraged them to "brag a little."[1] What Musk was saying to the audience listening in was that if you think like him or the other speakers and want to be part of such an elite team, come and work at xAI.

This launch also provided a window onto Musk's own deeply entrenched obsession with the meaning of life. Musk told listeners that his two best subjects when young were computer science and physics. He nearly pursued a career in physics, which he loves as a way to understand the nature of reality, but he opted instead for engineering.

Initially, he leaned toward computers as a way to make an impact, but then he shifted his focus to physical objects with SpaceX and Tesla, and later from atoms back to bits. Musk proceeded to riff on the fragility of civilization, consciousness, and how AI might one day shed light on mysteries like the existence of aliens and dark matter.

Musk also spoke of his hero and favorite philosopher, Douglas Adams, famous for the absurd joke that 42 is the answer to the meaning of life, the universe, and everything. Musk explained how Adams had taught him that the hardest part of understanding the universe is formulating the right questions. The tweet to announce the broadcast had even made a joke out of its date, noting that July 12, 2023, equated to "7 + 12 + 23 = 42."[2]

How would Musk's company differ from the other AI companies? He wanted it to be more like him. He aspired for his own biological "neural nets" to be maximally truth-seeking, and he felt that artificial "neural nets" should be developed in the same way. Why? "If the goal of AI is curiosity, aka understanding the universe," he posted on X, "then it will aide humanity, because we are more interesting than not-humanity."[3] Truth-seeking AI, he was convinced, would be the safest form of AI.

. . .

Musk is curious in every sense of the word. First of all, he is curious in the *strange* sense of the word. He named three of his children X Æ A-XII, Exa Dark Sideræl, and Techno Mechanicus, together with their mother, Claire Boucher. He sends thousands of tweets that enrapture his fans and appall his critics. He can be goofy, posting memes, and yet quick-tempered and callous. And he breaks all business conventions by running very flat corporate structures, which he replicates across multiple organizations, while sending up traditional executive titles by calling himself "Technoking," "Chief Twit," or "White House Tech Support."

But Musk is even stranger than we realize, because he is curious in the *inquisitive* sense of the word to such a degree that he calls it a religion. His curiosity about the universe directly motivates him to embark on grand missions to solve fundamental problems across communications, energy, transportation, and computation, and even to get involved in politics to take on beliefs that he thinks threaten his missions.

The way he accomplishes this is by immersing himself in the design and engineering of his products. He is curious in the old-fashioned *careful* sense of the word. He engages in the minutest details of the design and engineering of his products, both software and hardware. When describing the production of the Cybertruck, for example, he drew an analogy with LEGO, noting that it was his "favorite example of how extreme precision does not need to be expensive, *it is mostly about caring*"[4] [my italics].

The end products are often futuristic and strange, although, whereas *curious* once emphasized complexity and intricacy, his products are stranger in their simplicity, like his steel, straight-edged Cybertruck or, even more so, his Cybercab, which has no pedals or steering wheel.

Like many strange people, Musk is called names like *monstrous*, *grotesque*, and *freakish*, which highlight his differentness. His critics variously say that he is a huckster, a man-child, a sociopath, a megalomaniac, and a fascist. For all the weird things he does, though, it is his obsessive drive and creativity that truly make him a curiosity.

As physicist and entrepreneur Casey Handmer wrote, Musk is enigmatic because it is hard to relate to someone who "thinks in physics and math" and is preoccupied with problems that, in most cases, he is the "first person in history to ever encounter."[5] Accordingly, Bill Gates, for example, acknowledged that, "You can feel whatever you want about Elon's behavior, but there is no one in our time who has done more to push the bounds of science and innovation."[6] Jensen Huang, CEO and founder of Nvidia, also described Musk as being "singular in this understanding of engineering and construction and large systems and marshaling resources."[7] This is no ordinary person.

Musk's biographer Walter Isaacson summed it up when he wrote that Musk is "driven by mission more than any person I've ever seen, and it's not only mission, it's cosmic missions," and this comes from someone who has studied a wide range of people, including Steve Jobs, Jeff Bezos, and Jennifer Doudna. He says Musk's mission is "the most deeply ingrained thing in him," even though he knows that might sound naive.[8]

Journalist and Musk expert Tim Higgins identified this too. He wrote in *The Wall Street Journal* in 2024 that, to many young men, Musk is a hero because he represents something more precious than wealth: purpose.[9] In fact, Musk saw the article on X and replied, "What is life without purpose? But there is a purpose! It is to expand to the stars and thereby understand the Universe."[10] Agree with him or not, this is not how a regular businessperson speaks. It is key, however, to understanding what makes him tick.

. . .

Musk is so different from most other people that the only way to make sense of him is to consider him in his own terms. That is my goal with this book: to lay out the unique sequence of beliefs that make Musk such a curious person. There are nine beliefs, organized loosely around his philosophy of life, his companies, and his politics. A common theme among all nine is that Musk goes against the grain and never relents.

The list is subjective, but it draws on Musk's own words, across tens of thousands of tweets and scores of public interviews that he has given. This is not a straightforward task, as Musk's use of words can be very confusing. Most of the time he is surprisingly literal, and when he switches, say, from being serious to silly or from technical details to hyperbole, that is easy enough to follow. But sometimes it is not always so obvious whether he is being literal or ironic or rhetorical. His intent can be readily misconstrued and so one of the objectives of this book is to show on such occasions what he is "doing" when he is "saying" something.[11]

Each chapter looks at the context of his thinking, considering the influence of novelists, philosophers, politicians, fellow technologists, and public opinion on the X platform. This reveals that Musk can only be understood by looking at how his beliefs developed and how they build on one another. The order of the beliefs matters. Though each idea is key, how they are linked is more important.

The first third of the book—"The Convert"—focuses on three beliefs that shaped Musk's philosophy of life and how they mark him out as different to most people: seek meaning through better questions; assume you are wrong and try to be less wrong; and challenge yourself by loving humanity.

Musk firmly believes that "in order to be highly motivated, you have to have some philosophical foundation."[12] And he often describes Douglas Adams, Isaac Asimov, and the importance of physics as being foundational to his thinking.[13] He explains his three-point religion: the universe is the answer; we need to find the questions that will better make sense of it; and we must increase the scope and scale of human consciousness to do so. Yet few people really believe this because it sounds so bizarre. Musk himself describes his own thinking as niche and esoteric.

Sometimes Musk's philosophizing can sound like sci-fi storytelling, but I argue that he is for the most part sincere. We see how a combination of being on the spectrum and severe childhood trauma contributed to Musk's mixture of existential angst and hyperrational thinking. And we understand how they were reconciled by Douglas Adams's positive reframing of the question of life's meaning in a way that would lead to his lifelong obsession with human consciousness.

Part II of the book—"The Missionary"—focuses on how he gave creative expression to his angst and his rationality by applying three powerful, related beliefs: find purpose in creating; missions need corporations; and leaving Earth makes the universe more human. If Part I is about the making of his new religion, Part II is about how he puts it into practice. Musk may feel a lack of purpose from the belief that we humans are not created with any design, but he can find some meaning by designing and making things for others that have a life of their own.

Musk once denied he was really a businessman, claiming, "I'm sure probably lots of analysts on Wall Street would agree with that."[14] While he is not immune to the appeal of wealth and power, and has a monumental ego, he is first and foremost an engineer. It is his intensity and courage to defy received wisdom that combine with natural intellectual gifts to make him exceptional at building technology. Unlike most businesspeople, his companies are not simply a means to sell stuff and make money. Unlike most people who think of themselves as acting for humanity, he uses technology and markets. And unlike nearly everyone, he thinks of consciousness in a cosmic context and over the very long term, as symbolized by a city on Mars.

Part III of the book—"The Crusader"—focuses on how Musk went on offense to defend his core religious beliefs in society at large: put truth-seeking before tribe; protect the right to offend; and AI is inhuman—make it curious. Having practiced his religion in the real world of physics and markets, he takes affront at what he sees as untested secular religions that oppose his. In particular, he sees political correctness, compromise on free speech, and complacency about the risks of AI as failures of critical thinking, which undermine curiosity and creativity and are now being programmed into our technology platforms. Here

Musk's existential anxiety kicks in, and he anoints himself the standard bearer for rationality in American culture.

Musk's views, in turn, pushed him into politics, but he is not one of those businessmen like Michael Bloomberg or Mitt Romney who ran for office because they thought they would be great at governing. In that sense, he is more like Ross Perot. He feels the need to speak up when he perceives that everyone else has succumbed to what he considers to be groupthink: societies must maintain a field of play in which people like him—people who are different—are free to operate. As the launch of xAI shows, through it all, his mind is never far from the question of life's meaning, Douglas Adams, and the rational pursuit of truth, which may come as a disappointment to some on the right who are drawn to him in the mistaken belief that he thinks the way they do.

. . .

Taking all nine beliefs together, I contend that there is an internal consistency to Musk, from founding SpaceX and Tesla to becoming political, buying Twitter, building AGI, and even having fourteen children (and counting). Each of the nine beliefs is not unique to Musk, but the fervor with which he applies himself to each and every one of them is. Curiosity is the key to understanding him. It makes him hard to categorize, and harder still to emulate, but it is the only way to explain his extraordinary drive, self-belief, and inventiveness.

PART I

The Convert

"I continue to believe that this world has no supernatural meaning. But I know that something in it has meaning, and that is man, because he is the only being who demands meaning for himself."

—Albert Camus

Part I is about how Musk built a new religion. As shown in the following figure, it comprises three self-reinforcing beliefs. First, we must embrace uncertainty by asking questions about the universe rather than seeking certainty in answers. Second, we can reduce uncertainty and learn by testing our questions in the real world. And third, we must use our consciousness to increase the sum total of consciousness, allowing us all to ask better questions.

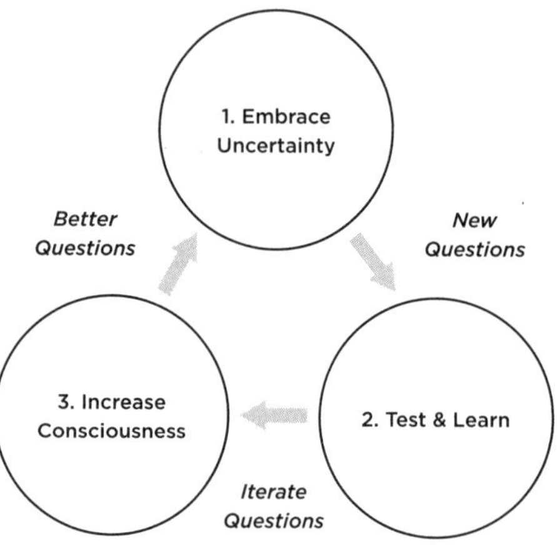

ONE

Embrace Uncertainty

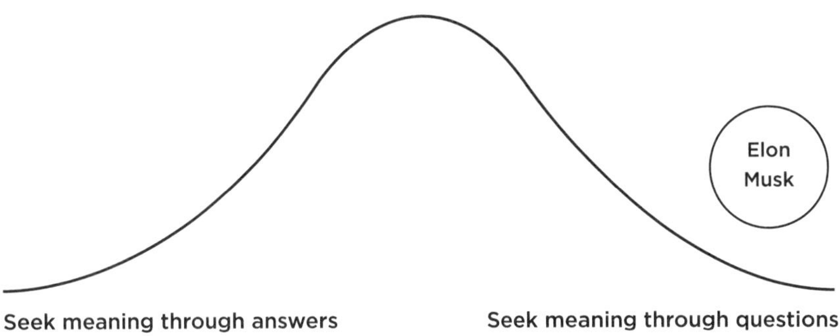

"My motivation, if I've got a religion of any kind," says Musk, "is a religion of curiosity . . . I'm trying to understand the universe or at least set things in motion such that, at some point, civilization understands the universe far better than we do today."[1] Musk became a convert to this religion at a young age. And like so many conversions, it was born of desperation. Musk makes no bones about it: "I had a very unhappy childhood. There were many years when I was very sad."[2] In his early teens, he was tipped into an existential crisis, and it had a major impact on his intellectual development. "I was raised by books," he says. "Books, and then my parents."[3]

Musk looked for imaginative ways to take his mind away from his troubles. Dungeons & Dragons, science fiction, superhero comics, *The Lord of the Rings,* video games, and computer programming were all forms of escape. He read continuously, including the *Collier's* and *Britannica* encyclopedias from front to back, and he explored all the religious and philosophical texts he could lay his hands on, from the Bible to the Koran, the Torah, Hindu scriptures, Marx's *Das Kapital*, and the works of German philosophers Schopenhauer, Nietzsche, and Heidegger. But they left him feeling desperate. Then he stumbled across the wisdom of Douglas Adams's *The Hitchhiker's Guide to the Galaxy* and everything changed.

A few years after it was published in 1977, young Musk picked up the book. One passage describes a difficulty inherent to galactic, electronic guidebooks: "The simple truth is that interstellar distances will not fit into the human imagination."[4] Adams illustrates this by writing, "Consider for a moment a peanut in Reading and a small walnut in Johannesburg."[5] Musk was living in Johannesburg at the time, and one can picture him feeling that the author was speaking directly to him. Musk read the book in early adolescence, a time when he was questioning the point of living, and he credits it with changing his entire way of thinking.

Adams was an occasional contributor to the BBC program *Doctor Who* and to the satirist ensemble Monty Python. His genius was to mix the two genres and replace a supersmart Time Lord with his everyman Arthur Dent, who finds himself on a voyage to the dawn of humanity and the end of time, playing the straight man alongside a cast of outrageous aliens.

Arthur Dent is an ordinary person to whom extraordinary things happen. He never had a burning desire to know the meaning of life, but he did complain of a "strange unaccountable feeling that something was going on in the world, something big, even sinister, and no one would tell me what it was."[6] He becomes an unwitting passenger, hitchhiking between spaceships and planets, on a journey with fellow travelers who are trying to make sense of life, the universe, and everything. Adams tantalizes the reader with the answer. Several times, they appear to get close, their hopes raised, only to be dashed.

The Hitchhiker's Guide to the Galaxy can be read on one level as a madcap comedy that shows the absurdity of life. For those looking for it, there is satire on religion, science, politics, and money. Musk, though, goes so far as to describe Adams as the greatest philosopher and his biggest influence. He even says *The Hitchhiker's Guide to the Galaxy* is a book on philosophy disguised as a book on humor. His interpretation was that Adams does not try to give the answer to life; rather, the point of life is to learn more in order to figure out what the actual point is.[7] All too often, we seek answers to the wrong questions because so much of what we assume to be reality is mistaken.

Adams shows how humans can be cursed by the presumption that we are the center of the universe and by the desire for higher meaning that this engenders. He makes fun of this by showing the universe from many different perspectives. Arthur, for example, is made to look back on Earth as it is blown up along with everything he loves. And we discover that Earth was, in fact, created by the alien species of Magratheans, and it wasn't designed for us at all. Earth is not even a planet but a computer, and humans are only the third most intelligent life-forms, after dolphins and mice, who are "not quite as they appear."[8] For we discover that the Magratheans were working for some hyperintelligent pan-dimensional mice—"the whole business with the cheese and the squeaking is just a front."[9] The laboratory experiment is truly on us.

We also meet the "mind-bogglingly stupid" Ravenous Bugblatter Beast of Traal, which sticks its head in the ground on the assumption that "if you can't see it, it can't see you."[10] We encounter the soul-destroying Total Perspective Vortex machine, which shows its victims how insignificant they are, living on "a microscopic dot on a microscopic dot" against the backdrop of the "entire unimaginable infinity of creation."[11] And from the Ruler of the Universe, no less, we learn, "My Universe is my eyes and my ears. Anything else is hearsay."[12]

The ensuing, unrequited desire for meaning, Adams suggests, is the cause of so much of the world's unhappiness, emptiness, greed, violence, and worry—for it's not easy to live with the uncertainty. To the overly curious human mind, the seemingly infinite nature of the universe can feel impossible to comprehend—like a "nothingth of a second," or traveling at the speed of light, or a band of monkeys randomly tapping out *Hamlet* on a typewriter, or the existence of sentient life itself.[13] But being unimaginable does not make these things impossible. Just as quantum physics says you cannot know position and momentum at the same time, just the range of probabilities, Adams tells us that you cannot know the question and the answer to the meaning of life at the same time, just the probability of life, which is virtually impossible.

The biggest joke of the book is about seeking meaning and certainty in absurd answers. In the distant past, a supercomputer took seven and a half million years to provide the answer to the meaning of life and, with "infinite majesty and calm," Deep Thought gave the answer "42." The two old men in front of the computer were flummoxed, so Deep Thought pushed back against their exasperation: "I think the problem, to be quite honest with you, is that you've never actually known what the question is."[14] When they told Deep Thought the question was about life, the universe, and everything, Deep Thought replied, "So once you know what the question actually is, you'll know what the answer means."[15] It turns out the answer had taken so long that everyone had forgotten what the actual question was, and Earth had been built as a huge organic computer running a ten-million-year research program to calculate the question that 42 was the answer to. In other words, the story becomes an answer seeking a question.

Adams gave young Musk a new perspective on the reality of his own desperately unhappy teenage years and a different way to think for a mind wrestling with unanswered questions. Far as it may seem from the world of Twitter, SpaceX, and Tesla, it formed the bedrock on which Musk would build all his other beliefs.

A Brutal Reality

Musk's attachment to *The Hitchhiker's Guide to the Galaxy* is unusual to say the least. It marks him as different from a very young age. Most people don't fixate on the meaning of life—especially as children—and of those who do, few fall deeply into despair, reject the entire premise of the question, and come out the other side. What, then, made Musk so desperate to find answers in the first place?

"Aggression turned inward" is a phrase that some psychologists use to describe depression, drawing from the work of Sigmund Freud.[16] When you get past his obsession with libido, Freud sheds light on the complicated emotions that people can feel when experiencing loss of the kind that Musk did. In *Mourning and Melancholia*, Freud explained how grief can combine with a severe lowering of self-esteem to cause deep depression and a loss of purpose.[17] It is hard to emerge from such a state due to the competing yet unresolved emotions that Freud called "the conflict of ambivalence." This may be caused, for example, by a sense of guilt for wanting to fight back against someone who is supposed to love you and/or a sense of shame from not being able to do so, to the point of unconsciously feeling that the punishment is deserved.[18] This is a powerful way to understand what happened to Musk.

He was a diminutive child, with a square jaw, a slender nose, and a toothy grin. It was a nose that was rearranged by a beating from a gang of boys at school: Musk was eating a sandwich when he was pushed down a flight of stairs, struck in the head, and then kicked repeatedly and viciously on the floor. His brother, Kimbal, who was there, said that one of them wanted to kill him. Musk was rushed to the hospital in Sandton, a short drive from the school, in a suburb of Johannesburg. He was unrecognizable from his cuts and bruises, and he spent several days in the hospital to recover. Many years later, he needed surgery on the cartilage in his nose to fix his breathing.

This assault had been a while coming. A group of boys had been harassing him since he joined the local state school in Bryanston after moving from Pretoria to Johannesburg. "The gangs at school would hunt me down—literally hunt me down!" he later recalled.[19] This was apartheid South Africa, where even fighting between the culturally English White boys—like the Musks—and the culturally Afrikaner White boys was common, and the threshold of violence that was accepted at such a school was high.[20] This was all the more so for boys who played on the school sports teams and who could act with impunity. Musk likens his upbringing to William Golding's 1954 novel, *Lord of the Flies,* about a group of marooned children who descend into savagery in the absence of any adult supervision.[21] He was subjected to the torment of knowing that he could be attacked at any moment, and there was very little he could do about it—the key ingredients for chronic stress. This went on for years.

A lack of social support exacerbated Musk's situation. He grew up in a suburb called Lone Hill, which was aptly named. "Elon didn't have friends," Maye Musk, his mother, recalled in an interview with *Vanity Fair*. "He was the youngest and the smallest in the class. It's sad as a mother to see it."[22] If he had been born three days later, he would have been the oldest child in the year below, but that was not to be.

This was a sports-obsessed culture, where boys won popularity on the rugby field while Musk, who describes himself as being "very nerdy," was to be found instead on the chess team.[23] And after getting his first home computer at the age of ten, he was far more interested in learning how to code than, say, studying the mandatory subject of Afrikaans. He fell outside of any clique.

Musk was also what we call today a "neurodivergent" child. Many years later, at the age of forty-nine, Musk would use the stage of the US prime-time TV show *Saturday Night Live* to reveal to the world that he has the neurological condition Asperger's syndrome, otherwise known as autism spectrum disorder. On another occasion, he said that Asperger's made him obsessed with the truth, and from the age of five or six, he felt strange because he realized that he thought in a way that was different from other people.[24]

Musk also found it hard to read the social cues that guide interpersonal interactions and allow most people to interpret what others are thinking and feeling and to adjust their behavior accordingly.[25] His own brother, Kimbal, would later say of him, "He is a savant when it comes to business, but his gift is not empathy with people."[26] Kimbal explains that he learned, with time, that he needs to tell Musk how he feels, because he can't otherwise expect his brother to register and process his emotions.[27]

As a child, Musk's condition could only have contributed to a feeling of isolation. This made him vulnerable to the kind of cowards who like to bully other kids. Being different from the rest meant he was without the protection of a larger group; the bullies made sure of that, for any friends he had were picked on for being associated with him. Meanwhile, his lack of support at school was not made up for by extra support outside. On the contrary, Musk later recounted, "I'd come home, and it would just be awful there as well." He had to face abuse on both fronts. It was, he says, "nonstop horrible."[28]

Musk's parents separated when he was six, and he spent the next two years with his mother and two siblings. In her autobiography, *A Woman Makes a Plan*, Maye alleges that her husband, Errol, demeaned her, beat her, and isolated her from her own family until she ran to them for safety. She describes him as a monster who made her life hell; he was violent and cruel in ways that didn't make sense.[29]

Musk was then given the choice of which parent to live with, and he chose his father, but he came to bitterly regret that choice. Errol was a forceful character, a brilliant engineer, a businessman with on-and-off success, and a womanizer. He had huge mood swings, Musk says, fluctuating between reality and fantasy and between love and cruelty. Errol says that he was autocratic with the children and gave them chores to do at home.[30] Musk and his brother, however, prefer to keep a veil over what happened. In 2015, Musk said that his father was good at making life miserable. Musk's words hardened after he learned that Errol had fathered a child with his stepsister in 2017. He told *Rolling Stone* magazine, "He was such a terrible human being . . . You have no idea . . . My dad will have a carefully thought-out plan of evil. He will plan evil."[31]

And so it was that, after Musk was nearly beaten to death, his father explicitly told him that he had provoked the attack and that it was all his fault.[32] How was a son supposed to react to that? Musk turned the aggression inward. He searched for answers about the outside world, and the deeper he dug for the meaning of life, the more the why became all-consuming. Why do humans exist if we are born only to experience a world that is unfair, to suffer, and to contemplate the oblivion that will follow when we die? In later life, he admitted, "I did have this existential crisis when I was around twelve about what's the meaning of life? Isn't it all pointless? Why not just commit suicide? Why exist?"[33]

At such a formative age, this curious boy, who viewed everything in a very literal way, struggled to compute the flaws he saw in his model of the world. Unlike others, he could tell himself not to fear the dark, as darkness is just the absence of photons that the human eye can see with a wavelength between ultraviolet and infrared radiation. But the scope of life, the universe, and everything was too much to process. It only made the depression worse. Years of torment wore him down and made the world seem like a dark place without hope. It was then that Douglas Adams appeared to help him understand how our reality is not always quite what it seems and why our heart and mind make it so.

Our Programming Bug

Musk was won over by Adams because he was funny, and not just that: he was absurdly funny. The search for the question that 42 was the answer to is perhaps the best example. It turns out that the question had been unconsciously printed onto poor Arthur Dent's brain wave patterns and when he went back in time and played Scrabble with some cavemen, Dent revealed the question by picking out letter tiles and laying them on the board to spell: "What do you get if you multiply six by nine?"[34] So not only was 42 the wrong answer; it was the wrong answer to the wrong question.

To Musk's logical mind, this illustrates that, instead of asking our own questions, we too often accept answers that we find around us without knowing the questions that first gave rise to them. "Once you know the right question to ask," he posted on X, "the answer is often the easy part, as my hero, Douglas Adams, would say."[35] This calls for out-of-the-box thinking, which he says is tantamount to "realizing you're trapped in a box created by others. Only then can you escape the box to another box. Repeat."[36]

Why do we even ask such questions? Douglas Adams showed Musk that primitive, early humans reveal our underlying nature, and this wiring remains with us today. Adams teases us that Earth is "an utterly insignificant little blue-green planet whose ape-descended life forms are so amazingly primitive that they still think digital watches are a pretty neat idea."[37] In fact, so many people today are miserable, seeking happiness in "small green pieces of paper," that many are "increasingly of the opinion that they'd all made a big mistake in coming down from the trees in the first place."[38]

Musk would adopt a similar view; however, whereas Adams uses a biological computer as a metaphor for the brain, for Musk this is the actual truth. Every emotion and every smell are, in fact, caused by electrical signals, and death is simply the loss of information that we call memory.[39] Or more precisely, we humans are an odd combination of, in his words, "a monkey brain with a computer stuck on top of it."[40]

Crudely speaking, the monkey brain is our limbic system, or our base drives and emotions, while the computer is our cortex, or our rational thought that allows planning and reasoning. It is our human fate that the wiring of one is entangled with that of the other. You only have to scratch the surface to find the ape lurking there. That's why half of Arthur Dent's guide was about sex and full of references to where humans could find a bar and drink alcohol. Or why, as Musk likes to joke, left to its own devices, the limbic part of a man's brain might spend 90 percent of the time thinking about sex and how to make it happen.[41]

An existentially anguished young Musk might, therefore, have been able to see that the monkey brain and the computer constantly sabotage each other. Rational, curious questions about pain and death are magnified by the limbic system in a way that can overwhelm the brain and cause chronic suffering. From Søren Kierkegaard and Fyodor Dostoevsky to Jean-Paul Sartre and Albert Camus, philosophers have described how the contemplation of the fragility of consciousness and the nothingness that will follow can give rise to the physical sensations of trembling, sickness, and weariness. Trying to understand not only life and the universe but also "everything" explodes the mind and exhausts the body.

The pioneering AI researcher Marvin Minsky captured this when he posed the question, "Why are people made to suffer so much? What functions could such suffering serve?" and answered it with, "Perhaps one answer to this is that the bad effects of chronic pain did not evolve from selection at all, but simply arose from a 'programming bug.' . . . We came to evolve a design that protects our bodies but ruins our minds."[42] This is like Adams's wonky equation 6 x 9 = 42—a software bug written in all human minds, which causes us to be anxious and often to perceive the world to be much worse than it actually is. Adams uses humor to show this in the form of Marvin the Paranoid Android, a misanthropic robot Arthur encounters who, despite having a brain the size of a planet, is manically depressed and does not know what to do with himself.

The teenage Musk knew such depression. He did not go through therapy—this was South Africa in the 1980s—but he evidently did manage to put himself through some form of self-analysis, which enabled him to reframe his thinking in a way that stopped him from attacking himself and redirected his aggression to the world around him.[43] In order to disentangle the thinking and the feeling, the most important step would have been for him to recognize that, in the history of human evolution, the body came first and then the brain (first emotional, then rational), and the brain's task is to keep the body alive, not—as is more commonly supposed—that the body is somehow there to allow us to be conscious and happy.[44]

Musk's computer told his monkey brain that it didn't know the answer to life's meaning—and that it was a dumb question anyway. As the French author Albert Camus wrote in *The Myth of Sisyphus*, "My reasoning wants to be faithful to the evidence that aroused it. That evidence is the absurd. It is that divorce between the mind that desires and the world that disappoints, my nostalgia for unity, this fragmented universe and the contradiction that binds them together."[45] Against the apparent infinity of the universe, the absurd is "lucid reason noting its limits."[46] One must reject both any logical rationale for taking one's life and also the intellectual suicide of believing any ideology that abandons reason.

The great physicist Richard Feynman came to a similar conclusion by a different route when he said, in a talk on the role of scientific culture in modern society, "We find that we do not know the meaning of existence; but in saying that we do not know the meaning of existence, we have probably found the open channel . . . To decide upon the answer is not scientific. In order to make progress, one must leave the door to the unknown ajar."[47]

Musk understands that it is uncomfortable for a lot of people to feel that they do not know the answer to the meaning of life, but he learned to use logic to accept this because his happiness depended on it.[48] Years later, Musk would write on Twitter, "Bringing anxiety/fear to the conscious mind saps it of limbic emotional strength."[49] We must confront our worries by facing them head on and then adopt what he calls a "cheery fatalism."

Adams helped Musk accept that everything he knew about the reality of the universe and himself was through the prism of the human mind, a vector that is neither rational nor emotional and neither good nor bad; it is all those things, both brilliant and unreliable. Accepting this can be a liberating thought. You don't need to blame the universe for your problems, nor do you need to feel ashamed that you are responsible for them. This is the human condition, which is our fate—and it is absurd. Musk could learn from Arthur Dent, who, amid the revelations from his journey, tries his best to find a nice cup of tea, stay sane, and take heed of the advice emblazoned on the cover of his guide to the galaxy—"DON'T PANIC."

It is not a coincidence that Douglas Adams used the medium of humor. It is the same reason that Sisyphus smiles. Charlie Chaplin summed it up best when he wrote in *My Autobiography*: "Through humor we see in what seems rational, the irrational; in what seems important, the unimportant. It also heightens our sense of survival and preserves our sanity. Because of humor we are less overwhelmed by the vicissitudes of life. It activates our sense of proportion and reveals to us that in an over-statement of seriousness lurks the absurd."[50]

Throughout his life, humor would be a tonic to Musk, and he would smile at the randomness of the universe, often reflecting on how fate loves irony. This is someone who named The Boring Company's inactive drilling machine "Godot," after Samuel Beckett's tragicomic play. Musk also launched a wheel of Le Brouère cheese into space in 2010 in memory of Monty Python's absurd sketch about a cheese shop that has no cheese. Such absurd humor is fundamental to Musk's character. It is the best release for his anxiety. Ironically, it also often conceals how heartfelt his sense of the absurd truly is.

The Ultimate Answer

Musk's embrace of uncertainty was eased by the humor that sugared the pill of the absurd and also by the life-affirming approach of Adams, which flipped the whole quandary of meaning on its head. The universe is not a problem to be fixed but an answer to be understood. It is *the* answer. This was an epiphany for young Musk. We may feel racked with doubts, but we should not feel unanchored in a vast cosmos. We don't need to go looking for answers; we need to find the questions. Musk could not be clearer when he said, "What's the meaning of life? And that's not even the right question to ask. It's like, how did we get here? Where's it going?"[51]

This struggle to find the right question is illustrated beautifully by Adams's portrayal of human history across the three phases of galactic civilization, namely the How, Why, and Where phases. Adams's retelling of our past, present, and future can help illuminate the way Musk thinks.

Adams begins with the ape-men of prehistory, who were preoccupied with survival and the question *How?* as in "How can we eat?"[52] They were nomads who lived in huts and had rudimentary language. They were highly intuitive and had no knowledge of the people, places, and things they did not encounter. But they knew what they needed to survive, which berries were poisonous and which they could eat, how to gather sticks to make huts, and how to hunt reindeer and keep warm with their skins. They understood the patterns of the rains, winds, and birdsong. They sensed the chaos of the universe, Adams writes, but it was a simple chaos.[53]

Adams's second phase is about inquiry and the question *Why?* as in "Why do we eat?"[54] Ever so slowly, humans moved into cold, damp, and smelly caves, and, like the cave-dwellers of Plato's allegory whose reality is the shadows of objects they cannot see, those who remained inside lost contact with the natural world outside. The more humans used tools to make clothes, food, weapons, and art, the more they could broaden their universe of lived experience, but the more they also made myths that separated them from nature and placed themselves at the center of everything. This, for Adams, made the chaos of the universe more complicated, and that, in turn, blurred their sense of reality.[55]

Musk truly believes that though our prehistoric ancestry may seem far from us today, it is deeply ingrained in us. He thinks we are wired for survival but that we have an evolutionary asymmetry. For all the advantages of the modern age, our limbic system causes us to struggle in an environment for which we are not adapted. We worry too much about the wrong things. We are more likely, for example, to be on the lookout for danger and to remember reasons to hate rather than to pay attention to positive news and remember reasons to love. This instinctual asymmetry had its uses—early humans who were complacent about lions did not survive—but today, it is often counterproductive, making us negative and vengeful when we involuntarily feel threatened by danger that is nonexistent.[56]

In the modern world, Musk thinks we are also more likely to fall into the trap of wishful thinking, which is innate to the human brain. "You want things to be the way you wish them to be," he says, "so you tend to filter information you shouldn't filter."[57] As social creatures, we are also vulnerable to answers that encourage us to conform so that we can coexist in ever-larger numbers. This, for Musk, is because our capacity for rational thinking is put at the service of the monkey brain. It might seem more logical for this to be the other way round, but instead our sophisticated computer is coopted to try to make us happy, to give us certainty and ideally the meaning of life. Or as Minsky puts it less charitably, we activate "mental parasites" in different parts of the brain to neutralize our "programming bug."[58] Unless you're Musk that is. Wishful thinking is not something that he is good at. The answers that satisfy most people just don't work for him, making the question *Why?* very bad for his sanity.

Adams's third stage of galactic civilization holds no more appeal, though. This is the phase of sophistication and the question *Where?* as in "Where shall we have lunch?"[59] By now, our lives are largely buffered from reality. This is Adams's decadent tribe of Golgafrinchans, who were transported, like Arthur, back to the dawn of civilization. Shorn of their leaders and doers, they are peopled by marketeers, hairdressers, telephone sanitizers, management consultants, and assorted middle managers who are incapable of making anything.

Some people might escape the question of life's meaning in this *Where?* phase but Musk is too restless. He is too curious about reality. He is the antithesis of the Golgafrinchans, whom Adams mocked for being so busy doing nothing that they were unable to discover fire or invent the wheel, and struggled to make it through the winter. He can escape momentarily via books and video games, but then he needs to be doing something.

If not Why? or Where?, Musk would have no choice but to turn back and go outside of the cave, to a life in "survival" mode, where he could explore and ask the question How? He thereby diverted his attention from inward to outward and embraced uncertainty: trying to see reality more clearly, looking at the universe from fresh perspectives (where we are not at the center), reimagining what might be possible, and discovering the simplicity from which the complexity emerges.

There is nothing original in this approach. It puts Musk in a school of thought that goes back via Albert Einstein and Baruch Spinoza to Galileo, who said in *The Assayer*, "Philosophy is written in this all-encompassing book that is constantly open before our eyes, that is the universe; but it cannot be understood unless one first learns to understand the language and knows the characters in which it is written."[60] Musk's route to this point of view through absurd humor, however, puts him in a category of his own.

. . .

Musk's journey in life from this point would not be easy. People like him can't entirely unlearn the question Why? And bringing one's fear of the dark out of the subconscious is not the same as overcoming trauma. Tellingly, Freud said that those people who succeed in turning their emotion outward and seek to act for all mankind, while asking for nothing in return, do so in part because they fear the hurt of losing a person who might love them back.[61] They also tend to substitute the harshness of the cruel figure of authority with exacting standards they impose on themselves and on others.

Musk's biographer, Ashlee Vance, wrote that Musk's life "might be an attempt to soothe an existential depression that gnaws at his every fiber."[62] Musk's friend and colleague Antonio Gracias, too, has said that when Musk feels threatened, his childhood PTSD hijacks the limbic part of his brain.[63] And his two ex-wives point to the enduring harm that Errol caused Musk when he was young. Musk himself would admit to Vance that his obsession with winning was probably rooted in some "very disturbing psychoanalytical black hole or neural short circuit."[64]

Melancholia can flip into mania. And a feeling of inferiority can be overcompensated for by a need for superiority in later life. But this is not the place to psychoanalyze Musk; suffice to say that he would continue to bear the scars of his childhood.

What we can say is that he was so much the better off for his encounter with Douglas Adams. The Englishman played a decisive role in helping the teenager realize that he was not the only person who saw the world differently and to reframe his uncertainty in a positive way. This belief compelled him to ask How? with a glass-half-full attitude and steered him on an adventure that would provide constructive outlets for his frustration.

Adams is the reason that Musk would speak of curiosity in a religious sense. It may sound ludicrous: a religion with no supernatural dimension nor any serious attempt to bind people together? But then again, Musk doesn't think like most people. While others might revere a higher power that provides an answer to their Why, Musk marvels at our blue-green planet with its ape-descended life-forms and asks How? He is also not simply a bit curious. Asked by a university student in 2022 about the day-to-day habit that made him what he was, he replied that it is important to be curious about how the world works; but not only that, one should be "somewhat obsessive about the curiosity."[65] Embracing uncertainty is undoubtedly the most significant of the nine beliefs in this book, as all the others build upon it.

Boiling It Down: Seek meaning through better questions

Most people question the meaning of life in a profound way only once in a while, when bad things happen to us. And then we are usually able to move on. We either start to feel better in ourselves or find something that gives us the answer we were looking for. Musk is different. His search for meaning can be summarized as follows:

1. Reality is rarely what we think it is. Looking at it from new and different perspectives can show that we too often look for answers to meaning in the wrong place.
2. How we feel about the world and ourselves shapes our thinking. So when a child who is still constructing their worldview is made to suffer, it can cause a full-blown existential crisis.
3. When the brain refuses to give the heart the answers it desperately wants to hear, the best option may be to accept that the question is absurd, to stop attacking oneself, and to try even to smile about it.
4. Once we stop panicking, our curious eyes may be opened to wonder at the universe and realize that the answers are already out there, waiting for the right questions.

TWO

Test & Learn

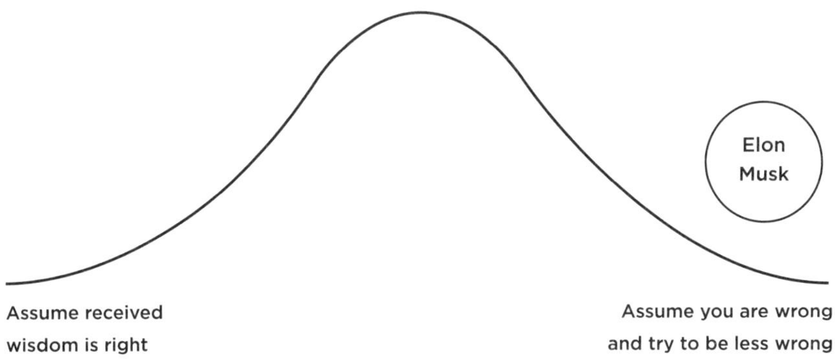

"I think it's possible for ordinary people to choose to be extraordinary," Musk explained in 2008.[1] How so? "They can choose to not necessarily conform to the conventions that were taught to them by their parents." It is a sentiment that resonates strongly with something Steve Jobs said fourteen years prior: "When you grow up, you tend to get told the world is the way it is and your life is just to live your life inside the world. Try not to bash into the walls too much. Try to have a nice family life, have fun, save a little money. But that's a very limited life."[2] Most people try to bash the innate curiosity out of children and make them conventional.

Not in Musk's case. Obsessed with how the world works, he knew from an early age that the universe might be the answer, but Johannesburg was not the place to search for questions.

Walls can be reassuring for a lot of people. Through childhood, we are immersed in the stories, customs, and traditions of our family, school, and tribe. This is where we belong, and it defines our identity. Adams spoke to this phenomenon when he wrote about the alien species from Olgaroon, who are born, live, and eventually die, strapped to a single "fairly small and crowded nut-tree."[3] But Musk could not live like this. The inhabitants of Olgaroon threw out anyone who was curious about life beyond their tree, and that is effectively what happened to Musk.

As a gifted but awkward boy growing up, the walls for Musk were the macho Afrikaner culture of apartheid South Africa, and they offered neither certainty nor comfort. His worldview had been fractured and he had been betrayed by those he should have been able to trust. Nor did he feel the binding effect of religion. That is why his brother, Kimbal, describes South Africa as being like a prison for someone like Musk.[4]

From a very young age, he fed his curiosity and wonder about the world by reading. He spent his teenage years expanding his secondhand knowledge of the world in a way that mingled physics, history, biology, and literature, just like the encyclopedias he read. This gave him a breadth of knowledge that in later life would help him create by cross-pollinating ideas from different fields.[5]

The time came, though, for him to wander and broaden his circle of experience. He could see very well that he was a creature of circumstance and that, while he could not change the time in which he lived, he could change the place. As Adams and many others have observed, most people seek local maxima—they climb the biggest hill in their neighborhood without realizing that if they descend the other side, they might find larger mountains with better views to be discovered. Musk knew this, and Canada would be the next step for him after South Africa.

The ultimate destination, though, was the United States. He had a romantic view of the country and would say in later life: "America is a nation of explorers. People came here from other parts of the world that chose to give up the known in favor of the unknown."[6] In North America, Musk first encountered people who saw the world differently and who—outside of his siblings and cousins—made him feel socially at ease. And at university in Ontario, Canada, he met fellow nerds who also loved video games and science fiction. There, too, he met his future wife, Justine Wilson, who would go on to become a writer of fantasy novels about angels and demons.

With all that said, Musk would still have felt that he was different, because no matter where he was, he still thought differently from others. He was obsessed with the truth and focused on How? questions, but he still had to learn a method for *how* to ask them. Curiosity is essential to learn and explore, but it is not enough. He could build his breadth of knowledge and expand his firsthand experience, but in and of itself, that was too passive. He needed a proactive approach that guarded against natural biases. This would be the scientific method.

Adams shows that we should ask our own questions instead of trying to make sense of the answers to other people's questions, but Musk then raises this to a new level. His extra step is to say that the more we understand the answer that is the universe, the more we will know what questions to ask, and the better the questions we ask, the better we will understand the universe.[7] It is a virtuous cycle. There may be no certainty in the world outside of the walls, but the goal should not be to feel certain about what is right but to try to be less uncertain and less wrong. Adams may have been the prophet of Musk's religion, revealing through *The Hitchhiker's Guide to the Galaxy* the article of faith that the universe is the answer to the question of life's meaning, but Adams did not transcribe the word of God. The scientific method, therefore, would be the rite of worship for Musk's religion. As the English man of letters Samuel Johnson wrote in 1751, curious people search after knowledge for the sheer love of knowledge, and science is "the daughter of curiosity" that helps them understand.[8] Posing new questions in a critical way allows us to sort through confusing information, with each question begetting more questions that might bring us closer to the truth.

This is precisely the approach that scientists are supposed to take. It's the language Galileo learned when he read the "grand book" of the universe. What makes it religious for Musk is that it keeps alive the question of life's meaning. Musk had taken his original cue from *The Hitchhiker's Guide to the Galaxy*, and he would take Adams's thinking even further. Adams believed that we humans cannot get our minds around things that are extremely improbable or hard to fathom. But Musk takes a more optimistic view, because he takes Adams more literally than even Adams had meant. If there is, in Adams's words, a "*virtual* impossibility" of understanding the truth of the universe, then there is, by definition, a "*finite* improbability" of doing so, however unlikely that might be.[9]

If we keep asking better questions as our understanding of the universe improves, Musk reasons, then ultimately we will get close to understanding the question that most approximates to "the meaning of life."[10] This approach enabled him to turn the "meaning of life" question into a series of scientific questions that may one day be tested in the real world. If we can keep repeating the process to a degree that becomes mind-boggling, then we may get ever closer to the finitely improbable. This is the physicist who dreams of the single equation that will unlock the mystery of the universe. It's a very, very long process to get that far, but there is still a process, and for Musk, that is what matters.

Keeping It Real

Thinking critically is not a deliberate choice that most people feel the need to make, but for Musk it is a must. It allows him to live with his uncertainty as it resists the twin temptations of wishful thinking and negative thinking. He knew this well because, when he was at his lowest ebb, he read the works of three dead German philosophers. To understand why Musk found Adams so appealing, it's instructive to examine why he might have found these popular philosophers so demoralizing.

Arthur Schopenhauer, Friedrich Nietzsche, and Martin Heidegger were the trio of irrationality that Musk discovered when he was looking for a way out of his existential crisis.[11] Born between 1788 and 1889, they rejected both the prevailing Christianity in Europe and the Enlightenment rationalism that had begun to undermine it. Many teenagers turn to them because of the way they speak up for the individual against blindly following the religious and ethical consensus of the day. But to Musk's mind, they were very depressing. The three of them witnessed in themselves the absurd way that the mind and the heart can sabotage each other, but they did not accept Camus's assertion that the absurd is "lucid reason noting its limits." Instead, they rationalized their own suffering to such a degree that they embraced irrationalism.

Schopenhauer became the most famous pessimist in philosophy. He believed there are universal truths that govern the laws of nature, but humans in essence have a "will to life" that is driven by ungovernable passions, not reason.[12] Influenced by Eastern religions and the notion that everything is conscious, he concluded that if our desires cause only suffering, we should try to be Buddha-like and compassionate. We should exercise maximum restraint, distract ourselves, listen to music, and ridicule our fate. Schopenhauer duly retreated from the world and other people to live alone with his poodle, Atman, and play the flute. This was not a blueprint for a twelve-year-old boy seeking inspiration.

Nietzsche wrote against the backdrop of Karl Marx and Friedrich Engels's *The Communist Manifesto* (1848) and Charles Darwin's *On the Origin of Species* (1859). He saw the Christian worldview collapsing in Western Europe, and he was appalled at the prospect of communists and English liberals scrambling to fill the void. Like his mentor, Schopenhauer, he believed suffering was at the root of human experience, but he ended up replacing Schopenhauer's pessimistic "will to life" with his own "will to power." Nietzsche reasoned that while life may be uncertain, one can at least try to master oneself, believing that "the ascetic ideal gave Man a meaning!"[13] This allowed him to divide the world into those who were strong enough to withstand suffering and do "great" things and those who were morally inferior and destined to submit to their will. He looked down on happiness, considered love a weakness, and opposed democracy and utilitarian ethics.

Nietzsche was less metaphysical than Schopenhauer, believing that humans need to triangulate between multiple perspectives in order to gain "objectivity." But he did not believe there are universal truths that are not subjective, and he was never far from the mystical. Like Schopenhauer, he also ended up becoming a recluse, making him equally unsuitable to be a role model for the disconsolate young Musk.

Martin Heidegger, the third German philosopher Musk had turned to, wrote about the contingency of existence, anxiety, and death in an unprecedented way. He constructed a vast abstract world of terms and—unlike Schopenhauer or Nietzsche—he was a poor writer.[14] Young Musk's eyes must have glazed over at the sight of his dense, elliptical prose.

For a child like Musk, who saw the world in a literal way and felt lonely, these philosophers could only have made things worse. They could not speak to a boy who had been brutally attacked. They rejected a higher power as an answer to the meaning of life but still tried to rationalize an answer to the question, and when they failed, they indulged in negative thinking. They went against the wise words of Viktor Frankl, who wrote in *Man's Search for Meaning*: "What is demanded of man is not, as some existential philosophers teach, to endure the meaninglessness of life, but rather to bear his incapacity to grasp its unconditional meaningfulness in rational terms."[15] Musk, as an adult, reread these authors and found them more manageable, but he was unchanged in his view that "it's just clear that they have real issues."[16]

When it comes to living with uncertainty, Musk is closer to the writer Albert Camus, who said of such thinkers, "These men vie with one another in proclaiming that nothing is clear, all is chaos, that all man has is his lucidity and his definite knowledge of the walls surrounding him."[17] They failed to realize that "this feeling of strangeness is shared with all men," and that when you rebel by living fully, you do so in solidarity with all other humans.[18]

By comparison, Adams's philosophy is even simpler, which is what Musk loves about it. You must resist the appeal of higher faith and the Germanic pull to irrationalism, for being rational is a vital part of what makes us human. You must question everything you thought you knew, and yet not become a skeptic, as you must imagine how the universe works and put your ideas to the test. In short, if you don't want to wallow in your own suffering, you have to look outward toward reality, not inward. And you must join together with others to do this. These positive sentiments would stay with Musk throughout his life and would lead him to launch a car into space in 2018 with the tweet: "Life cannot just be about solving one sad problem after another. There need to be things that inspire you, that make you glad to wake up in the morning *and be part of humanity*"[19][my italics].

The Physics Framework

Musk received a dual degree in physics and economics, starting at Queen's University in Canada and transferring to the University of Pennsylvania in the United States. He had carried forward a love of physics that he had gravitated to as a teenager, believing it was the most reliable guide to the truths of the universe.

Though a career in pure science was not for him, the "physics framework" became ingrained in his thinking, along with the conviction that the "mental tools of physics are a superpower that applies to anything, not just physics."[20] In a 2017 interview for *Rolling Stone* magazine, Musk expounded on the scientific method at such length that the journalist felt it necessary to lay out his full definition, as follows:

1. Ask a question.
2. Gather as much evidence as possible about it.
3. Develop axioms based on the evidence and try to assign a probability of truth to each one.
4. Draw a conclusion based on cogency in order to determine: Are these axioms correct, are they relevant, do they necessarily lead to this conclusion, and with what probability?
5. Attempt to disprove the conclusion. Seek refutation from others to further break your conclusion.
6. If nobody can invalidate your conclusion, then you're probably right, but you're not certainly right.[21]

This scientific method is central to Musk's doctrine and warrants closer examination. It brings us back to the world of Adams's early humans. Musk might have been drawn back into the survival phase of existence, but he was not going there without taking with him some of the Enlightenment know-how that came from the phase of inquiry. In pre-civilized times, humans had to rely exclusively on *common sense*, combining instinct, knowledge handed down from parents, and first-hand experience. They used ideas that worked for them until they didn't, and then they discarded them. This was a face-to-face world among family, friends, and neighbors that the Austrian economist Friedrich Hayek called the "micro-cosmos."[22] As they lived in bigger groups, spent more time in caves, and pondered the world they could not see, they entered the abstract world that Hayek called the "macro-cosmos." This was not the realm of common sense. As the great astronomer and science communicator Carl Sagan said, common sense works for the world that is visible, but beyond that, it is not applicable.[23] The "macro-cosmos" is the world beyond our lived experience, which humans have interpreted variously through literature, religion, and science.[24]

Here, the scientific mind steps outside of the cave and gets practical, pursuing a methodical approach to understanding what common sense cannot. That is how Musk thinks of it. "Physics has this problem," he says, of "trying to figure out things that are totally counterintuitive. And so, they had to have a framework for getting there. Quantum mechanics is incredibly counterintuitive. But it's true. So, physics developed a framework for figuring out things that aren't obvious. That's why I think it's the right framework."[25]

Unlike reasoning by convention or analogy to prior experience, the scientific method doesn't skip steps. It can be used to boil down and distill what you know about reality and then reason up from first principles to derive theories. Crucially, it then requires you to seek feedback by testing those theories in the real world. It is taxing to do this, and so Musk turns the practice into a kind of ritual. He would develop an uncommon sense for approaching problems in a nonintuitive way, and none more so than thinking "in the limit," which means to extrapolate a principle to imagine how it may behave when pushed to a very large or very small scale.

"Fundamental to the Scientific Method," Musk says, "is that the 'science' is always subject to question and never settled! Upon reexamination, we will discover that, in some cases, long-accepted 'scientific wisdom' was wrong."[26] That is why Karl Popper, one of the most famous theorists of the scientific method, said that the concept of science is no different to most human concepts in that it is built on a great myth.[27] It is not an exception in that regard. However, the myth of science is to combine theory with a critical attitude to theory, and that makes it unique. The scientific method instructs scientists to try to falsify their theories. That is why Richard Feynman answered his question "what is science?" by saying it is "the belief in the ignorance of experts."[28] Scientists must live with uncertainty, interrogate those beliefs that have been passed down to them, and recheck them from new direct experience.

Furthermore, a theory is not true simply because it has been confirmed. On the contrary, one has to try to disprove it by finding exceptions. Critically, it only takes one person or one finding to prove something wrong. Whether confirmed or not, the answer can be fed back into posing a better question in a recursive, open-ended way. Science is not the body of knowledge but the process of testing and learning. One must always seek negative feedback, in a way that practitioners of religion and literature typically do not.

Musk's go-to maxim therefore is to take the position that he is always to some degree wrong, and his aspiration is to be less wrong. It is a powerful way to reframe a negative sentiment in a positive way. And when he does refer to the truth, he always tries to qualify it by referring to truth with the least amount of error. In turn, he contends that you can assess someone's rationality if you "ask them to assign a probability to their argument being true vs false. Anyone who says anywhere close to 100% for a matter where there is subjectivity" does not realize how wrong they are.[29]

. . .

Musk would explore what the physics framework meant in practice once he went to San Francisco. There he joined like-minded people who shared his uncommon sense and were putting it to the test in the real world of making products. He would hone what he would call a "Silicon Valley operating system" with a "best idea wins culture."[30] And he would apply his "in the limit" thinking when, for example, considering how changes in unit costs, networks effects, and customer adoption might accelerate over time and scale in a non-linear fashion. Meanwhile, his approach to first principles thinking would be especially apparent in the interplay between design and manufacturing.

The legendary CEO of Intel, Andy Grove, wrote in the 1980s about the need to simplify before you automate. Musk would take this much further because he and his colleagues wasted too much time making a two-fold mistake: they manufactured products that included a part for which no one knew the purpose because no one could remember the question that that part was intended to be the answer to; and they then compounded the problem by trying to automate the production for an assembly that included said part. To guard against this, Musk developed a step-by-step checklist:

1. Question the requirements of the product (what's it supposed to do?) and make them less dumb.
2. Delete the number of parts and steps involved and observe what happens (add back parts and steps that shouldn't have been deleted, and, if this is less than 10 percent of the deletions, keep on deleting).
3. Only then, optimize by simplifying.
4. Only then, speed up the process.
5. Only then, automate.

Musk thinks of this mindset as a type of software, an algorithm that he tries to embed into the operating system of his companies.[31] Like the scientific method itself, this checklist builds in self-criticism to overcome lazy thinking, goes back to first principles, and is never finished.

The self-criticism is needed because it is counterintuitive to delete more than might be necessary. We are by nature too conservative and hate to take out something that we might later have to add back. In Musk's words, we have to make a "cortical correction" of our limbic system. This approach would shape his thinking on engineering, manufacturing, staffing, the regulatory system, and even government legislation.

Some might say that Musk went far beyond what Adams wrote in *The Hitchhiker's Guide to the Galaxy*, which is mocking of physics, and that Musk missed the subtlety of Adams's English humor. And they would not be wrong but for the fact that Adams more or less came round to Musk's way of thinking after writing the book. He came to this point of view via Madagascan rainforests, Richard Dawkins, and the process of evolution. Adams even thought that he may have stumbled on the ultimate answer: the fact that what survives, survives, or as he wrote in *Mostly Harmless*: "Anything that happens, happens. Anything that, in happening, causes something else to happen, causes something else to happen. Anything that, in happening, causes itself to happen again, happens again."[32] It's tautological, but Adams found it satisfying nonetheless. In due course, he would come to say that the scientific method was "the most powerful framework for thinking and investigating and understanding and challenging the world around us."[33] And when Adams died, Dawkins wrote, "Science has lost a friend."[34] A sense of the absurd and a scientific mind are not incompatible after all. Years later, in 2024, Dawkins would also say that Musk "has the welfare of the world at heart."[35]

2 + 2 = 4

It is precisely the contingent nature of scientific discovery that makes it so exciting for people like Musk. For as far as we know today, we humans are the only conscious beings who have the capacity to ask better questions by exploring the unknown. We might not be the center of the universe, but as Carl Sagan said, "We are a way for the cosmos to know itself."[36] To someone like Musk, who is without faith in a higher power, this makes science a human endeavor and makes him feel part of something greater than himself. Humans may not have certainty, but people like Musk have the capability to do something about this, to erode the uncertainty.

Very often the critics of rational thinking misunderstand what science actually is. The religious critique is well represented by the bearded Russian novelist Fyodor Dostoevsky.[37] Like Douglas Adams, he described how "mankind is comically constructed" with an errant equation in his existential novel *Notes from Underground*. Speaking of the scientists and engineers of the world—people like Musk—his protagonist declares, "Man has always feared this 2 X 2 = 4 formula, and I still fear it. We may suppose a man may do nothing but search for such equations, crossing the oceans and dedicating his life to the quest; but succeeding, really finding them—I swear he will be afraid of that. Really, he will find that if he finds them, he will have nothing left to search for."[38]

Dostoevsky described the limits of human knowledge—like Jobs and Camus—as walls. They give comfort to many, but those with a wont to over-think can only bash their heads against them. Unable to move forward and understand the world or to move backward and abandon reason, they are driven underground into depravity and sin because "reason is only reason and satisfies only man's intellectual faculties, while volition is a manifestation of the whole of life."[39] In the end, they would also have to admit that "two and two make five is also a very fine thing."[40] Not so for Musk, though. Curiosity is all about knocking down those walls of ignorance.

Dostoevsky's critique of rationalism ends up being similar to the three German philosophers whom the young Musk rejected. Desperate for certainty, he champions irrationality and glorifies suffering. In *Notes from Underground*, Dostoevsky writes that suffering is "the sole cause of consciousness," and consciousness is "infinitely greater than, for example, two and two makes four."[41] The only difference is that the Germans resort to negative thinking while the Russian engages in a leap of faith, which some would describe as wishful thinking. Both points of view demonstrate just how hard it is to live with uncertainty.

Musk does not consider that everything that has meaning needs to be scientific and verifiable. There is a place for imagination and emotion, which he describes in a typically unemotional way: "You need to feel life. The sensory experience of life. You can't get too caught up in the cold calculus of the cortex. You need to feel it in the limbic system, ask yourself, what does your heart say?"[42] With that said, Musk does not believe it is the job of the intellect to give the heart the answers that it wants. His critical thinking serves his curiosity about the universe, which is both emotional and intellectual and not one submitting to the other. It is concerned with exploration, novelty, discovery, the satisfaction of doing experiments, learning how things work, and solving problems.

Musk's curiosity is like a balloon that keeps him from going underground within his four walls, and the scientific method is like a weight that stops him from floating up toward the infinite. That's how to make the universe more human. He trusts in the process. This is a method one can use to ask whether one should exploit what one knows or move on to explore something better. And he is able to project this across generations and epochs to imagine the enormous potential of scientific discovery. The mysteries of the universe are just answers to questions that we have not yet thought to ask. Richard Feynman captured this when he wrote, "We are only at the beginning of the development of the human race; of the development of the human mind, of intelligent life—we have years and years in the future. It is our responsibility not to give the answer today as to what it is all about, to drive everybody down in that direction and to say: 'This is a solution to it all.' Because we will be chained then to the limits of our present imagination."[43] In order to progress, we must leave room for doubt.

Is it plausible that Musk could find meaning in the belief that we can make strides toward the questions that approximate to "the meaning of life"? Dostoevsky was being sarcastic when he said that scientists fear what they will do if they find their equations. He believed that people like Musk must submit to the immeasurably great and "twice two is four is not life, gentlemen, but the beginning of death."[44] Musk, however, fervently believes that the scientific method can help humanity over time to become less wrong, and so it does provide meaning.

First, he thinks, like Stephen Hawking, that questions about life, the universe, and everything were traditionally for philosophy, but philosophy has not kept up with modern developments in physics, and these questions must now be taken on by science.[45] Our mental models of reality can and must be tested in the universe around us. Adams, for example, joked that we humans feel that we are the center of the universe because we have a so-called anthropic bias, and our forebears were actually told that this was true by the "experts," until, that is, Copernicus came along in the sixteenth century with an alternative theory. In due course, Isaac Newton's laws of classical physics seemed to ask the right questions of the universe, within the dimensions of our lived experience, until, that is, Einstein showed that they did not apply over speeds and gravitational fields too large for humans to imagine. Einstein himself thought his theories were just approximations of better theories to come.

Second, Musk also believes, like Richard Dawkins, that we might better understand things that are improbably complex if we study not only the hierarchy of principles that govern how they work but also how they came to be.[46] We may discover the simplicity from which the complexity of life on Earth might have emerged, including ourselves, and thereby glimpse the natural beauty and elegance of the universe. For example, we may take it for granted today, but, thanks to the scientific method, we have an explanation for the diversity of life through the theory of evolution by natural selection, a mental model that did not exist for most of human history. Similarly, we now also know how genetic information is stored, copied, and passed on, thanks to our understanding of DNA.

This still leaves Musk with the big *why* question, the "first cause"—how the universe came to exist in the first place. How is no longer enough. Einstein searched for a unified theory that might answer this and reconcile gravity and electromagnetism, encompassing the new theories of quantum mechanics. To this day, scientists are still working on the same problem. But in Einstein's own lifetime, scientists came to the view that the universe has not existed statically for eternity and is actually growing. So it is more than likely that we are burdened today with mental models that we too will need to discard. Physicists like Stephen Hawking have suggested that we may live in a universe without boundary conditions and that we likely need to change the way we think about time.[47] This is why Musk mused about gravity, information theory, and dark matter when launching xAI: he believes that AI will be able to help us in these endeavors.

Third, Musk has faith that he will be able to get his mind around new models of reality that scientists may come up with. Science, after all, requires that theories be formulated in a way that makes them capable of being falsified in the real world. This includes, for example, the question of consciousness itself. On what dimensions do thought and emotions exist, ponders Musk. "I suspect there's more to it than atoms bumping into atoms," he has suggested.[48] How so? Was Schopenhauer right to think that consciousness and reality are one, and that science tells us nothing about metaphysics, as scientists like Erwin Schrödinger believe?[49] For now, Musk thinks not. He leans to the belief that consciousness is an emergent property of physics that can be properly examined in the realm of science.

Perhaps the attempt to build sentient AI will shed light on this, or perhaps, as science fiction writers have wondered, it will take millions of years.[50] If, however, new theories about the nature of reality do come along and are capable of being tested in Musk's lifetime, then his gut feeling would likely be that he would have the intellectual wherewithal to comprehend the scientific findings.

Fourth, Musk implicitly believes that his curiosity would be satisfied by getting close to understanding the nature of reality. Musk may be highly unusual in this regard. He might be in agreement with Camus that humans must resist the infinite and adhere to reason, but he parts ways with the French writer, who doubted that we would find any comfort in a hypothesis that could only be understood as a metaphor for reality.[51] Musk, however, believes there is some explanation for this universe and—like Einstein and Spinoza before him—he would be content to call this his God.[52]

In the meantime, humans have a lot of work to do. But for Musk, there is a way forward, provided we put the pursuit of truth before certainty and learn how to ask better questions. We don't need to be right; if we assume we are wrong, the mind is open, and we are more likely to remain curious and to learn. We just need to keep cycling through the physics framework, which for Musk has the spiritual quality of a mantra. He bows only to the measurable and the finite.

Boiling It Down: Assume you are wrong and try to be less wrong

Most of us believe most of what we are told most of the time. We call it "received wisdom," and it's right more often than not. But it's difficult to get smarter thinking this way, and Musk is obsessed with getting smarter. He is fanatical about thinking critically, which can be summarized as follows:

1. The more we interrogate the world, the better we may understand it and thereby ask better questions, provided we ask them in the right way and keep with the process.
2. We must avoid rationalizing our own suffering. It kills our curiosity, as it leads back to the question *why* and to negative thinking.
3. The scientific method is the best way to satisfy our curiosity. Uniquely among myths, it insists on the need for self-criticism because, whether right or wrong, we always learn.
4. Using our consciousness to better understand the universe can make us feel part of something bigger than ourselves, connecting us with generations of the past and the future.

THREE

Increase Consciousness

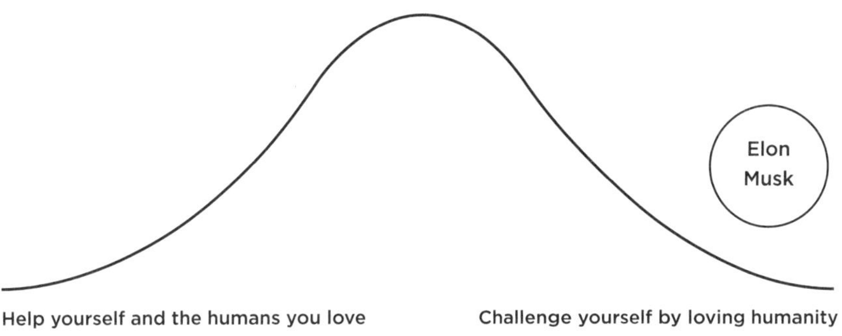

"Prometheus Unbound" was the caption Musk used for a post on Twitter in 2021 of a picture of flames roaring from the engines of one of his rockets.[1] Musk, who loves ancient history, evoked the rebellious Titan who defied Zeus by stealing his fire and giving it to humans. Four years later, Musk again posted the same caption next to a near-identical image.[2]

Fire is the obvious association Musk makes with his comment, but he would have been familiar with the deeper meaning of the myth. Originally a creation story in which Prometheus made humans out of clay and brought them to life with fire, the immortal God became a symbol for mortal humans in the plays of Aeschylus. He protects them from the king of the Olympian gods, who threw his thunderbolts down from on high. The fire represents the capacity of humans to sustain themselves. For, under his guidance, they would learn how to develop shelter, art, science, astronomy, agriculture, medicine, metallurgy, sailing, and writing. The fire also represents hope, because humans now had a reason to consider they might have a better future. Accordingly, Prometheus would later earn the epithet "philanthropic," as in "lover of humanity."[3]

Musk knows better than anyone how hard thousands of engineers must work to design, construct, and launch a rocket. And symbolically, they are also defying gravity, sending a thunderbolt back into the sky and toward the heavens. The sense of mission that this encapsulates represents the third pillar to his religion of curiosity, building upon his reverence for the universe and the scientific method: If the answer is the universe, and we can ask better questions by understanding it better, then to the degree we can expand the scope and scale of consciousness and knowledge, we should do that.[4] This is how we might get closer to the questions that approximate to asking what the meaning of life is. Musk was thereby able to construct a framework for moral action by making our universe more human. The goal is to be useful by taking "the set of actions that maximize the probability that the future will be good for civilization."[5]

Increasing the sum total of consciousness for Musk means both more people and smarter people who care about seeking the truth, testing, and criticism. The scope of consciousness encompasses different cultures with different ways of thinking and different points of view.[6] And it extends to a collective consciousness, as civilization enables individuals to become more connected and share their knowledge.

Musk was drawn to technology as a way to bend the arc of history because it brings with it the capacity to change the world during one's lifetime. It has a very leveraged effect on the ability of humans to change the future, usually for the better, though sometimes for the worse. This would be the way for him to channel his curiosity and put to good use his gift for critical thinking.

Musk loves J. R. R. Tolkien's *The Lord of the Rings* for the magical world it conjures, and even though he considered Tolkien somewhat skeptical about the impact of technology, Musk interpreted the books in a positive way. In this, he borrowed from Arthur C. Clarke's dictum (his Third Law) that "any sufficiently advanced technology is indistinguishable from magic."[7] To discover the limits of what is possible, one must go beyond them into the impossible (Clarke's Second Law), something which—unlike wizardry—becomes harder when one becomes older (Clarke's First Law).[8] Thereby a technologist is able to come closer to being a wizard than anyone else in the real world.

Alan Kay, the software theorist at Xerox's PARC, is said to have joked in the 1980s that "technology is anything that wasn't around when you were born." He spoke from experience, as he had helped pioneer the first graphical user interface that would help to make computers accessible for all. Douglas Adams thought of it in the same way, and in 2001, after observing the differing attitudes of his daughter and mother to innovations like email, cell phones, and DVDs, he came up with his own three rules for technology:

"Rule 1—Anything that is in the world when you're born is normal and ordinary and is just a natural part of the way the world works.

Rule 2—Anything that's invented between when you're fifteen and thirty-five is new and exciting and revolutionary and you can probably get a career in it.

Rule 3—Anything invented after you're thirty-five is against the natural order of things."[9]

By the time he left university, Musk would wholeheartedly embrace the implications of Rule 2. But Musk also stayed in Rule 2 well beyond the age of thirty-five. He wouldn't become like Adams's mother. He would keep chasing the magic, looking at science fiction to see what might one day become science, and then setting about trying to make it so. And he would demonstrate an uncanny ability to change his mind on what might become possible throughout his life.

Questioned by Life

Fifty years before Douglas Adams wrote about his three stages of galactic civilization, Sigmund Freud wrote *Civilization and Its Discontents*, an account that maps how humans seek purpose in life onto the history of civilization. Most people, he says, are not reconciled to the frustrations of the external world, and the very asking of the question of life's meaning forces them into answers that look away from reality, seeking happiness through some combination of the supernatural, purely intellectual or imaginative pursuits, distractions, or intoxication.[10] These were not for Musk, though.

He belongs to what Freud identified as "a small minority of people" who cannot turn to illusions. These individuals are able to reframe their anxieties in a positive way and test themselves in the real world. Perhaps thinking of himself and his psychoanalytic therapy, Freud said, "As a member of the human community one can go on the attack against nature with the help of applied science, and subject her to the human will. One is then working with everyone for the happiness of all."[11]

Such people are in a minority, perhaps, as most people naturally focus mainly on their family and friends. We do not think of loved ones as conscious beings per se, but to a literal mind like Musk's, that's what they are: our brains are biological computers made of hardware and software. He really does think in terms of consciousness, both individual and collective, and on how it might be enhanced. It sounds improbable, but when Musk went looking for something bigger than himself—long before he started his own family—he zoomed out to the level of the cosmos and the human race, and to a lesser degree perhaps than most people, on what happens in between. He was a socially awkward child who didn't know what a loving family looked like, and so it might have seemed a natural thing to do. Years later, when asked an open-ended question about love—romantic or otherwise—by podcast host Lex Fridman in 2021, Musk nervously made a few jokes and then duly replied by saying "foundationally, I love humanity."[12] This was his way of trying to break what he calls the generational transfer of trauma.[13]

Musk's chosen path matches up, too, with another Viennese psychologist: Viktor Frankl. Born in 1905, more than fifty years after Freud, he endured World War II in Nazi concentration camps, which he described in *Man's Search for Meaning*, a book Musk speaks highly of.[14] Frankl contended that humans are animated not by "a will to life," or "a will to power," but by a "will to meaning."[15] If suffering is unavoidable, then you must simply endure it; and even then, in spite of everything, life has meaning.[16] And, if your situation permits, you must go further and make sense of life by being on the front foot, facing outward to experience the world through its goodness, truth, beauty, nature, or by loving other people and creating works.[17] This led Frankl to say that "ultimately, man should not ask what the meaning of life is, but rather he must recognize that it is *he* who is asked. In a word, each man is questioned by life; and he can only answer to life by *answering for* his own life; to life he can only respond by being responsible."[18] It's the same change in mindset that President Kennedy invoked when he said, "Ask not what your country can do for you—ask what you can do for your country."[19]

By the time Musk was at university and turned the question of life's meaning back onto himself, he had already convinced himself that the universe was the answer and that we should seek to ask better questions, and so it was natural that he would demand of himself to explore ways to achieve this. This would direct him outward to the world, to other people, and to action.

Like Prometheus, though, Musk's mission was not to save souls, nor to save humanity, but to help humans save themselves. Aeschylus's tragedy was first performed almost 500 years before the birth of Jesus, and like Jesus, Prometheus came down to Earth and suffered for mankind. But unlike Jesus, who "set the world on fire" to purge humans of their sin, Prometheus gave humans fire to create, to be free of the darkness of their ignorance and of the night.[20] This is why Prometheus might appeal to someone like Musk—as he had to Byron, Nietzsche, Kafka, and Camus before him—not as a wayward god but as a heroic symbol of freedom. The tragedy of Prometheus tells us that life may not have purpose in and of itself, but we are endowed with the gift of consciousness, which gives life value. And if we take our destiny into our own hands, use reason, and create, then we have grounds to be hopeful.

Musk would turn to the science fiction writer Isaac Asimov to frame his role. In his 1942 short story "Runaround," Asimov drew up a list of laws to govern the conduct of robots so they would be helpful and not harmful to humans (i.e., protect humans, then obey humans, then protect self). He later realized there was an antecedent law that was missing, a law he called the Zeroth Law, which decreed that "a robot may not injure humanity, or through inaction, allow humanity to come to harm."[21] It was what Musk might have called a "cortical correction," which allowed robots to prioritize the interests of humanity as a whole over those of individual human beings when necessary. Intended for robots, it resonated with Musk since he thinks at the level of our species and feels that its future well-being is too often neglected.

Cycles of Civilization

From a young age, Musk wondered what the potential of human consciousness might look like, and his imagination was fed by both science and science fiction. The ambition he showed later in life can be traced directly back to this.

In 1977, Musk turned six and went to a movie theater for the first time to see *Star Wars*. He watched Luke Skywalker help the rebel army in its epic conflict against the evil Galactic Empire, and it made a lasting impression on him. The grandeur of George Lucas's space opera, in turn, owed a debt to the Foundation series of Isaac Asimov.[22]

Born in 1920, Asimov was a polymath who wrote more than 300 books, from science fiction to popular science to guides on Shakespeare, the Bible, and the ancient world. He said he never felt a sense of void nor any supernatural inclination—just a fear of planes, a love of enclosed spaces, and a passion for learning. He was immensely driven, though, and writing in his twenties, during World War II, he conceived of a history of a civilization set in the future that would become the Foundation series.

Musk read it when he was about ten years old, and he was riveted. Humans navigate the whole Milky Way, and all dimensions are huge. There are twenty-five million inhabited planets and a quintillion human beings (that's a billion billion). And the capital of the empire, Trantor, is a whole planet, covering seventy-five million square miles, with a population of forty billion people. The story is set in the distant future, twelve thousand years into the Galactic Era, although we're not told when that started. Asimov invites us to think of the entire universe as our home and to imagine a day when life has spread so far that people will have forgotten the planet that gave birth to humanity.

Musk was inspired not only by Asimov's space opera but by his concept of influencing the probability of outcomes through wise action. He mentions Asimov in the same breath as Adams in a 2018 tweet with the observation: "The future is a set of branching probability streams. Some actions by humanity have an extremely leveraged effect on shape & size of those streams."[23] This reflects the fact that the human experience of consciousness is shared not just with humans alive today but with all those who came before and all those who will come after us. And this, in turn, implies that the future potential of consciousness is linked to the health of civilization today—and, by extension, to our capacity for sound thinking.

Inspired by Edward Gibbon's *The History of the Decline and Fall of the Roman Empire*, the Foundation series was what Asimov called a history of the future.[24] It charts the parallel decline of the vast, decadent Galactic Empire and the rise of two Foundations guided by a dedication to knowledge over mysticism. It shows that the culture of civilizations matters.

The descent from empire into the Dark Ages could not be reversed until either a point of anarchy had been reached or opposing forces had built up sufficient strength. This was the role of the Foundations. They were created through the foresight of Hari Seldon, who reasoned that the Dark Ages could not be averted but that they could be shortened from thirty thousand years to one thousand years. Asimov describes the forces of decline over the course of four centuries. Like Gibbon's account of Rome, when the empire becomes too big, a chain reaction of events ensue: The periphery moves further from the center, communications falter, leaders become more isolated from the people, complacency sets in, fighting others turns to infighting, the powerful become corrupt, demagogues emerge, trade dwindles, resources are constrained, technology goes backward, populations decline, social fabric frays, mysticism spreads, there is "a damming of curiosity," and science breaks "into a million pieces."[25] This all happens in a self-reinforcing vortex.

The Foundations Asimov wrote of are living temples to knowledge, rooted in the scientific method and buttressed by common sense. They evoke the study of nature, reason, and Socratic debate, associated variously with ancient Athens, city-states, and the Greek islands. This spirit was lost in the Middle Ages as smart Aristotelean scholastics focused on the wrong questions in support of the Catholic Church, but it was rediscovered in the Arab libraries in Constantinople and Spain and would later pave the way for the Renaissance, the Reformation, and the Enlightenment.

Asimov also describes how the Foundations are steered through the different crises they are confronted with. Those who care about preserving knowledge espouse the importance of thinking from first principles and decry violence as "the last refuge of the incompetent."[26] Hari Seldon, for example, insists, "Scientific truth is beyond loyalty and disloyalty."[27] And Ankor Jael tells Hober Mallow, "Now any dogma, primarily based on faith and emotionalism is a dangerous weapon to use on others, since it is almost impossible to guarantee that the weapon will not be turned on the user."[28] This echoes the belief of Asimov's contemporary, Karl Popper, that irrationalism can lead only to violence, for if a problem cannot be resolved by reason or a more constructive passion, then the dispute must be resolved by force.[29] Furthermore, it is incompatible with any sort of humanism that might lead to freedom and democracy since it cannot acknowledge any form of equality before the law.

Asimov's epic tale would have a major impact on Musk. It signified what needs to happen for us to augment our collective consciousness. Musk sees himself as a technophile, but even more so, as a realist who does not want to engage in wishful thinking. And so, he says of the Foundation series, "The lesson I drew from that is you should try to take the set of actions that are likely to prolong civilization, minimize the probability of a dark age and reduce the length of a dark age if there is one."[30] Or as Asimov might have asked himself: If one was at the peak of the Roman empire when Marcus Aurelius was about to be succeeded by his mad son, Commodus, what actions could one have taken to limit the length of the Dark Ages in Europe and to hasten the arrival of the Enlightenment? "The lessons of history," Musk says, "would suggest that civilizations move in cycles. You can track that back quite far—the Babylonians, the Sumerians, followed by the Egyptians, the Romans, China. We're obviously in a very upward cycle right now and hopefully that remains the case. But it may not. There could be some series of events that cause that technology level to decline."[31]

Musk's curious mind would zoom out even further for a perspective beyond even Asimov and the Milky Way. He often speaks of the Great Filter theory, which offers a possible answer to the question posed by the celebrated physicist Enrico Fermi, "Where are the aliens?" If the universe is so old and so big, and human consciousness so recent, then why haven't we seen aliens? The Great Filter theory, originally proposed by the economist Robin Hanson, says that alien life would need to pass through several thresholds in order for it to visit us. Life on Earth has already passed many filters, including the existence of a planet it can inhabit, evolving from single to multicellular life with reproducing cells, moving from the oceans to the land, and developing a mammalian intelligence capable of tool-making. Modern civilization—which Musk dates to roughly 5,500 years ago, with the advent of writing—is the most recent filter, and it is incredibly recent, representing only one millionth of Earth's existence. It presents great opportunities for us to move forward, but it is also a treacherous time.

Asteroids and mega volcanoes aside, the next filters include getting off Earth and developing technologies safely so they do not cause our own extinction. For Musk, as for Asimov, we need to move beyond our tribalism so that we can continue to cooperate and use critical thinking in large numbers. And we need to continue to develop rockets and artificial consciousness safely and not in a form that we might turn against ourselves, like ICBMs with nuclear warheads and AI gone rogue. If we fail, we risk leaving the universe without any conscious life. We don't know that we are alone, but in the absence of evidence of aliens, we also don't know that we are not alone.

So for Musk, the way forward is clear. Civilizations do fail, and momentum is all-important. Musk believes that the rate of innovation either increases or decreases; it does not stay the same. There is no middle ground. You are either an "expansionist," who wants to grow the population, scientific knowledge, technology, and the economy, or you are an "extinctionist."[32] It might not appear to be the case now, but what happened to Asimov's Galactic Empire can happen to our human civilization if it stagnates and becomes decadent. This, after all, he observed was the fate of the three-thousand-year ancient Egyptian civilization that lost the general ability to build pyramids and to read hieroglyphics.[33]

Musk regrets that most people don't realize how good we have it today. It frustrates him that we take for granted the comforts and luxuries that modern civilization affords us due to the efforts of those who came before us. The only reason we idolize the past, he says, is because "happiness is reality minus expectations," and our expectations keep rising.[34] It's why he often says that you don't need to be an altruist to do things that are useful for society, because without civilization, life would be unimaginably worse.

This attitude also provides some context for why Musk became involved in politics later in life. When an erstwhile supporter criticized Musk for this in 2024, Musk retorted that he "labors under the illusion that western civilization is not at risk, when it clearly is. If America falls, nothing else matters, not stocks, not properties, nothing. All civilizations eventually fall, as history shows, but we want this one to last as long as possible."[35]

Musk then concurs with Karl Popper, who said that what matters is not to be optimistic about the future but to be optimistic about the present.[36] We do not know what will happen in the future, and being optimistic about it will do nothing to change the probability of a good outcome. Rather, we should have hope, and the best way to be hopeful is to be an activist for the future by being an optimist in the here and now. This means taking responsibility and trying to improve things, knowing that they might fail.

Making a Difference

It's one thing to feel questioned by life and to determine that you will act for humanity, but it's another thing to actually do it. For people like Musk, a big driver is the belief that if they themselves don't do it, then perhaps no one else will. This is the *inaction* part of the Zeroth Law: "A robot may not injure humanity, or through inaction, allow humanity to come to harm."[37] It's not that others cannot see the benefit of acting, but—consciously or unconsciously—they choose not to. Musk recognizes that this is the programming bug at work—we see reality as either better or worse than it is to some degree. A bad outcome can be ignored due to a blind hope that there is someone out there working on stopping it from happening. And a good outcome can be disregarded due to a pessimism that if it were possible, someone out there would already have made it happen.

Musk, though, turns on its head the idea that one person cannot make a difference to something as big as humanity. If you are curiously inquisitive, you will be drawn to the curiously strange, and the chance of making an impact can increase dramatically if you spend time on something that no one else is paying attention to. If something either good or bad seems improbable to most people, then that means it's at least possible and warrants attention. In the same vein, Google cofounder Larry Page said that you should actively try to work on what no one else is doing because you should aim to do things that would not happen but for you, invoking the economic concept of "additionality."[38] In other words, the best place to find your sweet spots may very well be where other people have blind spots.

Musk is motivated by the idea that he can make a difference by doing difficult things that others won't. He can become an instrument for advancing something bigger than himself, and this gives him a sense of agency. As Steve Jobs said, the curious person can live beyond those walls that give comfort to so many, once they realize one life-changing fact: "Everything around you that you call life was made up by people that were no smarter than you. And you can change it, you can influence it, you can build your own things that other people can use."[39]

The call to action is different for each person. Freud, for example, saw himself as studying the question of what humans reveal through their behavior about the purpose of their lives, and he sought happiness for his patients by applying his science to bring their neuroses into their conscious minds through therapy.[40] It may seem a long way from Musk, but what they share is a belief that it might be possible for the destiny of humanity to be nudged by individuals who shape their own destiny.

This explains some of the more colorful points of reference in Musk's mind. From the Foundation series, there are leaders like the mayor, Salvor Hardin, and the merchant prince, Hober Mallow, who stepped up in times of crisis. From *The Lord of the Rings*, there are Frodo and Sam, who left the Shire and ventured to the fire of Mount Doom. From revolutionary France, there is Napoleon Bonaparte—Musk read his *Last Will and Testament* as a child—who became first consul and then emperor. From the Marvel comics, there are the X-Men, who fought against Magneto. And from even *The Hitchhiker's Guide to the Galaxy,* there is the very English hero, Arthur Dent, whose "presence in the proceedings," Adams admitted, "make a difference to the way things turn out," even if he had no control over his life.[41]

Peter Thiel, one of Musk's cofounders at PayPal and an early backer of Mark Zuckerberg, went so far as to explain the high number of what he called "Asperger's-like" founders of the biggest tech companies thus: "If you're less sensitive to social cues, you're less likely to do the same things as everyone else around you. If you're interested in making things or programming computers, you'll be less afraid to pursue those activities single-mindedly and thereby become incredibly good at them. Then, when you apply your skills, you're a little less likely than others to give up your own convictions."[42] These founders thrive when they discover others who are ambitious to work with them. Think of Paul Allen and Bill Gates, Larry Page and Sergey Brin, Steve Wozniak and Steve Jobs. Elon Musk starting out with his brother, Kimbal, is no exception. Musk concurred with Thiel's point when he responded to a question on autism spectrum disorder in 2024, saying that a neurodivergent element can cause someone to be more curious about the nature of reality, more adherent to the truth, more willing to suffer criticism, and less desirous of simply fitting in.[43]

While autism spectrum disorder typically does not correlate with risk-taking or openness, it does correlate with seeing things differently and a capacity for critical thinking, which are key to success in technology. Above-average IQ is a big factor, but more important is the ability to look at things from different perspectives and in new contexts, which Alan Kay maintained was worth eighty points in IQ.[44] As Musk says, "Through most of our life we get through life by reasoning through analogy, which essentially means copying what other people do with slight variations. And you have to do that, otherwise mentally you wouldn't be able to get through the day. But *when you want to do something new you have to apply the physics approach*"[45] [my italics].

Some might think that people like Musk are odd for believing that they can affect the course of history, and they would have good reason to. Others may think that "long-termism" is an obsession with the future that puts humanity before humans, but they should not. For, in practice, most people will focus on the here and now and what is probable, because it is always easier to do so. The scientific method is a reminder, though, that knowledge is contingent, and it only takes one person to falsify a theory. For Musk, therefore, if you see the world differently than most people, and you think they are wrong, you shouldn't assume that they must be right and you must be wrong. Go back to first principles and check what you think. You could call it *thoughtful wishing* as opposed to *wishful thinking*.

In fact, for people like Musk, believing that you are an independent thinker who is in the minority can itself make you more defiant and rebellious because you fear the loss of freedom itself. Psychologists call this being *reactant*. The only way to not be passively resigned to consensus thinking is to actively challenge it. In Musk's case, he also learned as a teenager—once he had had a growth spurt and some basic martial arts instruction—that offense can often be the best form of defense and that if you punch a bully in the nose, they tend to pick on someone else next time. For the rest of his life, he would consciously choose to fight back rather than flee or freeze and thereby unconsciously submit to his fears.[46]

Believing, like Musk, that you might be able to change the world does require quite a large measure of ego for acting alone, and going against received wisdom requires a lot of self-belief. Asimov put it well when he wrote, "A person willing to fly in the face of reason, authority, and common sense must be a person of considerable self-assurance."[47] That's why, when asked about Musk, Berkshire Hathaway cofounder Charlie

Munger said, "Never underestimate the man who overestimates himself. I think Elon Musk is peculiar and he may overestimate himself, but he may not be wrong all the time."[48]

This was supremely demonstrated by the responsibilities Musk assumed in his nascent companies. This self-belief is one of his defining characteristics, especially in technical matters. When he failed to recruit a head of design and engineering on founding SpaceX, for example, he took on the role himself despite having no formal training, and when he judged that the early executive leadership at Tesla was not up to the job, he stepped in to run things, even though SpaceX was all-consuming.

Ego may be required to take on a difficult challenge, but it is often tempered by the hard-won knowledge that a sufficiently difficult challenge will mean a lot of failure. This is where Musk's cheery fatalism comes into play: It may seem highly risky and unlikely to work, but if it's important enough, then it's still worth a try. Musk makes the calculation that the low probability of succeeding is more than offset by the benefit achieved on the upside or the harm reduced on the downside if it does work out. This was Musk's attitude when he started both Tesla and SpaceX, putting the odds of each succeeding at no more than 10 percent.

. . .

The cutting edge of technology is defined by novelty, which means—by definition—no one can be experienced in it. This is where the magic occurs, and no one can reliably predict what will happen next. So, when everyone else is blind, having just one eye can make you a king. History tells us which areas of technology Musk would spend his life working on. What is significant is that they were very deliberately chosen. In each case, he chose to work on the internet, sustainable energy, and making life multi-planetary because he saw these areas as being at the vanguard of innovation, offering both excitement and opportunities to make a sizable impact on the world in his lifetime.

What is so unusual is that Musk would follow his curiosity single-mindedly as an engineer in not just one, but all three areas. But the overriding goal was the same: to expand the scope and scale of consciousness so that humans may flourish and discover the universe and its mysteries. And because he remained curious, he would add new missions like AI to the list further down the road, as well as the meta concern of maintaining what he regarded as a culture of curiosity to keep civilization in good health.

Boiling It Down: Challenge yourself by loving humanity

Most people don't think deeply about consciousness, be it our own or other people's. There is simply no need to, especially when young. Being alive and being conscious can be taken to mean the same thing, and so we think in terms of living humans and how we can help them, starting with ourselves and people like us. Musk, however, is different. He thinks about how he interacts with reality, his capacity to test and learn, and how this might operate at the level of humanity. His purpose in life can be summarized as follows:

1. The more consciousness we have and the smarter it is, the better the chance we have to ask the questions that might make sense of the universe.
2. Asking ourselves how we are going to make the future less uncertain is the best way to stop searching for certainty in the universe.
3. Civilization has long been the engine of critical thinking. To sustain this, we must keep innovating and testing or risk sliding back into irrational thinking.

4. Life is short, so we must be deliberate if we want to maximize the chances of greater consciousness. It only takes one individual to show that something is not impossible, so focus on the thing that you believe most people are wrong about.

PART II

The Missionary

"The best way to predict the future is to invent it."

—Alan Kay

Part II is about how Musk applies his religion. The following figure comprises three ways that Musk believes he can reduce uncertainty, increase consciousness, and thereby find meaning. Consciousness can only be augmented by creating, and markets can help creators do this at scale. The ultimate challenge for expanding consciousness will be to explore the universe beyond Earth.

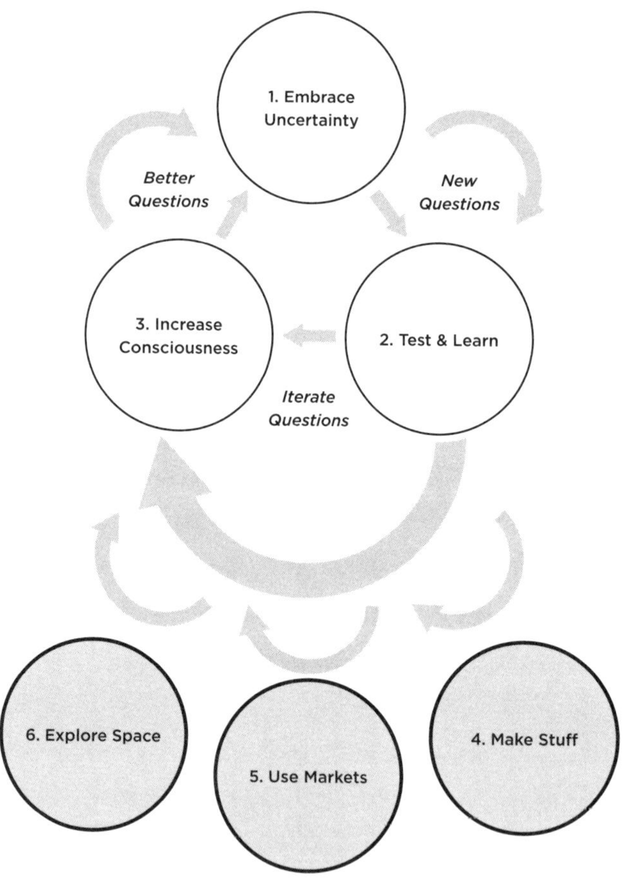

FOUR

Make Stuff

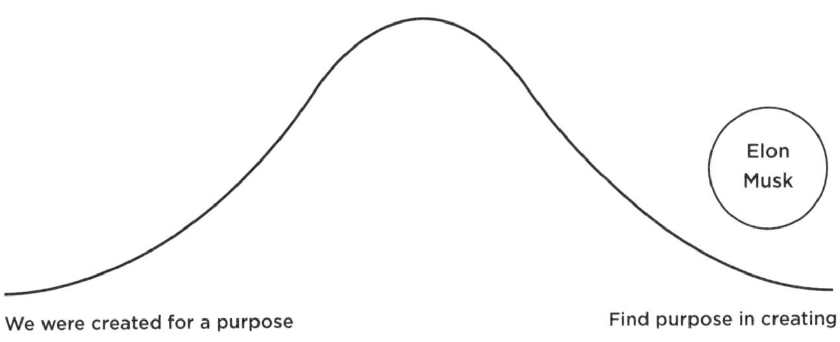

"If you don't make stuff, there's no stuff," Musk said in an interview with podcast host Joe Rogan. He was venting his frustration about those who take for granted that new things will just come along. Such people, he said, are detached from reality as they have "this absurd view that the economy is some magic horn of plenty, like it just makes stuff."[1]

Musk knew from his firsthand, brutal experience of building services and products for others that everything we use exists because some group of people came together to create it. It's implicit in Jobs's realization that "everything around you that you call life was made up by people no smarter than you."[2] Except that Musk wouldn't use that kind of false modesty. "Smart is as smart does" for Musk.[3]

Using that metric, Musk is probably one of the smartest people alive, at least in the field of engineering. His curiosity led him in his twenties to his calling to increase the scope and scale of consciousness, and thanks to the same curiosity—combined with large doses of ambition and determination—he succeeded in his aim by becoming a prolific creator.

In the beginning, Musk used to create for the sheer curiosity of discovering new things. He had a childhood that you might call "free range," and like so many original minds, he was largely self-taught. He read a lot, but he wasn't to be found only in the library. His father was an electrical engineer, and when left alone under the care of the housekeeper, Musk had plenty of opportunity to rummage through the garage and take things apart. Physics and chemistry did not exist for him only in books. He was the type of boy who was curious about how a light switch worked and came to understand the wiring of the whole house. He would take the chlorine used to clean the swimming pool and mix it with the brake fluid for his father's car to create a fireball, and he would assemble makeshift rockets using charcoal, potassium nitrate as an oxidant, and sulfur as a stabilizer.[4] While most of his peers were playing rugby and dating, he was nurturing a love of technology.

Fortunately for Musk, the early 1980s were also the years when personal computers came into the home. He saved up and, with Errol's help, bought a Commodore, which was one of the reasons, Maye says, he chose to live with his father. He recalls that "the second I saw a computer, you couldn't drag me away from it! I immediately pulled two all-nighters teaching myself to program. No pushing is required when kids love something."[5] The computer only had five kilobytes of memory, but that was enough. The child who loved to play early arcade games started to write his own. Coding was the perfect fit for his highly logical mind.

Next came the ambition. When most of us take a job, we sell our time to an employer and compress our play into pastimes to pass the time on the weekend. Not Musk. He did consider a career in video games. While at university, he interned at a start-up in Palo Alto, where he wrote code for a computer to read video from a disk while running a game at the same time. In a case of fate loving irony, the name of that video game company was Rocket Science Games. As a keen lifelong gamer, Musk had huge regard for the entertainment value of video games, but he was faced with a pivotal question. He could either be the kind of person who made games with spaceships or be the kind who built the real thing. The gamer in him might have said to himself, *Do I want to be a player maximizing my agency or a non-player character (NPC), controlled by the computer, operating in the background? Furthermore, do I want to be playing intensely, head-to-head against players (PvP) or in a more pedestrian way, playing against the environment (PvE)?* Musk was all PvP.

Musk very nearly went to work in the field of science. While working nights at Rocket Science Games, by day he was interning at Pinnacle Research Institute, working on an alternative energy storage system to batteries, and he was set to study this as a postgraduate at Stanford University. The research was important work, but Musk realized that it neither suited him temperamentally nor allowed him to maximize what he had to offer.

Musk's ambition would demand that he go into engineering and work incredibly hard at it. In the realm of the internet, he was a one-eyed king, and he had the gumption to work for himself, teaming up with his brother, Kimbal, to start Zip2. The company connected customers with stores and restaurants in their zip code and then gave them the directions to zip there. The Musks managed to buy a local business directory, gained access to mapping software, and set about putting the directory online, linking it to the maps and making them navigable for consumers.

This proved to be a capability that was attractive to media companies, and the Musks would end up selling the company to Compaq. He was developing a mastery of his craft.

In 1999, Musk set up X.com, which had the goal of bringing banking online for consumers. Along the way, he discovered there was a lot of value in being able to make payments digitally by email if you could authenticate bank accounts, especially for customers in e-commerce. After merging X.com with Confinity to create PayPal and selling it to eBay, Musk could have called it a day. But each time, he raised his level of ambition. "The idea of lying on a beach as my main thing sounds like the worst," he has said. "I would go bonkers. I would have to be on serious drugs . . . I'd be super-duper bored. I like high intensity."[6]

Instead, his religious drive really kicked in, and he pursued it with a zeal that was fanatical. The renowned start-up investor and essayist Paul Graham singled out *determination* as the most important ingredient to be a successful founder, and he said it "consists of willfulness balanced with discipline, aimed by ambition."[7] Graham notes that the love of what you're doing—when it's like play—is very important for creating, but at some point, working hard to make products for other people requires more than the intrinsic enjoyment of making things—namely determination. Herein lies the secret to Musk's formidable powers of creativity.

Musk had a lot of talent and ambition and was buoyed by the success of Zip2 and X.com, but a lot of people with those attributes would then have chosen the beach. Along with his curiosity, determination is the trait that makes Musk stand out, precisely because of the dynamic between willfulness and discipline. Musk's determination might be seen as the outward turning of that inner aggression. This fits neatly with Graham's belief that willfulness is a mixture of stubbornness and energy. The act of creating, in turn, demands a discipline from Musk that harnesses his energy and channels his defiance in a positive way.

Musk himself explained candidly to Andrew Ross Sorkin, "Even in happy moments when a kid, it just feels like there's a rage of forces in my mind constantly . . . now this productively manifests itself in technology and building things for the most part."[8] So great is his willfulness that it requires a level of discipline that is extraordinary. Discipline does not always correlate with openness and curiosity, but with Musk, it does. He has his religion, and so there is only one mode and that mode is hardcore. "Working hard to make useful products & services for your fellow humans," he wrote on X, "is deeply morally good."[9]

What's more, Musk learned that making stuff is incredibly satisfying. He would demonstrate, *par excellence,* that when you attach heartfelt meaning to the process of creating, you can become a great creator, and the act of creating itself can provide an unmatched sense of meaning. Musk may not have thought in terms of increasing consciousness when he started Zip2, but by the time he started SpaceX and Tesla, he certainly did.

Giving Birth

Musk uses a definition of *engineering* borrowed from Theodore von Kármán, the man whose name is used for the line that marks the end of Earth's atmosphere and the beginning of space: "Science is discovering the essential truths about what exists in the Universe, engineering is about creating things that never existed."[10] Musk also likes to make statements like, "The first step is to establish that something is possible; then probability will occur."[11]

This notion of something out of nothing is captured by Peter Thiel in his book *Zero to One*, which describes the essential characteristics of great start-ups. He says that copying others is going from 1 to *n*. Even science starts at 2, with things that are experimentally repeatable.

Creating in the form of technology, however, goes from "zero to one." It is a singular act that happens only once. And from there it can be 10x or 100x better than what already exists, to the extent there is less competition.[12] As if to underscore the existential nature of creating, it turns out that Thiel is quite theological in his view. While he doesn't talk about it much, Thiel is a Lutheran who believes that God created humans in his likeness and that the resurrection of Jesus gives hope to humans; through our faith, we may overcome our sinful nature, stop desiring what others have, and live in peace.[13]

Musk, too, is religious about creativity but only in the rebellious Promethean sense that relates to human destiny. Unlike most people of faith, he does not find meaning in the fact that there is a higher intelligence that designed the universe for humans, placing us at its center. Douglas Adams felt that it became natural for most humans to think this way once they started to create tools that served a function. We then created God in our own image as someone who designed for us this world, tailor-made for our needs.[14] For Adams and Musk, however, the opposite is true: meaning is to be found in using our intelligence to make tools that help us better make sense of our universe.

Adams even said, in 2000, that creative excitement had gravitated from the insurgent, intelligent wit of Monty Python and 1960s rock music "to science and technology: new ways of seeing things, new understandings of the universe, continual new revelations about how life works, how we think, how we perceive, how we communicate."[15] Early motorists used to "start up" their car engines by igniting the fuel, and now young people with a creative spark were launching "start-ups," building something from nothing in their parents' garages.

Musk would agree with Adams that we understand life, the universe, and ourselves by creating, be it through art or through science and engineering. We learn not by receiving knowledge passively but by solving problems in a way that demands creativity. Just as we learn from understanding how things came into being, we learn by the actual process of making. Adams gave the examples of the heart, which we better understood once we invented the hydraulic pump, and the process of evolution, which we better understood once we invented the computer.[16]

For Musk, the best example may be AI. He understood that "much of AI is about compressing reality to a small vector space," because he had made video games, and this process was "like a video game in reverse . . . Physics formulas are the rendering rules."[17] As Musk spent more time making AI, he increasingly thought of humans as using biological neural networks. When thinking about self-driving for Tesla, for example, he thought of the roads as having been designed for biological neural nets and eyes, and this made him focus on the use of silicon neural networks and cameras—but not LiDAR technology—for Tesla's self-driving AI.[18] In turn, this reinforced his conception that "humans are basically a big data stream of photons in that produce a tiny data stream of motor commands out."[19] And sure enough, in 2025, xAI would start making video games.

If curiosity is what leads the inquisitive person to create, then creating helps us see how the three meanings of *curious* are linked. First, whether inquisitive people are trying to fix a glitch in their world model or just playing, they encounter novel situations that prompt them to ask new questions, and this creates the possibility for answers that are original.

Second, as Musk emphasizes, the curious person pays careful attention to tiny details, and this requires—just as Musk says of fear—bringing the subconscious into the conscious. We notice when things appear flawed, but it takes a lot of mental effort to sit with the problem and study what those flaws are.[20] Interestingly, this is an attribute highlighted by Charles Darwin. He possessed a love of nature and science, mixed with insatiable curiosity and a healthy amount of ambition, but he described his abilities as moderate with a notable exception: "I think that I am superior to the common run of men in noticing things which easily escape attention, and in observing them carefully."[21]

When making things, Musk goes on, we tend to fall back on methods, materials, and tools that are familiar because that's the easiest thing to do. What we should do, however, is go back to first principles, imagine what the near-to-perfect product is, and then work backward, selecting the methods, materials, and tools necessary to get the atoms into that shape.[22] It is when you are in those tiny details trying to solve problems that you are forced to come up with new solutions.

Third, when you create products that may never have been seen before, they often have a strange quality that causes people to marvel and wonder how they were made. One of Musk's companies, Neuralink, for example, made a brain–computer interface that allowed a paralyzed man, Noland Arbaugh, to play a video game just by thinking. That was in 2024, and it seemed like magic.

Sometimes curiosity is characterized as *intuitive* rather than *rational*, but this is a false dichotomy. When you are deciding what to test and learn, you do not know the answer beforehand, and so you have to go with what you feel. But this does not mean the process is irrational or uncritical; rather, gut feeling is informed by experience. Musk believes that physics can be counterintuitive, but he practices critical thinking so much that he has developed an uncommon sense for it that seems almost intuitive, at least compared to other people. This is also why he says you must like or preferably love what you are doing because you will still be thinking about it when you are not working and even when not conscious of doing so.[23]

While not all creativity is scientific, when curious people like Musk apply the scientific method, they start to create. They are not simply making empirical observations. They have to make conjectures that they can test in the real world. As Darwin wrote of himself, he had "a fair share of invention" and could not resist forming hypotheses on every subject, albeit he willingly discarded them "as soon as facts are shown to be opposed."[24] Karl Popper went further, writing, "Experience is creative. It is the result of free, bold and creative interpretations, controlled by severe criticism and severe tests."[25] Science is itself the knowledge of the universe that humans create. Yes, we discover it, but as Popper says, "Discovery is a creative art."[26] Or, as Adams wrote, "It's impossible to divorce pure science from technology: they feed and stimulate each other."[27] This, for Musk, is the means by which we can get closer to the questions that approximate to the meaning of life.

Musk knew he was, by nature, a technologist and not a scientist. Per the original Greek meaning of technology, which encompasses everything from engineering to art, medicine, and music, he was a skilled craftsman who applied his knowledge through his work. His contribution would be to use his physics framework to engineer the tools that would, in turn, advance scientific knowledge. And he believed that the line between the two was blurred anyway, noting, "Engineers invent new technologies. Along the way, they may come up with new reality compression formulas, like Nikola Tesla."[28]

. . .

If making babies is the most natural way to augment consciousness, one might also say that technology is a force of human nature. Just like doctors make people healthy and musicians make music, engineers make things that have a life of their own and can go on to replicate themselves. That's how Musk thinks about it. There is a continuum. And it's not just about the scale of consciousness. Just as children increase the scope of their consciousness by being curious, testing their environment, and learning, technology can increase the aggregate scope of consciousness across generations by fueling cultural development and an ever-growing body of knowledge.

Musk certainly thinks of civilization in terms of both demographics and technology. Accordingly, he tells us, “Kids are the best. I’m doing my best to encourage more people to become parents and ideally have three or more kids, so humanity can grow. The population collapse in most countries is a tragedy. Sales of adult diapers should never exceed sales of baby diapers!”[29] He also chides people whom he thinks are smart for not having kids, including Richard Dawkins, saying, “Ironically, for someone who knows so much about evolution, Dawkins only has one child. That is a >50% generational suicide rate.”[30]

Musk’s perspective is similar to that of Friedrich Hayek, the dry economist. Hayek believed that the “purpose” of human beings is to reproduce. “Life exists,” he wrote, “only so long as it provides for its own continuance.”[31] And the optimal way to achieve such human flourishing is by growing the economy, which in turn requires that people actually “make stuff.”

And Musk doesn’t stop there. He hates anti-technology “eco-warriors” who say we should have fewer children and return to nature. He elaborated, in 2022, when he announced on X: “Realized what I have in common with environmentalists, but also why they’re so annoyingly wrong: They are conservationists of what is, whereas they should be conservationists of our potential over time, our cosmic endowment.”[32] And he rebuked the much-loved primatologist Jane Goodall, saying, “She is so wrong. Arguing in favor [of] reducing humanity is arguing for genocide. The unborn have no voice.”[33]

Musk, in turn, invokes the legend of Prometheus and says of his creations: “SpaceX, Tesla, Neuralink, Boring Company are philanthropy. If you say philanthropy is love of humanity, they are philanthropy.”[34] As if to prove the point, Musk has sometimes spoken about Tesla and

SpaceX as though he were their parent. He said, for example, "When you put your blood, sweat, and tears into creating something, building something, it's like a child."[35] In due course, he would speak in the same way about building AI.

Expanding Scope and Scale

When Musk left university in 1995, there was a lot of hype about the internet, but he could sense that its full potential was still not recognized by most people. Musk was seventeen years of age when Tim Berners-Lee invented the World Wide Web, and by the time he graduated, the Web was becoming accessible through browsers, portals, and search engines to anyone with a computer, a modem, and a landline. This meant that the internet for Musk fell under Adams's Rule 2 of technology (invented between fifteen and thirty-five years of age), and he could be one of the pioneers.

Musk was not alone in seeing this, but he had a predictably unusual perspective on it. "It wasn't like, 'Oh, I want to make a bunch of money,'" Musk recalls, but the realization that "with the internet, anyone who had a connection anywhere in the world would have access to all the world's information, just like a nervous system. So humanity was effectively becoming a super-organism and qualitatively different than what it had been before. And so I wanted to be a part of that."[36] Collective consciousness could be expanded in the digital realm and be made accessible to all, and helping build this out would be exciting.

Musk, therefore, is doubly unusual in the way he derives intrinsic meaning both from increasing consciousness and from the act of doing so by creating. It's not something you would remark about, say, Bill Gates or Mark Zuckerberg. But you might say this about Steve Jobs. Neither Musk nor Jobs believed in the intelligent design of the universe, but in different ways, they fervently believed that consciousness was special and that computers might somehow reveal the potential for human consciousness.

When you look more deeply, the similarities between Musk and Jobs help us make sense of Musk as a creator. Walter Isaacson wrote biographies on both Musk and Jobs and described them each as having "demons."[37] In Jobs's case, he struggled with the fact that he had been given up for adoption by his biological parents. Isaacson said that, throughout Jobs's life, he had a "compulsive search for self-awareness" and for calm, which always eluded him.[38] Both he and Musk felt the ephemerality and chaos of existence. This is true of a lot of people, but what distinguishes Musk and Jobs from so many others who feel that way is how they managed to respond in a constructive fashion. Instead of embracing irrationalism, they rebelled against the human condition by trying to put a dent in the universe. They broke those rules that stood in the way of their creativity.

Jobs shared with Musk the goal of using his consciousness to grow the consciousness of us all by assigning a special role to creating. He thought that "one of the things that really separates us from the high primates is that we're tool builders . . . what a computer is to me is it's the most remarkable tool that we've ever come up with and it's the equivalent of a bicycle for our minds."[39] The computer can amplify our talents far beyond our inherent abilities, and it can free us from drudgery to do much more creative work. Musk would agree for both computers and AI, although in the case of the latter, it might also be true to say that our minds are the bicycle and the AI is riding us.

The two men also share the same obsessive drive to change the world.[40] They knew they were different from most people and embraced it. Jobs celebrated this idea in Apple's classic 1997 "Think Different" advertising campaign, which proclaimed that there is a certain kind of genius who can push forward the human race because they "are crazy enough to think they can change the world." He imagined himself in the company of creative "geniuses," from Bob Dylan and John Lennon to Albert Einstein and Mahatma Gandhi to Ted Turner and Richard Branson. Musk has his own heroes, but the sentiment is the same.

Undaunted by the difficulty of the challenge, they, too, share a single-minded intensity in the way they try to bend reality to their visions. For Musk and Jobs, this meant starting companies that were an extension of themselves. Paul Graham, for example, recognized this similarity in 2015 when he wrote of Tesla that "there is obviously a Jobs-like force behind the product."[41] They did so even if that meant not caring about being liked, to the extent that they were also both ousted from the companies they founded (PayPal in the case of Musk). And yet they were able to attract brilliant people to work with them and achieve things together that many thought scarcely possible.

The way that each of them went about their creating was very different, though. For Jobs, the act of creating was a spiritual matter. He believed that "design is the fundamental soul of a man-made creation that ends up expressing itself in successive outer layers."[42] Converting ideas into products gave form to a spiritual essence, and it could elevate other humans. Like Musk, Jobs went back to first principles to clear his head of received wisdom, but he had a very different take. He was not devout, but he practiced Buddhism throughout his life, and he was convinced of the transcendent nature of consciousness.[43] His idea of thinking from first principles was more to adopt a "beginner's mind" and to listen to that childlike voice within.

Musk, on the other hand, is religious about identifying key axioms in an analytical way and reasoning up from them. He is obsessed with Douglas Adams, science fiction, the scientific method, and space travel, in which Jobs had minimal interest. Jobs, by contrast, emphasized intuition, believing it to be innate but lost in the West. He sought to combine the imagination and vision that come from intuition with the best of Western critical thinking. He wanted to help others be like him, to appreciate simplicity and beauty, and to add to the stream of consciousness. Taste and originality were his truths, and he saw himself as a guru. He was a hippy, not a nerd.[44]

With all that said, Jobs was at pains to emphasize the importance of effort. Similar to Musk, Jobs was not into metaphysical navel-gazing. He was like Schopenhauer but without the pessimism, downplaying the more ego-less aspects of Eastern religions. And he made a nod to Thomas Edison's adage that "genius is 1 percent inspiration, 99 percent perspiration," when he alluded to "the disease of thinking that a really great idea is 90 percent of the work."[45] Rather, the idea is just the beginning, and it takes a lot of craftsmanship to get to a great product, "keeping 5,000 things in your brain" and organizing them to get what you want. "It's that process," he said, "that is the magic."[46]

Musk would go even further than Jobs, saying that genius is more like 99.9 percent perspiration when you include manufacturing, and still more when you can do so and be cash positive.[47] Musk, too, has strong views on simplicity of design and ease of customer experience, but he has had to worry a lot more about costs and, therefore, the engineering that happens inside the box. Musk likes to be on the factory floor and insists that the designers be there too to help drive innovation. That's why he contends that he knows more about manufacturing than anyone alive and why, for example, after visiting SpaceX in 2012, Richard Dawkins described him as "the new Steve Jobs PLUS Steve Wozniak."[48]

Their routes were different, but Musk and Jobs ended up at the same place, creating cultures in their organizations—for both ran more than one business—that focused solely on building products that were not just good, or great, but insanely great in order to uplift humanity. Love them or hate them, you could not ignore them.

Maker as Identity

Musk's first wife, Justine, gave a TEDx talk in 2017 in which she spoke of visionary people, using Musk as one of her main examples.[49] She said that they may be called "geek or outsider, socially awkward, weird, a little different, odd one out," but they stay true to the way they see the world and become the living embodiment of what they do. She described Musk's mentality as that of someone who belongs to a tribe of engineers, even though he seems to be a businessman.

This notion of self-identity as an engineer is key to understanding Musk. From the beginning of his career, he would define himself as an engineer, as someone who made things. This reinforces both his capacity to work hard and the meaning he derives from it. At Zip2, for example, Musk was happy to be the CTO and chairman and to bring in a more experienced CEO, until, of course, he thought the new CEO and then his successor didn't follow his desired product road map for the company.

This dynamic continued throughout Musk's career. Again at X.com, Musk and his investors recruited a more experienced CEO, Bill Harris, while he focused on product. After the merger with Confinity, Musk did step in to replace Harris, but he continued focusing on product until he was pushed out of the company. In 2021, Musk again showed his contempt for titles and the chain-of-command approach to creativity by bestowing on himself the title of Technoking of Tesla. And after he acquired Twitter, in May 2023, he announced the appointment of new CEO Linda Yaccarino to run commercial and advertising, so he could transition to executive chairman and be free to concentrate as CTO on product, software, and servers, as well as being "Chief Twit." He never changed his view that "signal is engineering, management is noise."[50]

Musk's extreme approach to making things is captured by business author Jim Collins in his classic book *Good to Great.* The book is about companies and what it takes to survive and outperform over the long term, but some of the qualities map onto Musk himself.[51] Three characteristics, in particular, are worth examining more closely.

First is what Collins calls the "hedgehog," which is the need for a mission that is big and simple. It is a Greek allegory that was revived by the British philosopher Isaiah Berlin.[52] The hedgehog knows one big thing—it can roll into a ball of sharp spikes—as opposed to the fox, who knows many things but none as big as the hedgehog's. The hedgehog has both clarity and inflexibility of thought. Musk may not have agreed with Nietzsche's "why" of life, but he would agree with his dictum that "if we possess our *why* of life we can put up with almost any *how*."[53] And his big and simple why was to understand the nature of reality better by increasing the scope and scale of consciousness. This manifested itself through the internet, sustainable energy, a self-sustaining Mars base, and AI, but the mission was one and the same.

Second, there needs to be determination to persevere for any sufficiently ambitious goal. Collins says, "Confront the most brutal facts of your current reality, whatever they might be," and "retain faith that you will prevail in the end, regardless of the difficulties."[54] This means being neither an overly optimistic person who thinks reality is better than it is (things will turn out well when they don't) nor an overly pessimistic person who thinks reality is worse than it is (there is no hope). Collins gives credit for this to the stoic message of Admiral Stockdale, who was the highest-ranking naval officer to be imprisoned and tortured in the "Hanoi Hilton" during the Vietnam War. His defiant realism is similar to the "tragic optimism" shown by Viktor Frankl. Both call for a commitment to truth-seeking and asking questions.

What this means in practice is that when you have little control, you have to focus on what is within your control. And then you must be honest with yourself and adapt to your situation. As Musk says, "Start somewhere and then really be prepared to question your assumptions, fix what you did wrong, and adapt to reality."[55] There is no pass or fail, just testing and learning and changing course, per the scientific method. And in the meantime, you need a lot of resilience. Musk knew this all too well, often quoting his friend Bill Lee, who says that for the first few years of a start-up, you have to just "stare into the abyss and eat glass."[56]

Third, Collins speaks of "a consistent system with clear constraints," combined with "freedom and responsibility within the framework of that system."[57] The two go together. Poets, painters, and philosophers across the ages have said that freedom needs constraints. They are necessary inputs for creative output, and it is no different for Musk and his engineering. It comes back to curiosity and determination. You have no choice but to apply yourself to the task at hand, having faith in the process, taking risks, and constantly adapting, day after day. Collins uses the analogy of the flywheel. Potters push the wheel with their feet, and it builds momentum and stores the energy as it spins so that they can mold their ceramics as they turn steadily in their hands. With consistent effort, the creators are able to give form to action, and the act of creating forces them to stay in the present.

A creator like Musk wants to be always turning the wheel, and the activity of creating becomes something by which he defines himself. Musk did not choose a life of luxury, distraction, and wondering what restaurant he was going to eat in next. He chose instead to learn to endure, more or less, nonstop, short-term pain if he believed it was meaningful and contributed to outsized long-term gains. And it certainly took its toll, for stress becomes chronic when it persists for too long.

There is obviously good reason why self-help books for companies are not generally applied to human beings. Justine Musk also noted in her talk that it is often painful to be a visionary like Musk because what they do is "bring light to the dark and they show us the universe."[58] Musk's religion of curiosity may have been his salvation, but it could at times be overwhelming. Since he pushed himself to the limit, it was inevitable that he would sometimes fall off the edge. Musk himself says, "I don't think you'd necessarily want to be me . . . I don't think people would like it that much . . . it's very hard to turn it off," adding, "It's like a never-ending explosion."[59]

Musk gave an interview, for example, in June 2008, in which he explicitly said that he wanted to throttle back his intensity within no more than a year, as his eldest twins had turned four.[60] It was not meant to be, however. Over the coming months, he separated from their mother, Justine; watched SpaceX's third rocket blow up; and stepped in to become the CEO of Tesla. He was pushing himself relentlessly, especially when Tesla was in what he described to Walter Isaacson as "survival-or-die mode," which lasted from 2007 to 2020.[61]

Musk has described how his work—always shifting between different companies—has fried his mind and left him with emotional scars. In particular, he has spoken of coming close to a nervous breakdown both in 2008 when Tesla and SpaceX faced bankruptcy and again ten years later. It was in that context in 2017, that he responded to a tweet asking whether he was bipolar by saying, "Maybe not medically tho. Dunno. Bad feelings correlate to bad events, so maybe real problem is getting carried away in what I sign up for. . . If you buy a ticket to hell, it isn't fair to blame hell . . ."[62]

Making stuff, it turns out, is not a panacea—not when you are maniacal about it as Musk is. Naturally, his personal life suffered greatly as a result. He was often nomadic, spending half the week in the Bay Area, for example, sleeping at friends' houses or in hotels; he did that for a full fifteen years. And, years later, he described SpaceX's facilities in South Texas as being "a monastery for technology."[63] It is not surprising, therefore, that Justine Musk noted that visionaries can make lousy husbands who are impossible to live with.[64] Musk did remarry—to English actress Talulah Riley—but they, too, ended up divorcing not once but twice, albeit on amicable terms.

Musk's work did not stop him from having a family life—far from it—but marital harmony was too much to ask for, since Musk was betrothed to making stuff. For he wasn't just curious but obsessively so. And as Samuel Johnson wrote, when curiosity is your "first passion and the last," it can only be satisfied "by more rapid flights, and bolder excursions."[65]

Boiling It Down: Find purpose in creating

Most people find meaning in life from the joy of becoming parents and do not feel a great need to create beyond that. Musk has done the former to the extreme, but he has also had a strong need to do the latter. He doesn't believe we have a divine "maker," but he has been able to assign meaning to the things he has made. His approach to creativity can be summarized as follows:

1. If we want to have the best chance of making a wide impact, we have to create something new and be very determined about it.
2. Creating can provide an intrinsic sense of meaning—we may struggle with the lack of intelligent design in the universe, but we can find purpose using our intelligence to design and build products with a life of their own.

3. Because of 1 and 2, there is a double meaning in creating when our creativity is aligned with the mission to increase consciousness in a way that is self-reinforcing.
4. Being a creator—an artist, an engineer, a founder—can become an identity. This can provide structure, assigning value to doing hard things, but it can also be quite overwhelming.

FIVE

Use Markets

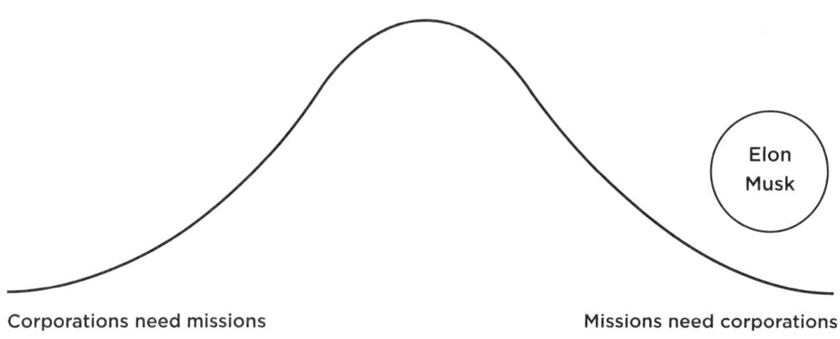

"Elon starts with a mission and later finds a way to backfill in order to make it work financially. That's what makes him a force of nature."[1] So said Reid Hoffman, PayPal alumnus and LinkedIn founder, before he and Musk fell out. Musk thereby somewhat turns Jim Collins's hedgehog concept on its head. Collins argued that for-profit companies can go from "good to great" if they have an ambitious sense of mission, as this brings focus and purpose. For Musk, the process works in reverse: Clear ambitious missions benefit from for-profit companies. You start with what he calls the "holy grail"—the long-term potential, which inspires everyone—and then you earn your keep and make money so that you can fund development.[2] Earning your keep, it turns out, becomes very important as it enables for-profit companies to use markets to become vehicles for risk-taking creativity in a way that nonprofit organizations cannot.

Warren Buffett, chairman and CEO of Berkshire Hathaway, identified Musk's novel approach in 2023, remarking that "he dreams about things, and his dreams have got a foundation . . . It is a dedication to solving the impossible and, every now and then, they will do it."[3] Buffett was also honest enough to admit that it required a fanaticism that he did not possess.

This is an unusual way to speak about running a company, but so is Musk's attitude to markets. The story of SpaceX will be told in Chapter 6, so we will focus here on Tesla as a prime example of how Musk marries technology and business to achieve his missions.

Musk thinks of civilization in terms of the fundamental ratios of silicon to biological compute and of energy consumed/produced per person.[4] In that context, the internal combustion engine struck him as a curious thing. We drive around in cars that carry fuel in a tank and burn it to create the pressure to turn over the engine. The fuel comes from dead organisms that lived millions of years ago and were sustained by energy radiated from our sun, millions of miles away. We have been extracting these hydrocarbons from the ground since the Industrial Revolution, and we have used them to develop mass transportation, capital goods, and computers, and yet at the turn of the twenty-first century, we're still pouring gasoline.[5]

Energy has long been a prominent theme in science fiction. Asimov, for example, saw that nuclear power was the big revolutionary development of the 1940s, and this technology became a winning factor for the Foundation compared to neighboring barbaric planets that used "chemical power," namely coal and oil. But Musk's question was simpler. Why don't we capture solar energy directly, store it in batteries, and release it as electricity to power our vehicles? Furthermore, oil is nonrenewable and will run out at some point; it's just a matter of time. Not to mention the untold harm that carbon emissions may cause over time if not reversed. This is not good for human consciousness.

Musk wasn't alone in thinking about electric vehicles (EVs). Companies like General Motors, with its EV1, and Honda, with its EV Plus, developed new platforms in the 1990s. They could have been corporations that harnessed a sense of mission to transform the industry, but in the end, they gave up on manufacturing and supporting these models. Meanwhile, Toyota launched the Prius model in the United States in 2000, which was popular with the environmentally conscious drivers of California, but it used hybrid technology, employing both an electric motor and an internal combustion engine. The prevailing view then was that oil would last for another fifty years or more and that someone would figure out an alternative somewhere down the road.

Musk was not puritanical about this. When he sold Zip2 in 1999, he didn't hesitate to spend a large amount of money on a gas-guzzling McLaren F1. But he did know a thing or two about energy storage, and when he came across the company AC Propulsion, he knew he had to be involved. The company had developed an electric power train technology but lacked the desire to commercialize it into a road car. So Musk framed a new mission. "The fundamental intention of Tesla, at least my motivation," he later recalled, "was to accelerate the advent of sustainable energy."[6]

In the five years following university, Musk had honed his ability to use markets as a way to create software products that would accelerate technological change and reach a large audience. He was now ready to take this experience and self-belief and apply his founder-led start-up mentality to the physical world of atoms.

The global transportation infrastructure is huge, and optimized for hydrocarbons, so changing it would require a lot of capital for the new technology to achieve impact at scale. Fortunately for Musk, he developed an exceptional gift for combining applied physics and business. He would remark of himself that "I make the spending decisions and the engineering decisions in one head," which takes away the tension between the two as "my brain trusts itself."[7]

Musk has also explained his mindset by contrasting Nikola Tesla with his peer, Thomas Edison. Tesla Motors had been named after Nikola Tesla, the inventor of the AC induction motor architecture that the company uses, but Musk says that of the two inventors, he is the bigger fan of Edison. Unlike Tesla, Edison succeeded in bringing his inventions to market and making them accessible to the world. Indeed, Edison created multiple industrial businesses that would become the core of General Electric.[8]

Musk's principal concern was not to build a large company but to raise the capital required to achieve a sizeable impact. This is evident in the road map that he publicly laid out as early as 2006. It showed how Tesla's first car, the Roadster, would pave the way for a whole family of electric vehicles:

1. Build sports car.
2. Use that money to build an affordable car.
3. Use that money to build an even more affordable car.
4. While doing above, also provide zero-emission, electric-power generation options.[9]

There is an echo of this master plan in the IPO prospectus of Facebook, which sums up Musk's position very well: "Simply put: we don't build services to make money; we make money to build better services."[10] The company's profit is not an end in itself, and it really bothers Musk whenever it is portrayed in a negative light, as profit, for him, is no more than the difference between the value that customers willingly pay for a product and the cost of making it.[11] Musk himself acknowledged, "If something has to be designed and invented and you have to figure out how to ensure that the value of the thing you create is greater than the cost of the inputs, then that's probably my core skill."[12]

For Musk, the profit motive is what enables his companies to develop technology and to deploy it at scale in order to deliver on the mission. This means hiring brilliant people who are inspired by the ambition and the difficulty of achieving it—not just good people but the best. And it requires a lot of capital—financial, human, and physical. The company must invest in design and development to create the highest quality products so that it can sell enough at a high enough price to save some money to reinvest in building the next generation of products, all the while keeping costs as low as possible. And until profits are big enough, it must attract funds from external investors on the basis of its potential for future profits.

Musk succeeded in doing all of these things at Tesla, such that, by the end of 2023, the business had delivered over 1.8 million cars in the year, representing about 20 percent of global battery electric vehicle sales.[13] In so doing, he had changed the direction of an entire industry.

Musk's approach challenges the common bifurcation of organizations between privately owned for-profit companies versus governments and nongovernmental organizations (NGOs), which put public good before profit. People who want to do good in the world appear in all shapes and sizes. Highly empathetic people may devote themselves to people they know in their community. Scientists may do research for the pure intellectual reward it provides. Competitive people may be drawn to the challenges of the business world. Righteous people may be drawn to the world of nonprofits, finding a sense of purpose that is often absent in business. Musk, however, stands out in his own category. His priority is to be "useful at scale," which he believes is "the hardest thing in the world"[14] And he is convinced that, if you are serious about it, you cannot ignore the role markets can play.

Navigating the Uncertain

Missions aim high, but start-ups, by definition, go from zero to one and begin small. Musk tries to bridge this gap by making use of markets to grow while learning on the job. He does so by focusing long-term on the mission and short-term on the product, in keeping with his belief that a company is just "a bunch of people" who come together to create a product or service and "there's no such thing as a business, just pursuit of a goal—a group of people pursuing a goal."[15]

"If your customers love you," Musk likes to say, "your odds of success are dramatically higher."[16] Whether customers find his cars useful, for example, can be measured very bluntly by how many they buy. Until 2023, he famously spent no money on advertising, with the rationale that "brand is just a perception, and perception will match reality over time. Sometimes it will be ahead, other times it will be behind. But brand is simply a collective impression some have about a product."[17] That's why Musk seeks constructive feedback, and quickly, explaining: "I think it's very important to have a feedback loop, where you're constantly thinking about what you've done and how you could be doing it better. I think that's the single best piece of advice: constantly think about how you could be doing things better and questioning yourself."[18] This is the scientific method in action.

Musk understood the critical role markets play in helping his teams to test and learn. One can say that he used them to guide his curiosity and creativity. That certainly aligns with the view of Paul Graham, who wrote that curiosity can be "both the engine and the rudder of great work."[19] Graham wasn't writing specifically about start-ups, but he captures the way great leaders at the helm of companies change course based on the feedback they receive. This is true for all great product-focused founders, and none more so than Musk.

He has started nine corporations—Zip2, X.com, SpaceX, Tesla, SolarCity, The Boring Company, Neuralink, OpenAI, and xAI—and of all of them, only one—OpenAI—was a nonprofit (and ironically, it proved to be financially unviable as such; see Chapter 9). Musk's curiosity has been the engine for all of them, but to date Tesla stands out as the company where his curiosity has been most in demand to steer the boat and deliver at a massive scale.[20]

Very few environmentally conscious people in 2004 would have thought that a business was the way to reduce carbon emissions, and by the same token, few conventional businesspeople would have seen the long-term potential for Tesla. When Musk did so, teaming up with Martin Eberhard, Marc Tarpenning, JB Straubel, and Ian Wright in 2004 to commercialize AC Propulsion's proof of concept, the tzero, it was because he was an engineer with a mission who understood what markets could do for him.

Musk knew the team did not know how to build a roadworthy EV. That was the brutal fact of the matter. But he also knew that no one else really knew how to either. The Tesla team had the ambition and the determination to do this, and, provided they thought critically and never gave up, they had a chance. Because they knew it would probably not work, they tried all the harder. And, as a result, they created the first serial production, commercial, lithium-ion battery car sold to consumers.[21] Over time, the rigors of the market would give the engineers access to the distributed knowledge of hundreds of thousands of customers.

As with the universe, the answer was out there—they just had to ask the right questions by making great products. And while they did they not have the optimal team when they started out, success in the marketplace allowed them to attract the best talent.

At any point in time, Musk didn't have all the details figured out. John Carmack, an engineer who, like Musk, has worked on challenging software and hardware problems, characterizes Musk's approach to engineering as "to simply identify the next obstacle on the critical path and efficiently crush it from first principles, largely letting the problems of tomorrow be solved tomorrow."[22] When, for example, his teams were working to retrofit the Roadster onto a Lotus chassis and to address its fundamental range and charging constraints, they did not know how they would design a ground-up EV design for the Model S luxury sedan, and when they were doing that, they did not know how they would build the affordable mass-market Model 3 (not to mention future platforms for SUVs, pickups, and semitrucks).

This was the right approach. If they focused initially on the cost of lithium-ion batteries or the need for a large charging network, they would never have started. By the time they were ready to build the Model 3, however, sufficient progress had been made for a low-cost, mass-market car to be feasible. And along the way, they incorporated software that updated over the air (OTA). Step by step, they progressed with the mission.

. . .

Musk's approach to achieving the mission by focusing on the product evolved as his companies scaled. Manufacturing was one of the problems that Musk had entrusted to the future, and he considered it to be the hardest. This was the reason Musk became CEO in the first place. He had wanted to exert influence as chair and by being the overarching force in business and product strategy, which would have allowed him to spend more time at SpaceX. But when Musk concluded that the founding CEO, Martin Eberhard, was unable to manage manufacturing costs, he decided that he had to be replaced. Musk would later say that prototypes are "a piece of cake" compared to the low unit-cost production needed to do profitable, large-scale manufacturing.[23]

In 2016, Musk explained that "Tesla engineering has transitioned to focus heavily on designing the machine that makes the machine—turning the factory *itself* into a product."[24] Tesla wasn't able to ramp up production of the Roadster, Model S, and Model X until at least three years after they revealed the prototype for each, and they were each at least a couple of years late. With the Model 3, Musk aimed to accelerate the timeline, but by the end of 2017, he had landed the company in "production hell." No sooner had the company emerged from this in 2018 than it was plunged into subsequent logistics and servicing crises. One by one, the teams at Tesla overcame each challenge.

The engineers at Tesla were always making mistakes and learning from them to get better. Musk's personal ethos is similar to the Japanese production culture, which he incorporated in his own factory operations, known as *Kaizen*, which means "continuous learning." Musk started out, for example, with an approach to manufacturing that was "automate, accelerate, simplify, and remove" before he realized that the sequencing was completely the wrong way around and settled on the reverse order, as described in Chapter 2. Over time, the intense scrutiny of manufacturing would reinforce his belief that "the best part is no part."

Markets brought an extra discipline that pushed first principles thinking. Products needed to be designed with the cost of sourcing and production in mind, and, more often than not, that meant not outsourcing but bringing the production of parts in-house, in what is known as "vertical integration." Here, Tesla followed a different path to Apple, which had applied those same Japanese techniques in the United States but by 2004 had largely outsourced manufacturing to China. Not Musk. He obsessed instead on what he calls the "idiot index," which is the ratio of the cost of a component in relation to the cost of the materials needed to fabricate it.

Tesla tackled problems as they arose and, in so doing, developed new technologies to overcome those challenges. Traditionally, car companies buy in parts, which they assemble, and sell the finished cars through dealerships, making much of their money through servicing and repairs, but Tesla would take a contrary approach and do everything. This would come to include supply parts, batteries, the castings, all the software, the marketing, the charging network, battery storage for homes and the grid, solar panels, and more. Every time the engineers at Tesla had a technology challenge, they looked to solve the question internally, knowing that every problem could be turned into a potential opportunity. So long as Tesla was scaling its product offering, it was creating new possibilities. Tesla had become what Musk calls a "technology tree," a term common to strategy and video game players.[25]

By about 2021, Musk viewed Tesla as having largely fulfilled its original mission to accelerate the shift of the auto industry to EVs. He maintained that Tesla had done so by a decade or more. If the oil-driven economy had once been unsustainable, there was now a sustainable alternative. As a result, Musk said that even if other car companies came along and made better EVs than Tesla, he would still consider that he had been successful.[26] Sure enough, a lot of new competition did come along, especially in and from China—and most notably in the form of BYD. But, in truth, he was just getting started, as the tree kept sprouting new branches.

Never Too Big to Fail

Musk knows his business history. Markets can help deliver grand missions, but the journey is a long and arduous one. Once again, offense is often the best form of defense. Companies must prioritize innovation to navigate the uncertainty, and this becomes harder with size, making culture all-important. Tesla is a prime example of this.

Musk is fond of the smartphone analogy. "Tesla is technically a car," he once said, "like an iPhone is technically a phone."[27] And by 2024, he said car companies that don't embed self-driving capability in their vehicles will be like the Finnish company Nokia, which went from being "king of the hill" to a manufacturer of niche products. As a result, he told investors that they should only buy Tesla stock if they believed the company's future lay in AI and robots.[28]

Musk was confronting the challenge of Adams's Rule 3 (invented after thirty-five years of age) and doing his utmost not to be a casualty of what the economist Joseph Schumpeter called the "creative destruction" of capitalism. For the history of business is littered with stories of companies like Xerox, IBM, and Kodak, which once dominated and then faded away. Since then, Google missed social media, Microsoft missed mobile, Nokia missed smartphones, Intel missed GPUs, and Apple missed AI. Closer to home for Musk, GM squandered their nascent lead in EVs, and Boeing became so complacent with its sole-source, cost-plus contracts that it ignored the case for reusability in rockets.

The institutional memory of an established company can work against it. This is where Arthur C. Clarke's First Law kicks in and penalizes those who have been around the longest. As Musk loves to point out, people find it very hard to change their minds, especially when they are older. Meanwhile, investors say they want their companies to be castles that are protected by moats, and they focus on broadening those moats. In industries with a slow-moving landscape—think Coca-Cola and Pepsi—this can last for a long time. But with the spread of software, ever more sectors are vulnerable, and sooner or later, there comes a paradigm change with a new technology that is not just a little bit better, but 10x better. We forget this because of Douglas Adams's Rule 1 (invented when born) and our assumption that trains and electric light bulbs are a part of the way the world works, even though they were once cutting-edge technologies.

Musk knows this all too well, and it makes him instill a culture of innovation that is self-consciously "hardcore," to the point of seeming counterproductive to outsiders. He knows that, in the long run, markets reward those companies that stay at the forefront of innovation. Those that don't keep evolving fail to survive. "Smaller companies are generally better at innovating than larger companies," says Musk. "It has to be that way from a Darwinian standpoint because smaller companies would just die if they didn't try innovating."[29] If you're not about to kill someone, then someone is about to kill you.

It's one thing to conceptualize this, but it is another thing to do it. For there is what the renowned business strategist Clayton Christensen described as the "innovator's dilemma," a concept that was very influential on both Jeff Bezos and Steve Jobs.[30] The dilemma is that when there is a new technology that has not yet reached the market or where the market is still very small, a company would seem to be harming itself by developing new products that might one day cannibalize its core business. You're spending money on something that your salespeople cannot sell and that your shareholders cannot see the payback on. You have to go against the grain, as the time when you most need disruption is when things seem to be going very well. What Christensen highlights is that it is not just bad companies that fail to do this; it's true of good and even great companies.

Jobs resisted the "against the natural order of things" aspect of Adams's Rule 3 technologies (invented after thirty-five years of age) with his belief that there is a cycle of destruction and rebirth, and the only way to stay ahead of this is to have a "beginner's mind." In his own way, Musk, too, is intrinsically driven by his mission to increase consciousness rather than simply beating the competition, and he excels at it because he focuses not simply on innovation but on the *rate of innovation*.[31] This is why Musk pushes Tesla and SpaceX so hard, moving so quickly from one model to the next-generation model. Yes, he misses his own deadlines, but in setting them, he creates internal and external expectations to strive for. And the more he tests, the more he learns.

Andrej Karpathy, Musk's former head of AI at Tesla, describes how Musk created a culture at Tesla that is set upon fighting organizational entropy. He even says, "Elon is a very efficient warrior in the fight against entropy."[32] That is why, nearly twenty years after it was founded, "he basically runs the world's biggest start-ups . . . Tesla is actually multiple start-ups." In short, Musk's philosophy allows him to outcompete the competition by competing not with them but with himself. And it's not for everyone. It's not democratic. Karpathy says that this mentality needs someone who is very smart and who has a big hammer to champion such an approach. The leaders who have flourished under Musk at Tesla—JB Straubel, Franz von Holzhausen, Ashok Elluswamy, Lars Moravy, Tom Zhu, and Drew Baglino, to name a few—have all embraced this mentality.

But if you are not all in, you are out. Musk believes that not only does innovation need to be encouraged, but lack of innovation needs to be punished.[33] If you are not making the boat go faster, then you are making it go slower, or in Musk-speak: "The outcome of any given company is the vector sum of the people within it. Improve the alignment of the individual vectors and their amplitude and the outcome will improve accordingly."[34]

. . .

Musk is a master at leading markets to keep his missions on track. Long before AI capabilities, cloud computing, and chip technology made self-driving cars feasible, Musk saw the huge potential. He had been curious about the potential for autonomous cars, like his good friend Larry Page (who would develop this as Waymo within Google), and a 2012 encounter with the British AI company DeepMind drove home the prospect of imminent, exponential growth (discussed further in Chapter 9). So, while customers weren't asking for autonomous cars, that's what Musk would start building for them.[35]

In its own right, Musk saw that self-driving technology had the potential to reduce deaths from road accidents—over one million globally a year—while also creating billions of hours of free time for motorists and perhaps even increasing vehicle utilization fivefold by developing a shared rentable fleet.[36] It also made EVs more attractive, which would help accelerate their wider adoption. Musk's rationale was even simpler, though. Again, thinking in the limit, he firmly believed that self-driving would one day happen; it was just a question of time. So Tesla had to lead the innovation and become more valuable or miss the future and watch its value head toward zero. There was no dilemma for Musk. He would not make the incumbent's mistake and miss autonomy in the way Big Auto had missed EVs in the 1990s.

So in 2013, Tesla announced that an intense effort was underway to develop self-driving technology for cars, such that they might one day be operated without the need for human intervention and be ten times safer. For Musk grasped that he would have the biggest fleet and therefore the most data on which to train Tesla's AI neural networks. This, in turn, would allow his teams to develop the best and safest self-driving capability. Tesla would be building its own superorganism, with its brain in a data center and nerve cells in each car. This was its differentiated strategy to beat competitors, Google/Waymo foremost among them.

Like most people in the industry, Musk underestimated how difficult self-driving would be, especially the last 1 percent, which is critically important in terms of human safety and regulatory approvals. In hindsight, he missed all his announced targets, observing, "generalized self-driving is a hard problem, as it requires solving a large part of real-world AI. Didn't expect it to be so hard, but the difficulty is obvious in retrospect. Nothing has more degrees of freedom than reality."[37] Meanwhile, Apple, Uber, GM, and Ford had given up, and he was still going. Undaunted, he set about trying to solve real-world AI. And in 2024, the company unveiled the Cybercab, which had no pedals or steering wheel, despite huge pressure for him to launch the "even more affordable car" of the original timeline. Nearly all the executives and investors of Tesla thought this was madness, given that the AI technology and regulation didn't yet exist. But Musk followed his intuition and owned the decision. He knew that he might be proven wrong, but, as a private-sector company, he could take that risk. Musk believes in the power of superlatives and precedents, and he knew that if his bet on the Cybercab paid off, the car would be remembered in a hundred years' time.

Along the way, Tesla kept on growing its technology tree, from building semiconductor chips to processing lithium. Musk also unveiled the Optimus program of humanoid robots, realizing that if Tesla had the best real-world AI capability, it could also apply this to robots. In 2025, Musk predicted there would one day be twenty billion bipedal robots globally—one per person on average with more for industrial use—and it would be "the biggest product of all time by far."[38]

Time and market feedback will tell whether he is right.

Risky Business

The market for a company's shares matches buyers and sellers and allows investors to price risk in the same way that the market sets the price for the company's products. In general, the more risk you take, the greater potential there is for upside and also for downside, and Musk's companies epitomize this. Markets allowed him to go from zero to one and grow from there by orders of magnitude, with the fatalistic acceptance that it might all come to naught. They provided incentives for the best risk-taking talent to join and thrive in a risk-taking culture, and they enabled him to attract investors willing to take on a wide distribution of possible outcomes. Those investors backed him because he convinced them he was a risk worth taking, and this was informed not only by his track record of success but also because he put his own personal capital at risk. Latterly, he was able to remain a meaningful shareholder in his companies because the value investors placed on the companies grew with their success in the marketplace, so he could raise additional equity capital at ever-higher valuations.[39]

Tesla is the best example of Musk's use of risk capital. At the very beginning in 2004, he underwrote the company's development of the Roadster for $25 million over two years, but he ended up having to put in approximately three times that amount personally.[40] He pushed the pace so hard because when the company lost money, it literally lost his money. By 2008, he had used up what remained of his PayPal proceeds, and with SpaceX facing similar trouble and the Great Financial Crisis mounting, he barely raised the outside money necessary to make payroll and avoid bankruptcy. In the end, GM and Chrysler needed to be bailed out by the government, but Tesla survived.

Tesla remained on life support through 2013, and periodic infusions of funding were required to keep the business operating at the pace that it did, including from Daimler-Benz, Toyota, public shareholders, and the US Department of Energy.[41] In desperation, Musk even talked to Google about a possible deal to backstop the future of the company.[42] Years later, Tesla was still not out of the woods, as again in 2018, the company was less than ten weeks from collapsing, given manufacturing problems with the Model 3, prompting Musk to reach out to another possible buyer, which this time was Tim Cook at Apple.[43]

These near-death experiences fade in the memory, but Musk's 90 percent estimate of Tesla failing seemed realistic for many years. In the end, it was able to sell enough cars whose output value was greater than their input value. By 2019, Tesla generated more cash than it spent, and as a result, in 2020, it was able to raise over $12 billion at a market valuation averaging over $400 billion.[44] Critics decried the wealth this created for Musk personally, but he had used markets to play a very high-risk game to advance his sustainable energy mission, and he—together with his investors, consumers, and the entire sustainable economy—won big.

. . .

By now, it should not be a surprise to learn that Musk is a huge advocate of markets. Sometimes markets fail and then for-profit companies are infeasible; but otherwise, he says, "I am a big believer in the market system," adding that "it is just the collective will of the people."[45] It's a view that goes directly against the presumption that the smartest people at the center can possibly know what is best for everyone. In that, Musk is aligned with Adam Smith, who said it is a conceit to argue that the "man of system" can design civilization, moving pieces across the "chess-board of human society."[46]

Musk is also aligned with Friedrich Hayek, who expanded on Adam Smith, saying that social engineers at the center can never have as much knowledge as that which is distributed among the population at large. Not only do free markets connect buyers and sellers, but prices act as indirect signals that allow for the transfer of knowledge. And they allow anyone who thinks differently and loves to innovate to get started, test at a small level, and scale up with experience. For Musk, as for Smith and Hayek, society as a whole benefits.

Musk is not against regulation in the public interest. On the contrary, he considers it vital to create a level playing field in which regulators act as referees enforcing the rules. If you want to achieve energy transition to combat climate change, for example, don't get involved in the market; rather, price externalities such as carbon and let markets do the work. The problem with capitalism is not too much competition but too little, and this is a failure of regulation. It is not the market that is the problem, but the fact that it is not a free market. "Socialism vs capitalism," Musk says, "is not even the right question. What matters is avoiding monopolies that restrict people's freedom."[47] And that applies to both for-profit and nonprofit corporations because, for Musk, governments are no more than corporations in the limit that happen to be funded by taxpayers.

In Musk's mind, governments inherently tend toward monopoly since they are centralized and lack a feedback loop with users. Confident in their good intentions, officials make assumptions about what the people want because they don't have a way of asking. Nor are the individuals who sit at the top of these bureaucracies able to see the consequences of their actions, from which they themselves are insulated. They may not be paid as much as their risk-taking peers in the private sector, but their jobs are typically more secure and high in status. In other words, to quote Nassim N. Taleb, they lack "skin in the game."[48]

For Musk, the consequence of having no feedback loop, is that the people in power at the center become removed from reality. Instead of taking risks all the time, they take huge risks infrequently that have not been tested at a smaller scale. In Musk's words, "There's not really a cleansing process for a government short of a catastrophe."[49] And because the cost of their capital is so cheap, they become complacent about how they incur costs and allocate capital, prompting Musk to say socialism "shifts resources from most productive to least productive, pretending to do good, while actually causing harm."[50] Endeavors like the Manhattan Project or the Apollo Space Program are exceptions that prove the rule, since there was, in each case, an external, galvanizing geopolitical threat.

Excessive government intervention, therefore, is very harmful in Musk's eyes because the distortion of markets results in less choice for consumers. Products and services will typically be more expensive, less varied, lower quality, and slower to arrive than those made by private companies competing in a free market. For Musk, similar dynamics exist with both crony capitalists and so-called government-funded non-governmental organizations (NGOs). Musk may be exaggerating—and taking a dig at Bill Gates since he shorted Tesla stock—but he says that no more than 20 percent of philanthropic assistance reaches the ultimate beneficiaries.[51]

For Musk, organizations that exist in markets have to fight entropy to survive while those without competition are not allowed to die. As a result, the people who work there end up serving the interests of the institution rather than the people they are supposed to serve. Bureaucracy and vested interests grow. That's why Musk endorses the approach of the American economist Milton Friedman, which he summarized as: "The worst results come from people spending other people's money on a different group of other people. That is the government!"[52]

Musk also shares Friedman's view that unfunded government spending is morally wrong. It causes inflation, imposes a burden on future generations, and can put the solvency of the entire country at risk. This would be the primary driver behind his mission for the Department of Government Efficiency ("DOGE"), which was established in January

2025 with a goal of cutting federal spending by 15 percent to halve the annual $2 trillion deficit.

Commentators compared the cuts that Musk made via DOGE to those that he made at Twitter, which was a reasonable comparison to make as, like the government, Twitter also had to service the interest on a huge amount of debt. Musk did not disagree either, writing on X that under his ownership, "Twitter added far more features with fewer people. What really matters for improving American's standard of living is shifting people from low productivity jobs in government to high productivity jobs in industry. Many more people needed in manufacturing!"[53] He believed DOGE could cut waste and fraud without affecting critical services. And he felt that technology was key to this, declaring, "My goal is to fix government IT!" and adding, "This is harder than getting a rocket to orbit. Actually."[54]

And so it proved. Despite his efforts, the amount of savings that DOGE was able to make was quite underwhelming (less than $200 billion by the time Musk left in May 2025). This was the backdrop to Musk's opposition to President Trump's "disgusting abomination" of a budget bill that formally increased—not decreased—the annual deficit: those people who supported it were, for Musk, undermining the work of DOGE and jeopardizing the public finances of the nation.[55]

Before this confrontation overshadowed everything else, Musk had stirred up a great deal of controversy due to the disruptive way the DOGE team went about their work, and it caused direct damage to the Tesla brand. As Musk might have seen it, he still made great products, but the collective impression of them fell behind the reality for swathes of the customer base in the United States and Europe on account of his political activity.

This did not change his view on markets, though. He told his employees they had to keep making autonomous cars and humanoid robots that others find useful and love. This would help to create a solar-powered future with a highly sustainable and productive economy.

One day in the future, the role of markets may change. In a world of so-called abundance, Musk envisages cheap energy, billions of robots to do our physical labor, and AI to do our intellectual work, and in such a world, money will not matter.[56] Until then, however, he believes that free markets will remain the best way to incentivize creativity, allocate resources, and keep the forward momentum of civilization on Earth and beyond.

Boiling It Down: Missions need corporations

Most people think for-profit organizations exist to make money and nonprofit organizations exist to spend that money. More recently, companies have tried to reposition themselves as "mission-driven" or "purpose-driven." Musk is different. He starts with a mission and sells products so that his engineers have the means to make better products. His approach to markets can be summarized as follows:

1. Technology can be married with business to achieve great things. Money is not an end in itself but a means to pay for talent and invest in innovation.
2. Markets are such an effective way to scale, as one can test the value of products not only against the laws of physics but also against the wants of customers—two feedback loops with reality.
3. One must be both reactive to the market and proactive via a culture of innovation that demands self-criticism and creative disruption.
4. There is no substitute for free markets when it comes to allocating capital to proven risk-takers and creating prosperity.

SIX

Explore Space

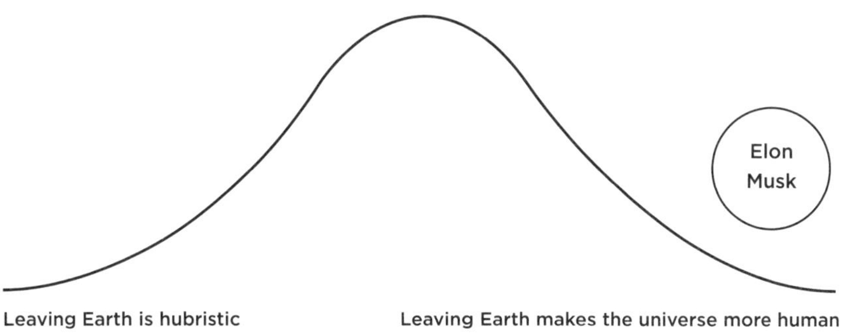

"A new philosophy of the future is needed. I believe it should be curiosity about the Universe—expand humanity to become a multiplanet, then interstellar, species to see what's out there."[1] Musk posted this at the age of fifty-one, in the summer of 2022, when SpaceX's rocket development was progressing at pace. It is perhaps the most literal sense in which Musk wants to try to increase the scope and scale of consciousness.

The foundations of the SpaceX dream were laid more than twenty years earlier. As was the case in Musk's childhood, the contemplation of his mortality was again the backdrop for some life-changing decisions.

Musk had a brush with death at the start of 2001, when he was twenty-nine. He took a trip with his wife to Brazil and South Africa and caught a life-threatening case of malaria. Musk has said that he was only thirty-six hours from dying after twice being misdiagnosed. He spent ten days in intensive care, lost forty-five pounds, and took six months to recover. He had plenty of time to think, but he did not fall down an existential hole. Instead, he thought about what he wanted to do with the rest of his life. He had the freedom and resources to do almost anything he wanted, including never having to work again. And it was to the frontier of space that he was drawn, pulled by his fascination with the meaning of life and the universe.

Musk had spotted an inconvenient truth. It was supposed to be the destiny of our species that humans would go out and explore our solar system. President Kennedy's beacon call to go to the moon in 1961 had led to an astonishing period of innovation. NASA launched programs named after legendary figures of classical mythology—Apollo and Gemini—that did the once-impossible and put humans on the lunar surface. No sooner had the goal been achieved, in six missions between 1969 and 1972 (seven including Apollo 13), than then-President Nixon scaled back the program. A decade later, as the Cold War came to an end, the ambition to send humans beyond Earth had dissipated. It should have been Adams's Rule 1—a natural part of the way the world works—but it was not.

In Musk's mind, the NASA Space Shuttle program that followed the Apollo program was an implicit lowering of ambition. Yes, it serviced the International Space Station (ISS), but that circumnavigated our planet without leaving its orbit. Human consciousness remained tied to Earth. The destiny he wished for was not manifest, and no one else seemed to realize this. There was a presumption that someone somewhere was working on crewed missions to deep space. Except that wasn't the case; not where you would expect at NASA, or anywhere else. For Musk, the opportunity to move forward was there, and it had to be taken.

Neither building a rocket nor starting a for-profit company was part of Musk's original plan. He wanted to buy a rocket so that he could launch a capsule that would land on Mars and grow plants. It was to be called Mars Oasis. He imagined the whole of humanity watching by video link as the seeds germinated and a blaze of green shoots appeared through the red soil. Life would blossom on another planet. This might provide the inspiration that Musk felt was greatly missing. It would be the ultimate precedent and superlative. Musk's plan was to serve humanity in this way and then be on to his next venture.

There was a problem, however. He couldn't buy a rocket in the United States that would make it to Mars for less than $50 million, and Musk thought he would need two or more. Despite his great wealth, this was far above his budget. So he was forced to go to Russia in search of a couple of ICBMs that could be reconditioned for a peaceful payload and an interplanetary destination. Unfortunately, the Russians did not take him seriously and the Mars Oasis concept had to be scrapped.

This whole saga did set Musk thinking, though. It was not that the technology to go to space didn't exist; it was just that it was too expensive. Russia had lost the Cold War, and yet it could produce Soyuz rockets at half the cost that American companies could. Meanwhile, the demand for satellites looked set to increase—something that Musk was well aware of, having been a part of the internet communications boom. Might there be a way to create a business, working with NASA, that would allow him to develop rockets in the United States and also open up human access to the solar system?

Musk was thinking differently about space. "My original motivation for MO [Mars Oasis]," he wrote, "was based on the notion of 'where there is a will, there is a way.' However, I now think it is the other way around. As evidenced by the attention given the Shuttle tragedy, the dream of space is an integral part of the American identity. So if people think that there is a way to get to space, they will take that path. We need to show that it exists."[2] Musk believed that commercial rocket companies could be built on the foundations of NASA in the way that companies like Google and eBay were built on the internet, which was originally funded by the US Department of Defense through the development of ARPANET.[3]

And so it was that SpaceX was born in 2002. The idea of setting up an independent space company to compete with the likes of Lockheed Martin, Boeing, and Northrop Grumman seemed to most people a sure-fire way to lose money. Musk's friends tried to discourage him. But that did not dissuade him, because he already knew it was likely to fail. The difficulty was the point. As President Kennedy said in 1962, "We choose to go to the Moon in this decade and do the other things, not because they are easy, but because they are hard."[4] And for Musk, it wasn't just about building a company; that was just the backfilling to make the mission work financially.

. . .

Eighteen years later, in 2020, at Cape Canaveral in Florida, Musk would watch one of his Falcon 9 rockets launch two humans into orbit. The mission to the ISS would also be the first to send humans into space from US soil since 2011. Within a year of SpaceX being founded, Space Shuttle *Columbia* crashed, and the decision was subsequently made to phase out the entire Space Shuttle program. Fittingly, the astronauts named the SpaceX Dragon capsule, which docked with the ISS, *Endeavour*, after the shuttle they flew their first mission on and after the command module of Apollo 15, which landed on the moon in 1971, the year Musk was born.

Musk was obsessed with space and SpaceX, even more than

electric cars and Tesla. How do we know this? Musk was attacked on Twitter in 2021, together with Jeff Bezos, by Bernie Sanders for being immoral on account of his wealth.[5] At the time, most of his wealth was in the value of his Tesla shares, yet his reply was, "I am accumulating resources to help make life multiplanetary & extend the light of consciousness to the stars."[6]

Out of the Cradle

In an alternative history, Musk could have remained CEO of PayPal after X.com and Confinity merged, pursued his desired consumer banking strategy, and not sold to eBay. Years later, in fact, after buying Twitter and renaming it X, he would look to incorporate digital payments into the platform and to create a so-called everything app. What, then, would have happened to Musk's love for space exploration? Would he have had time to look at the NASA website and see that it had no concrete plans for travel beyond the ISS? Would he have just paid the $50 million for the rockets to establish Mars Oasis and never created SpaceX?

When imagining a parallel life of Musk, there is an intriguing case study in the life of Jeff Bezos, the man who created an online retailer even bigger than eBay. Born seven years before Musk, Bezos was old enough to remember when Neil Armstrong stepped onto the moon in 1969. Bezos would go on to create a massive space company, Blue Origin, as well as an internet satellite business, Project Kuiper, that sits within Amazon. And in 2021, he even personally crossed the Kármán line.

Like Musk, Bezos is a very smart and driven businessman who loves solving hard and important problems. Early on, he, too, saw the giant potential of the internet connecting humans and changing society forever. Bezos self-identifies as an inventor and has a mentality of always being in start-up mode, or "Day 1" as he likes to call it. He is obsessed with three things—the customer, inventing technology, and being long term—and given our social human nature to be otherwise, he is zealous about the need for Amazon to have an explicit "best idea wins" approach to truth-seeking.[7]

Bezos, too, grew up on authors like Isaac Asimov, Robert Heinlein, Jules Verne, and Frank Herbert, and he is a huge fan of *Star Trek*. He is curious and passionate about the pioneering spirit and engineering challenge that space represents. At university, he initially majored in particle physics before switching over to computer science and electrical engineering. And by the age of thirty-five, in 1999, Bezos duly hatched the idea that would become the independent company that is Blue Origin.

We shall never know if Musk would have started SpaceX if he had never left PayPal and become an online banking billionaire. But we have good reason to think that he might have. The passion behind SpaceX is visceral. Most people don't realize that he was working on Mars Oasis some three years before he invested in and became chair of Tesla. And he continued to build SpaceX even though he had to divide his time between the two companies. Above all, Bezos spent a relatively small fraction of his net worth on Blue Origin and did not expect it to make a profit any time soon, whereas Musk invested over half of his net worth to start SpaceX—$100 million—even though it had to reach profitability to become self-sustaining, something that had a very low chance of happening.[8]

With all that said, what Musk and Bezos share in common—that passion for space that sets them apart from most other people—is much greater than what sets them apart from each other.

Musk likes to quote the Russian rocket pioneer Konstantin Tsiolkovsky, who wrote around 1900: "Earth is the cradle of humanity, but you cannot stay in the cradle forever."[9] This mentality taps into Musk's religious view that the universe is the answer, and if we can increase consciousness sufficiently, we may one day be able to ask questions that make sense of that answer. For millennia, curious humans have looked to the night sky with wonder and awe and endlessly asked questions, from what causes the movement of celestial bodies, to where are the aliens, to what is dark matter? The human project is to explore the unknown. If we are curious and think critically, we may be able to unlock some of the remaining mysteries of life, the universe, and everything. *Curiosity* was even the name of the robotic rover that NASA sent to Mars in 2011 to study the planet's geology and atmosphere.

For Musk, space is also the greatest adventure. What moment in history was more exciting than Neil Armstrong saying, "One small step for man" to an enraptured global audience? Now humans must span out into our solar system, then different star systems, and perhaps, one day, different galaxies. He imagines us discovering perhaps ancient alien civilizations and formulating those questions that we do not yet know to ask. Exploration, in turn, will drive technological innovation, which will allow humans to pursue scientific inquiry and explore even further.

This potential, which assigns a central role to human consciousness, is reflected in the optimistic view of AI pioneer Ray Kurzweil: Our ability to be creative with minds and hands will give us the ability to accelerate our evolution with technology "until the entire universe is at our fingertips."[10] And it speaks to the view that Musk shared with Feynman that the scope and scale of consciousness has unknown potential. As Musk, the founder, would put it, "Human civilization is still a tiny startup in the grand scheme of things."[11]

What makes humans special, for Musk, in the context of the whole universe is not that we live on Earth but that we may be the only creatures with high-level consciousness. Musk even asks what percentage of our solar system's energy could be harnessed for intelligence. This references the Kardashev scale, which measures civilizations depending on whether they have harnessed all the power of their planet (Type I), their sun (Type II), or their galaxy (Type III). To date, he believes we are less than 5 percent toward Type I.[12] "Becoming multiplanetary," he reasons, "is a critical step on the Kardashev ladder."[13]

Setting Mars as the North Star, therefore, brought tremendous clarity for Musk and his teams. The moon is crucial, and a lunar permanent base may be an important step in the development of Mars planning, but Musk downplays its importance. He argues that, compared to Mars, the moon would be vulnerable to any calamity affecting Earth, and it lacks a carbon dioxide atmosphere that could be used to produce methane rocket fuel for Starship, but the overriding fact is that we have already been there. It would be going backward, and so he leaps right past it.

Musk's excitement on this point would be infectious. His vision allowed him to collaborate with brilliant people who also liked to do hard things, perhaps even more at SpaceX than at Tesla. Leaders of SpaceX, like Gwynne Shotwell, Tom Mueller, Hans Koenigsmann, and Mark Juncosa, share the credit with Musk for the company's successes. In particular, Gwynne Shotwell has been essential as she freed up Musk to focus on engineering by running the company's day-to-day operations. Musk does have a reputation for being very difficult to work for, which is deserved, but it is also true that these men and women would otherwise likely have been doing work at other aerospace companies that would have been a lot less exciting.

Bezos shares Musk's profound passion for space exploration, but it is qualitatively and quantitatively different. His rationale for Blue Origin goes back to a belief that he wrote of in high school: "The earth is finite, and if the world economy and population are to keep expanding, space is the only way to go."[14] He even did an interview on this subject with the *Miami Herald* when he was eighteen and then went to Princeton, where one of the professors was Gerard O'Neill, whose views had been important in shaping his own.

By the mid-1970s, O'Neill wanted to build a positive case for space development, which led to his book *The High Frontier: Human Colonies in Space*.[15] Also influenced by Tsiolkovsky, O'Neill believed that humans could build a new sort of utopia in space, freed from the land constraints of a planetary surface and the competition for resources that causes. He tried to garner support by showing that the science largely existed to do this. He described how orbiting space stations could be built using the resources of the moon. They would not have sufficient gravity to sustain regular human life, but this could be overcome if the stations were designed as cylinders and made to spin. It just needed to be built out, and for this, he advocated the involvement of private enterprise.

This vision captured the imagination of young Bezos. He thought of Earth as a home planet that we can protect, hence his company's name, Blue Origin. Activities like mining and heavy industry could be moved not offshore but off-planet, leaving Earth to be zoned for residential and light industry. Like Musk, he thought in terms of energy consumption but came to a different conclusion: that this would constrain the human population on Earth and result in too many solar panels. Then he looked at the problem from the point of view of an industrialist, seeing for himself a role to make space access possible so entrepreneurs in the future could build on it in the way he had with Amazon via the internet, the postal service, and the payments network.[16] This could scale to the point where the solar system could support a trillion humans, which would also mean, in his words, a thousand Mozarts and Einsteins.[17]

Musk, by contrast, thought colonies in free space made no sense. He likened the concept, on Twitter, to trying to build the United States in the middle of the Atlantic Ocean. "In order to grow the colony, you'd have to transport vast amounts of mass from planets/moons/asteroids."[18]

Cost was not a priority for O'Neill, but it is if you think like Musk. Cost invalidates a lot of ideas for him, like space mining and space solar panels, which beam power back to Earth. That is why Musk speaks of the need to be both spacefaring and multiplanetary and has done so since the very beginning of SpaceX. He's an unashamed planet chauvinist, the charge that Asimov admitted to when exposed to O'Neill's thinking.[19] When the planets come ready-made with the mass to provide gravity and resources, why would you start anywhere else?

Filling the Void

On a mild Tuesday afternoon in February of 2018, Elon Musk was at Cape Canaveral to witness the maiden launch of his latest and largest rocket, the Falcon Heavy. Four minutes after liftoff, the rocket reached space, and its nose cone came off to reveal his own cherry-red Tesla. The car was driven by a mannequin called Starman, who listened to David Bowie's 1969 classic "Space Oddity," and written on the car's circuit board was "Made on Earth by humans."

Musk was forty-six years old, and he paid homage to the two writers who had helped him as an unhappy child to stop going over the meaning of life in his head and to start making things for other people. On the dashboard of the Roadster was a sticker that read "DON'T PANIC," a tribute to Douglas Adams, whose books had helped a younger Musk to unpick the *why* of life. And in the glovebox, etched in glass, was the Foundation series of Isaac Asimov, who had inspired him with the *how* of life through his science fiction.

This is the other side of Musk's philosophy of curiosity. Exploring space is existential for Musk in a way that it is not for Bezos. This is how he embraces uncertainty and keeps himself busy pressing on the flywheel. This is why, for all of Steve Jobs's hippy sensibilities and disinterest in space, Musk is wired in a way that is closer to Steve Jobs than Jeff Bezos. Compared to Musk, Bezos is a chilled-out guy. So it is instructive to compare the different demeanors of the two men.

There was a period in Bezos's twenties when he said he was very scared of his mortality.[20] But in general, he does not give the impression that he is attacking the world as a way to rid himself of the aggression within. He is grateful for the upbringing that he enjoyed. He was high school valedictorian and is especially effusive when it comes to family. "One of my great gifts is my mom and dad," Bezos has said. "My admiration goes to those people—we all know some of them: I know I do—who had terrible parents but so admirably broke that cycle, pulled out of it, and made it work. I did not have that situation. I was always loved."[21]

Bezos describes his philosophy of life as having a "regret minimization framework," which is to say, make decisions to do or not do things so that you will not look back later in life and have regrets.[22] This included, in his fifties, stepping down as CEO of Amazon, divorcing, remarrying a glamorous television presenter, moving to Miami, and building a four-hundred-foot yacht.

Musk has endorsed Bezos's wish to have no regrets, but it's a mindset that calls for a calmness that is foreign to him.[23] He takes on more and more work, at a mounting cost to his physical health and emotional well-being. And there is an insecurity that reveals itself when he gets into unnecessary spats with other successful people, be it Bill Gates, Mark Zuckerberg, Reid Hoffman, or Bezos himself.

When Musk talks about space, the emotion is unmistakable. He displayed this at a TED Talk in 2017. "I think it's important to have a future that is inspiring and appealing," he said. "There have to be reasons that you get up in the morning and you want to live. Why do you want to live? What's the point? What inspires you? What do you love about the future? If the future does not include being out there among the stars and being a multi-planet species, I find that incredibly depressing."[24] The excitement is palpable, but it is tinged with that despair. And he is even blunter at the end of the interview, saying, "I'm not trying to be anyone's savior . . . I am just trying to think about the future and not be sad."[25]

Becoming multiplanetary is, for Musk, a crucial Great Filter for humans to traverse, making the first step of leaving Earth's orbit absolutely paramount. We must explore the universe, but we must first make sure that we survive in order to have a chance of doing so. Ensuring human access to space, therefore, is a prudent collective insurance plan for human civilization. All in all, it is just astonishing to him that, after roughly 4.5 billion years of life on Earth, humans succeeded in achieving access to space in the twentieth century and then decided it was no longer a priority.

It may be that conscious humans only walk on the Earth today because small mammals had an evolutionary window when a large asteroid wiped out the dinosaurs, but Musk knows there will be more where that rock came from. Consciousness is fragile for Musk. The way his mind works is that if consciousness had taken 10 percent longer to evolve relative to the 4.5-billion-year history of Earth, it would never have come to exist, as our oceans will boil in 500 million years. There is not much we can do about that, but there's plenty more we can and should do to make sure that the entire evolution of life on Earth has not been for nothing.

Some experts, like Stephen Hawking, put the odds of the human species being wiped out at no less than a 1 percent chance per century, whether by natural disasters, deadly viruses, superintelligence, or maybe just ourselves. That's per century, meaning the chance of it happening on an annual basis is highly improbable, and the chance of it happening over a time frame of 10,000 years is highly probable, unless humans do something about it. Since the development of AI accelerated after

Hawking's death in 2018, the odds may have gone up significantly. As Adams might have said, something that seems to be a "virtual impossibility" has, in fact, a "finite improbability" of happening.

And so for Musk we must seize the moment now and with urgency. This is where Asimov's cycles of civilizations come in. Space innovation started decelerating after 1972, and should that trend continue, it is possible that the window to get to Mars might close altogether. When asked on X how long our civilization would last, Musk replied that it "needs to retain its current technology level until Mars is self-sufficient, which could be achieved within ~20 years. If we become multiplanetary and then multistellar our civilization will last millions of years. If not, maybe just a few hundred years."[26] In another post, he declared, "We must build Terminus."[27] Terminus was the improbably remote and barren planet that Hari Seldon chose as the location to establish a Foundation, his center of knowledge and learning that might turn the tide of history. Mars is Musk's Terminus.

Finally, there is perhaps an existential aspect to Musk's craving for space exploration, which relates in some way to the prospect of death. It is a subject on which even Musk's rational brain can offer no words of comfort. Its limbic strength remains even when it is brought into consciousness. As the physicist Sean Carroll wrote in *The Big Picture*, "facing up to reality can make us feel the need for some existential therapy. We are floating in a purposeless cosmos, confronting the inevitability of death, wondering what any of it means."[28]

The heavens have inspired not only questions for the curious, but also answers for those in search of meaning, from worshipping the sun to interpreting the omens of comets to tracing their fates through astrology. The night sky can evoke another feeling too. As the French polymath Blaise Pascal wrote in the seventeenth century, "The eternal silence of these infinite spaces fills me with dread."[29] When William

Shatner went up to the edge of space in Bezos's New Shepard rocket, he was traumatized by the contrast between life on Earth and the blackness that surrounds us. "All I saw was death," he recalled.[30] It's the dread that Arthur Dent felt when he saw the Earth blow up and everything he loved with it. For Musk, too, "We are microbes on a dust mote in a vast emptiness overwhelming dominated by the sun."[31] And he genuinely feels that "our collective light of consciousness is a tiny candle in a vast darkness."[32] He doesn't fear aliens. On the contrary, "The scariest answer to the Fermi Paradox is that there are no aliens at all."[33] Then we are alone.

Space exploration may offer a way, however, to confront and rebel against the prospect of death. "We're only adrift if we choose to be," says Carroll, citing Albert Camus's allegory of Sisyphus to illustrate how one can find meaning in one's task and make the universe more human.[34] For Musk, we may not be able to overcome our mortality (and, unlike some other billionaires, life-extension is not one of Musk's passions), but perhaps one day, we might stare into the abyss and not be afraid, as there will be human eyes staring back at us.

The philosopher Hannah Arendt wrote in *The Human Condition* that the Russian launch of the Sputnik satellite in 1957 was the most important event in human history, and not in a good way. Citing Tsiolkovsky, she said launching a man-made object into the universe was a modern renunciation of what it means to be human.[35]

Musk's view could not be more opposite. Prometheus brought fire down to Earth for us, and while we remain mortal, we can use the fire to harness solar energy, to increase consciousness, and to make rockets that will take us beyond Earth. That is why, when he alluded to Prometheus on Twitter, he described the Greek god as "unbound."[36] This was deliberate and significant. Aeschylus wrote three plays, of which only the first, *Prometheus Bound*, survives. The immortal god is condemned to eternity in chains and suffers, bound to a rock, tortured by an eagle. But Musk unbinds him. Like Percy Bysshe Shelley and Friedrich Nietzsche before him, Musk looks ahead to the final, lost part of Aeschylus's trilogy, where the errant Titan may have found some reckoning with Zeus. In that sense, Musk faces the darkness with defiance.

Prometheus Unbound

It is hard to think of anyone more different from Musk than Mary-Jane Rubenstein, professor of religion and science in society at Wesleyan University. In her book *Astrotopia*, she criticizes Musk, together with Bezos, for being rich, White, Christian, scientific-minded, heterosexual men (she is a self-declared postmodernist, feminist, queer atheist). She mocks their need to launch phallic missiles into space. She writes too of "'a new scientific method' that values the knowledge systems of Indigenous peoples, the dignity of nonhuman life-forms, and the integrity of the land" with a goal of achieving a cosmic justice that draws upon Afrofuturist, feminist, and mystical communities.[37]

What would Musk say? He wasn't replying to Rubenstein, but he might as well have been when he posted: "It is unfortunately common for many in academia to overweight the value of ideas & underweight bringing them to fruition. For example, the idea of going to the moon is trivial, but going to the moon is hard."[38] As Nassim N. Taleb might put it, Rubenstein does not seek to test her words in the real world and so lacks skin in the game. By contrast, on setting up SpaceX, Musk made himself study textbooks on the elements of rocket propulsion, such as aerodynamics, thermodynamics, astrodynamics, and structural mechanics. He would later say, "SpaceX does more meaningful, cutting-edge 'research' on the advancement of rockets and satellites than all the academic university labs on Earth combined. But we don't use the pretentious, low-accountability term 'researcher.'" His preferred term is "Engineer."[39]

Whether or not you empathize with Musk's quest for meaning or are persuaded by Rubenstein's cosmic justice, no one would even argue that her "new scientific method" might succeed in getting rockets into orbit, never mind something seemingly so on the edge of human possibility as reaching Mars. In that sense, as a for-profit company devoted to a grand mission, SpaceX showcases Musk's ambition in a way that eclipses even Tesla.

The mission of SpaceX is a supreme example of going back to first principles and thinking in the limit, and it all stems from the goal to be multiplanetary and spacefaring. Since the early days of the company, Musk wanted every decision at SpaceX to be looked at through the prism of whether or not it would make a self-sustaining civilization on Mars happen faster. For it is not just about getting there: Musk reasons that human civilization on another planet must be self-sustaining, meaning that, in the event of a calamity, it could survive without contact with Earth. He reckons—and the estimates do change—a city of at least a million people will be needed for that and at least a million tons of cargo. Illustratively, that would mean an average of one thousand rockets each carrying one hundred people every second year (Mars and Earth only come into alignment every twenty-two months) to complete the task over two decades.

The next threshold question for decision-making is how to reduce the dollar cost of taking a ton of payload into orbit. It's not the mass or the cost that matters, but the ratio of the two. Musk estimates that SpaceX will need to reduce the cost to transport a person or a ton of payload to the surface of Mars by approximately 10,000x, from approximately $1 billion to approximately $100,000. SpaceX will also need to churn out rockets and boosters at scale, starting at one per month, rising to ten per month over time. If SpaceX can do that, then the cost of a city on Mars with a million people would total roughly $100 billion in real terms, spread over twenty-plus years.[40]

Musk saw that building a city on Mars would require SpaceX to engineer a spacecraft that did not yet exist: something so new, it would redefine what was thought possible. That would be Starship: a rocket that could carry one hundred people and one hundred tons and would one day have a thrust more than three times greater than that of the Saturn V.[41] It would be the largest flying object ever. It would be able to take off from Earth, refuel in orbit, fly to Mars, land on the surface, take off again, and return to land on Earth. Scaling to such a degree would be incredibly expensive, so the rocket would need to be not only very large but fully, reliably, and rapidly reusable. Here, SpaceX had already reimagined the accepted standards of the space industry and looked to commercial airplanes as the benchmark. An airplane is not disposed of after each transatlantic flight but refueled and turned around. Musk wanted to do the same for rockets. SpaceX therefore needed to make huge strides in rocket technology, combining reuse, size, and the capability to safely carry humans.

Such a challenge would demand every shred of creativity that Musk and his teams could muster. That is why he describes reusable rockets as operating "close to the ragged edge of physics."[42] Or, in his inimitable way, "If this was a video game, the setting is to extreme difficulty."[43] Nature does not make it easy. The Earth is a very dense planet because of its iron core, which makes its gravitational force very strong for its size. This holds Earth's gases in a thick atmosphere, which can sustain life on the surface but also causes tremendous drag on a spaceship trying to escape. Rockets must go straight up and then turn to travel at about twenty-five times the speed of sound to reach and stay in space, given the rotation of the Earth. Less than 5 percent of the weight of the rocket at launch ever makes it onto orbit, given all the fuel and oxidant needed to get it there. This is the reason why NASA's motto is *Ad astra per aspera* (through hardship to the stars).[44] It is just the sort of challenge for someone who has extreme ambition, willfulness, discipline, and curiosity.

The number of crashes SpaceX experienced in its history of rocket development is testament to the difficulty, including all of the first three launches, which left the company on the brink of bankruptcy. But Musk did not shy away from this. Time was money and he pushed a high drumbeat of launches. In that sense, every launch was a test flight because, successful or not, you could learn from it.

Musk's relative lack of resources early on compared to Bezos actually proved to be an advantage, as it forced him to create a for-profit corporation that competed for business. Unlike Tesla, which entered a crowded automotive market, there was no existing commercial market for space travel. Musk's goal was singlehandedly to establish one. This meant starting in the US small-to-medium-payload market with SpaceX's Falcon rockets. Musk was happy to pitch SpaceX in the no-frills workhorse segment, equivalent to Southwest Airlines in the airline industry.[45] He learned how to build a rocket with a low-cost base and to demonstrate reliability before expanding his addressed market and moving to larger rockets and the transportation of supplies and crew to the ISS.

Blue Origin had access to Bezos's deep pockets, but this ended up hindering its developments. While this was partly by design from Bezos (who even chose the emblem of a tortoise for his company), by not competing for NASA contracts, Blue Origin missed out not only on contract funding, but also on the extreme pressure to innovate and the experience of making orbital vehicles. As a result, SpaceX reached orbit in 2008, whereas Blue Origin did so only in 2025, by which time SpaceX had already done so more than 400 times.[46]

John Carmack, whose company Armadillo Aerospace once developed reusable suborbital launch vehicles, praised Musk for committing the amount of money that he did and then going for "orbit or bust."[47] He was willing to crash rockets knowing he had to maintain the rate of innovation to survive and to learn from those crashes. The likes of Blue Origin and Virgin Galactic, on the other hand, spent more money on not getting to orbit than Musk did with Falcon. Carmack concluded, "While it would have been poetic if space industrialization . . . grew out of one of the tiny little teams attending Space Access, @SpaceX is still very much the stuff of dreams, and Heinlein is smiling."[48]

Along the way, Musk also built out the technology tree, as he did with Tesla. The Falcon's revenue would be supplemented by a new business line announced in 2015. Starlink operates an enormous constellation of low Earth orbit satellites—carried to orbit on SpaceX's own rockets—which provide internet connectivity to subscribers in low-density, non-urban areas. By 2025, SpaceX was projected to generate $15.5 billion in income, helping drive the company's valuation to $350 billion, with about three-quarters of the income expected to come from Starlink.[49]

Musk had gone full circle, having started out his own career connecting humans digitally with information, travel directions, and payments. SpaceX was not only about providing humans with low-cost access to orbit but also providing humans on Earth with low-cost access to the internet, from airlines and cruise ships to armies, researchers in Antarctica, protesters in Iran, schools in the Amazon, and increasingly direct to smartphones. "By enabling high-speed, low-latency and affordable Internet globally," Musk posted on X, "Starlink will do more to educate and lift people out of poverty than any NGO ever."[50]

The tortoise might one day catch up with the hare now that Bezos has reallocated much more time from Amazon to Blue Origin and—since 2017—has been spending $1 billion a year. This would drive Musk crazy, but he knows that competition is good in the long run and has even publicly wished for Bezos to get more involved.

. . .

His critics say that Musk—the man who "loves humanity"—has a savior or messiah complex because of the purpose he finds in building his companies. Jemima Kelly at the *Financial Times*, for example, called him "a hypocrite, a sycophant, a charlatan, and a fabulist."[51] But this misses the point, because those tendencies are associated with delusion, and whatever you might think about Musk, his companies are anything but delusional. One may question how beneficial they are to humanity, but it is hard to deny that Musk's companies have redefined the sectors in which they operate.

Musk is also accused of being obsessed with Mars to the detriment of Earth—to a greater degree than Bezos—but in his defense, he doesn't say that it should be prioritized over all the important issues on Earth; he simply says that less than 1 percent of global resources are devoted to this, and that is not enough. It shouldn't be as much as Medicare, he likes to joke, but it should be more than we spend on lipstick.[52] He is accused, too, of sponging off the United States government, but SpaceX actually saves American taxpayers a lot of money by being much cheaper and more effective than its competitors, like Boeing's Starliner and NASA's Space Launch System (SLS). Finally, even if SpaceX fails to develop a Starship rocket that makes possible a city on Mars, Musk knows that it will still have been a worthwhile endeavor. Writing on X in 2024, he noted that "the absurdly ambitious nature of the goal nonetheless results in the creation of alien-level technology that is crushingly better than competitors who merely aim for Earth orbit."[53]

Like Tesla, SpaceX has missed most of its self-imposed deadlines, but as its teams like to say, they turn the impossible into the late. As of 2025, it has launched more than fifty humans into space, including the farthest from Earth in over half a century. It has been an extraordinary chapter in the history of engineering. And it all originated from that existential crisis, Douglas Adams, an obsession with the truth, the ruthless application of critical thinking, and the dream of a shining city on a distant planet.

Boiling It Down: Leaving Earth makes the universe more human

Most people think that solving problems on Earth is more important than exploring space. For Musk, this is the wrong question. We can and should do both. It is not hubristic to reach for the stars. This is obvious to him when you think on a big enough timescale. On the contrary, it is hubris *not* to leave Earth. Musk's view on space can be summarized as follows:

1. The window to accelerate human access to space is now open, and we should act without delay to lower the cost of reaching orbit.
2. Spreading out into the solar system may be the single best way to increase the scale of human consciousness over the long term.
3. For those who imagine consciousness as a candle flickering in the void, building rockets is an opportunity to combine the existential passions of creating and spacefaring.
4. Large rockets that are fully, reliably, and rapidly reusable are the fastest and cheapest way to make civilization multiplanetary.

PART III

The Crusader

"Civilization has not yet fully recovered from the shock of its birth—the transition from the tribal or 'closed society,' with its submission to magical forces, to the 'open society' which sets free the critical powers of man."

—Karl Popper

Part III is about how Musk goes into battle for his religion beyond his own efforts to increase consciousness through his companies. As shown in the following figure, it comprises three additional beliefs that seek to reinforce Musk's three core beliefs. He opposes dogma, which he thinks threatens civilization by putting feel-good certainty before uncertainty-busting curiosity. He champions free speech so that no beliefs can escape criticism. And he seeks to build AI that will expand silicon and human consciousness in a symbiotic way.

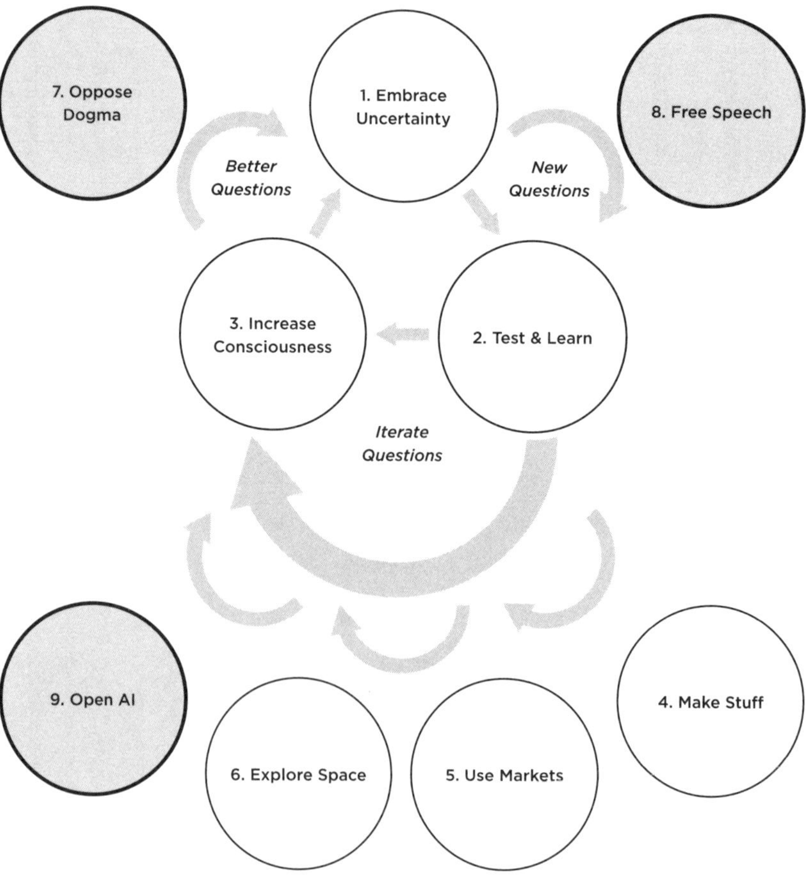

SEVEN

Oppose Dogma

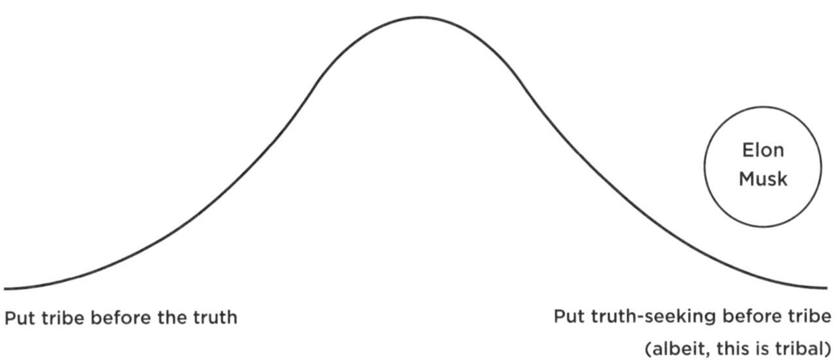

"Engineering is fun for me," Musk wrote in 2024, "whereas politics and posting on controversial issues feels like putting my hand on a hot stove—mega pain. The reason I do the latter, admittedly ineptly at times, is because I think it is necessary to counteract corrosion of civilization."[1] What did he think was causing this corrosion? "The woke mind virus," which Musk had declared two years prior, "has thoroughly penetrated entertainment and is pushing civilization towards suicide. There needs to be a counter-narrative."[2]

In short, this is why Musk got into politics. Though he may have preferred to work on Starship and self-driving cars, he was built to go against the grain, to resist conformity, and to show everyone else where he thinks they are wrong. This was not, as has been suggested, a midlife crisis. Surely he was not unchanged by the astronomical rise in his wealth, which increased tenfold in less than two years (2020–21). But, agree with him or not, he likely saw himself more in the mold of one of his heroes, Benjamin Franklin: a successful scientist and entrepreneur who was drawn into the realm of public service.[3] In Musk's case, his physics brain applied to society at large the same principles he tried to apply to himself.

While a dogma is a belief that cannot be questioned, Musk's dogma—the scientific method—is that you have to question your beliefs; this is the only thing that cannot be questioned. So when he encountered the ideology of "wokeness" in his late forties, with its identity-based worldview, he had an allergic reaction. It dared to claim immunity from his religion by placing tribe before truth, and so he assigned to himself the role of providing a counternarrative.

"Wokeness" first came to Musk's attention in 2019. Until then, the word was little known outside the Left and served as an expression of defiance and solidarity among Black and minority groups that had experienced discrimination. By 2019, the word had entered mainstream usage, adopted both by White liberals who looked at society increasingly through the prism of race, gender, and sexuality and by their critics on the Right, for whom the term had a negative connotation.[4] This was, in part, catalyzed by President Trump taking office in 2017. Just as the Republican Party became radicalized by the Tea Party when President Obama was elected, the Democrats increasingly embraced identity politics when Trump emerged as a candidate and then became president. The activism intensified in response to some of Trump's brazen divisiveness and flouting of accepted norms, and it was further boosted by the unprecedented government intervention caused by the COVID pandemic and the explosion of the Black Lives Matter movement, following the murder of George Floyd.[5]

To Musk's mind, the identity-based worldview is plainly illogical. Fundamentally, his interpretation is that anyone who is not White, male, straight, and wealthy should be seen as a victim, and anyone who is White, male, straight, and wealthy should be seen as the problem. And then, for Musk, identity-based activists say that someone such as himself cannot know the truth of someone with a different identity because he lacks their lived experience of a society organized around systems that marginalize people who are not like him. Like the dogma of traditional religions—which cannot be questioned because the truth is revealed by the divine—their personal truth cannot be questioned. This reading of the ideology was never going to sit well with someone who cherished the scientific method as ardently as he did.

This was also a very personal matter for Musk. In 2022, one of his eldest twins, Vivian Wilson, legally changed her name and gender, which is possible under Californian law if, for example, you believe the gender assigned to you at birth, based on your biological sex, does not reflect your true identity. In the public filing she also stated that she wanted to have nothing to do with her father. Musk blamed this on her Santa Monica high school, Crossroads, which he said filled her head with Marxist views, including hating him for being rich.[6] He maintained that "I have very good relationships with all the others."[7]

Musk made the claim on X that his son was "born gay and slightly autistic, two attributes that contribute to gender dysphoria" and that he was manipulated by adults into believing that gender-affirming care for adolescents (puberty blockers and hormones) would be the answer to his problems.[8] Musk considers that he knows what it is like to be a troubled teenager and agreed with J. K. Rowling on X, saying, "Almost every child goes through some kind of identity crisis during puberty," but troubled teenagers are vulnerable to brainwashing by those who tell them what they want to hear.[9] "It is deeply wrong," he alleged, "to make them permanently infertile with 'puberty blockers.' If they still wish to transition as adults, provided they are fully informed of the risks, they can then make decisions as consenting adults."[10]

Musk himself signed the necessary medical papers, claiming he did so without understanding what he was doing, so perhaps he, too, felt responsible.[11] In any event, he later said, "My son, Xavier, is dead," alluding to the concept of *deadnaming*, when you call someone by their pre-transition name.[12] "Killed by the woke mind virus," he went on, "so, I vowed to destroy the woke mind virus after that."

In Musk's eyes, identity-based activists claim the moral high ground and then zealously censure anyone who dissents. This induces compliance by a silent majority who don't really understand the identity-based ideology, and that allows it to spread quickly. Musk used the pejorative term "mind virus" to describe "wokeness," since viruses spread without resistance from one living organism to another. Gad Saad described this phenomenon in his book *The Parasitic Mind: How Infectious Ideas Are Killing Common Sense*, which Musk has extolled. What makes something parasitic is that it is hosted in another body to survive, but it causes harm to its host and will keep doing so until it kills itself by killing its hosts until there are none left.[13] But Musk considered himself immune. So speaking out against "wokeness" became a crusade for him that must be won at all costs. "Unless it is stopped," he wrote, "the woke mind virus will destroy civilization and humanity will never [reach] Mars."[14]

For Musk, the only way to resist was to think for oneself because, as Steve Jobs once said, dogma is "living with the results of other people's thinking."[15] That's why Musk asked on Twitter in 2021, "Who wrote the software running in your head? Are you sure you actually want it there?"[16] This is especially important for him when it relates to children. Young people, he says, must be taught critical thinking, as this "creates a mental firewall to allow children to reject concepts that are not cogent." It is like having a personal "anti mind-virus defense system."[17]

Musk felt that identity-based activists achieved the compliance of so many because they took advantage of our tendency to conform, to signal virtue to the tribe, and to avoid confrontation. He thought that they "weaponized" the natural empathy response for their own purposes.[18] When people put pronouns in their bio to indicate "allyship," for example, he saw only that "the woke mind virus ate your brain."[19] The intolerance spread because of the threat of being called out for opposing "social justice" and being ostracized. But Musk didn't care. He was not so encumbered by the usual empathy response.

He felt that he had the measure of identity-based activists, and that not enough people were doing anything to stop them. To use Isaiah Berlin's phrase again, he might have thought of them as "hedgehogs"—those who have a simple, organizing theory of the world that they internalize with a fervor that is religious.[20] And it didn't matter that most people were indifferent to their ideology. As Nassim N. Taleb has written, norms can be established not only through a process of consensus-building but through the dictates of a minority group if they are both intolerant and well organized.[21]

Perhaps Musk saw the "hedgehog" quality in identity-based activists because he is a "hedgehog" himself. He is fanatical about his religion of curiosity and truth-seeking, and he is intransigent about the central role for criticism. So a clash became unavoidable. Musk thought that the identity activists had started it by creating "an artificial mental civil war" or "holy war," and he would not back down.[22]

It might make him unpopular, but that would only be proof to him that he was right and that everyone else had taken the easy option. He had over 200 million followers on Twitter, over $200 billion of net worth, and a sense of purpose in his life. So if anyone could take the hit and speak up for the silent majority, he felt that he could and should. "This is a battle to the death," he wrote on X.[23]

This, in turn, led Musk into politics. He had previously supported Barack Obama, Hillary Clinton, and Joe Biden in 2012, 2016, and 2020, respectively, and considered himself liberal on social issues and right-leaning on economic matters. But no longer. Identity-based activism was not the only factor.[24] President Biden had built his career on his support for labor unions, which Tesla opposed, and he went to lengths to snub the company in 2021 and 2022.[25] Musk also felt that Starship's progress was tied down with red tape. But he viewed these as symptoms of a more serious malaise: The left-wing ideology that he said had turned the Democratic Party into a "party of division & hate."[26]

Truth vs. Tribe

While identity-based ideology is generally perceived to be about power and social injustice, for Musk it was linked directly to his underlying philosophy. He knew the process by which he came to his "physics operating system" and his search for better questions, and he knew how this set him apart. So it was natural for him to reflect on whether contemporary culture supported people like him and their endeavors, especially when he was told that his identity made him the problem and that he didn't understand the truth.

In this sense, Musk followed a very similar sequence of thought processes to Karl Popper (whom we met in Chapters 2, 3, and 4). Born in Vienna in 1902, Karl Popper was a melancholic child who developed a boyish desire to understand the nature of reality. He was fascinated by the concept of infinity, and his curiosity led him to develop his theory of scientific knowledge and the desire always to try to be less wrong. In 1937, the year before Hitler occupied Austria, he fled Vienna because, though he was raised a Lutheran, he had Jewish ancestry. Given the times, he turned his attention to politics and the origins of totalitarianism, and in 1946, he published *The Open Society and Its Enemies*. He argued that people with dogmatic beliefs are too certain of their ability to predict the future and leave no room for new ideas that might come along and be put to the test. No different than the way an individual gains knowledge, a society learns too from an open-ended process of creativity, criticism, and error correction, which allows the best ideas of the day to win and the worst ideas to be killed off before they become too big.

Popper's diagnosis of the origins of closed thinking also aligns with Musk's reckoning with the absurd and the philosophy of Douglas Adams. For Popper, there is an acute feeling of loss for the unity of the tribe that happened when humans started to think critically and felt a separation from the natural world. Popper called it the "strain of civilization," echoing Sigmund Freud's *Civilization and Its Discontents*.[27] While he questioned the science behind Freud's theories, Popper agreed that the comforting walls of the closed pre-civilized era were eroded, creating tension, disunity, uneasiness, and a new need for higher meaning. Ever since then, he went on, we have been more aware of suffering and the imperfections of life and more dissatisfied with a world that cannot live up to our moral ideals and dreams of perfection. It is here that religion steps in to offer the comfort of belonging to a group as a sort of synthetic version of a tribe.[28] And if it can't be spiritual, then secular will do.

The "shock" of civilization's birth that Popper described, therefore, is akin to the desperate search for the meaning of life that Douglas Adams portrays. Musk knows very well the void of meaning that people can experience. He tried to respond with "Don't Panic" and by remaining open-minded in order to resist wishful thinking and the need to conform. But equally, he knows how hard this is for other people. "There seems to be an innate need for religion," Musk has observed. "Many atheists simply adopt another belief system (e.g., wokeness) that is essentially a religion."[29] And he sees this new ideology as a direct competitor to his own religion: "Nature abhors a vacuum," he wrote on X. "Woke is absolutely the religion that occupies the space previously held by Christianity."[30]

For Musk, as for Popper, secular religions need to recreate the tension between good and evil that characterizes traditional religions. The followers are offered a route to salvation in this life, if not the next. That is why intellectuals, usually informed by their own suffering, ask themselves how they can fix the unfairness of the world. Popper wrote about fascist intellectuals who define their own national or racial groups relative to others and Marxist intellectuals who define the working class by its struggle against the ruling class. The identity of the tribe is always defined in opposition to another tribe that has wronged them. Based on the same analysis, Musk found identity-based politics of all persuasions inherently negative, humorless, and misanthropic, noting: "Both the far left & far right have a lot of hate. One could simply replace the word 'far' with 'loathing,' as they have that emotion a lot, whereas most people, who are moderates, do not."[31]

Traditionally, Popper argued, the Right offers the strongman who can restore the myth of a better past, and the Left offers the myth of a better, classless future. The past is rewritten respectively according to bogus laws of nature (race) and economics (class), which are, in turn, used to prophesy the future. But these are forms of closed thinking. They use pseudoscience to justify social engineering. They look for evidence to confirm their theories, and they suppress any disproof that might undermine their creed. On this Musk was in emphatic agreement. "I find it remarkable," he said, "that sociopolitical views, even among very smart humans, are almost always a function of tribal belongingness, rather than reason."[32] The group then becomes the answer to everything. "It's truth v tribalism," he said, as people are so reluctant to change their minds.[33]

In the case of identity-based ideology, Musk contended that "the fundamental axiomatic flaw of the woke mind virus is that the weaker party is always right."[34] This means that if "the oppressed are always the good guys, then . . . the strong are the bad guys."[35] Musk utterly rejected this. He agreed instead with Aleksandr Solzhenitsyn that "the line dividing good and evil cuts through the heart of every human being" and not between those who have the privilege of being in the majority and those who do not.[36]

For Musk, there was a kind of self-delusion among identity-based intellectuals and activists that caused his operating system to short-circuit. In the extreme, they proffered a myth that whatever feels authentic to you is your truth, and anyone who says otherwise is imposing their truth. Conversely, if you have privilege, you just need to acknowledge your guilt, be quiet, and listen. This notion that we each have an essence and our own truth draws on philosophers such as Nietzsche and Heidegger and was despised by Musk, no less than Popper. The French philosopher Michel Foucault took it even further, preaching that there is no self and no reality, just a truth constructed by people with power at the time you have the misfortune to be born. More recent schools of thought have drawn on this approach to argue that any abstract concept is a social construction, that every social phenomenon is systemic, and that truth is a purely subjective experience.

To Musk, therefore, there is an Orwellian aspect to the identity-based worldview, in the way it asserts that there is no basis for agreeing on what is true.[37] As Orwell wrote in *Nineteen Eighty-Four*, "In the end the Party would announce that two and two made five, and you would have to believe it. It was inevitable that they should make that claim sooner or later: the logic of their position demanded it. Not merely the validity of experience, but the very existence of external reality, was tacitly denied by their philosophy."[38] For Musk, this is simply a device for inoculating an indefensible belief from criticism.

Go Woke, Go Broke

How bad could group-based identity activism really be for Musk? He did not mince his words when he said, "At its heart, wokeness is divisive, exclusionary and hateful. It basically gives mean people a shield to be mean and cruel, armored in false virtue."[39] In Musk's view, "wokeness" may seem well-intentioned, but it caused all sorts of harm that was not at first obvious. In particular, Musk said that identity-based activists claim to be fighting racism and sexism, but they simply replace them with other forms of racism and sexism.[40]

Musk saw the identity-based worldview as a fundamentally zero-sum game in which there are only winners and losers. Everyone should be classified according to their identity, for that is the main driver of how much social power and privilege people possess. Those who have it repress those who don't, and so the task is simply to correct the unfairness until "social justice" is achieved. Musk's analysis aligns with that of Friedrich Hayek, who damned the concept of "social justice," alleging that it is deliberately nebulous to make it difficult to object to and serves only to justify the cutting up as opposed to the growing of the pie.[41]

Given the nature of Musk's own religion, his ethical and rational objections to identity-based ideology were one and the same. That is why he approvingly quoted Frank Herbert, who wrote in *Dune*,

"Respect for the truth comes close to being the basis for all morality."[42] But it is hard. "Most people (maybe all?) are instinctively moral relativists," Musk said. "If you're perceived as being in the group, you can do no wrong, whereas those outside the group can do no right. This instinct can be overridden, but requires a strong commitment to truth over convenience."[43] What this implied was that "morality should be considered in the absolute, as both the strong and the weak are capable of right and wrong."[44]

Musk was insistent that it is not about what you do, nor who you are; signaling virtue to your tribe might feel good, but true virtue, he likes to say, is caring about the reality of goodness instead of the perception of it.[45] It's more important to judge people on the consequences of their actions—"deeds done"—than on the intentions behind them.[46] And he seemed to acknowledge his large ego and at the same time forgive himself for it in his ironic tweet: "If I am a narcissist (which might be true), at least I am a useful one."[47]

Musk's ethics have some similarities with those of philosopher Paul Bloom, who wrote in *Against Empathy* about how compassion can be quite rational while empathy can be misguided and exploited, as it is intrinsically irrational.[48] Musk takes a slightly different tack, though. "The good interpretation of the woke movement," Musk said in 2024, "is that we want to have empathy for our fellow human beings. And, of course, we want to have empathy for our fellow human beings. I strongly believe we should care about humanity and we should care about the future. But we need to have empathy that is deep, not shallow. Shallow empathy is caring about criminals, but deep empathy is caring about the victims of the criminals."[49] It ties in with the view of Hayek that some of the more benevolent aspects of human nature do not scale beyond individuals and families to large communities with many strangers.[50] Indeed, Musk often provides examples of empathy that are so exaggerated they are "suicidal" for civilization, a phrase borrowed from Gad Saad.[51]

Musk's views are broadly utilitarian but not to be confused with those of the effective altruism movement, where the emphasis is on making money to do good rather than doing good by making things.[52] He once joked on X, "affective autism > effective altruism?"[53] Nor is it to be confused with the views of Ayn Rand, author of *Atlas Shrugged* and *The Fountainhead*, who wrote in praise of individuals who drag society up by acting in their own self-interest. Musk has described this perspective as being sophomoric: "It's a counterpoint to communism and useful as such, but should be tempered with kindness."[54] Rand's philosophy also rests on the idea that enlightened individuals know the objective truth, which runs completely counter to Musk's view that we are always wrong and should try to be less so.

The way to increase consciousness, for Musk, is through a "positive-sum" game, where one person's gain does not result in another person's loss. If the identity-based worldview is for him fundamentally closed to learning and change, his own worldview is one in which society is open to testing and learning, using the dogma of scientific thinking and the error correction afforded by democratic elections and free markets. Musk would agree with the Swedish historian Johan Norberg, who wrote, "Liberalism is not based on ignoring the meaning of life but on believing that more people have a chance to find that meaning if they have the freedom to search for it."[55]

Musk also asserts that we should stop treating people based on the notion that they are members of racial, gender, or other groups; instead, we should treat everyone as individuals, equal before the law. His positive-sum society is built up from the level of the individual, endowed with the gift of critical thinking, to their families, friends, associates, and finally to strangers. To find meaning, therefore, at the level of the group is anti-individual, which makes it anti-science and anti-merit. Popper called this "inhuman," and Musk calls it "anti-human."[56] Terrible mistakes have been made in the past, Musk accepts, because all people are capable of evil. But if "civilization" is responsible for the way that humans have dehumanized other humans who were not like them—slavery, segregation, male-only suffrage, homophobic laws, etc.—then it is also "civilization," acting through the democratic process, that has eliminated many of these practices.[57]

For Musk, the concept of diversity, equity, and inclusion (DEI) is a lose-lose strategy, which he argues makes both the strong weaker and the weak weaker. He believes it is wrong to promote diversity based on group identity when what is needed to solve problems and create is divergence of thinking. Based on his experience, the most talented people who like to work on hard problems will only want to work for organizations that are dogmatic about recruiting the best talent and developing the best ideas.

The corollary of this view for Musk is that any organization—including the government—that subscribes to DEI will inevitably become bloated, which, in turn, distances decision-makers from the front line, making them disconnected from the consequences of their actions; they have no stake in the outcome of what they do and little ability to listen to feedback. This aligns with the view of Taleb, who wrote, for example, in *Antifragile* that bureaucrats, academics, and executives all not only lack skin in the game but are "fragile" and break when there is stress, whereas citizens, artisans, and entrepreneurs are "antifragile," as they become stronger when stressed.[58]

Perhaps the worst part of DEI, for Musk, is that it can encourage a kind of learned helplessness. Informed by his own experience, he is convinced that if you don't take risks and test yourself, you become weaker. Again he aligns with Taleb for whom the willingness to try and fail is courageous, writing in *Skin in the Game*, "Courage is the only virtue you can't fake," because whether or not you get hurt, you take the risk of getting hurt.[59]

This analysis of DEI lines up too with the work of Jonathan Haidt, a social psychologist whom Musk has praised. Haidt started out a liberal, made a concerted effort to understand conservatives, and ended up writing with Greg Lukianoff about what they called the "coddling" of an anxious younger generation in America. Lukianoff and Haidt, too, disagreed with the notion that good and evil are divided into groups, with the belief that emotions should be pandered to, and with the anti-Nietzschean view that "What does not kill me makes me weaker."[60] They argue that young people who are overprotected struggle to handle any loss of control, unpredictability, criticism, or hostility. It is the diametric opposite of the macho, hardcore, PvP cultures that Musk champions at Tesla, SpaceX, and his other organizations.

Musk shares with Haidt the view that a "weak makes right" ideology encourages people to blame their problems on society instead of exercising personal moral responsibility.[61] That's why Musk often retorts to his critics that they are "takers not makers."[62] He feels that by not selecting on merit, DEI patronizes many people by assuming that they would not want to compete on merit. And, in so doing, it denies them the opportunity to feel the satisfaction of making progress in the face of difficulty, which for him is the essential ingredient for building character, for learning, and for creativity.

Hedgehog vs. Hedgehog

Musk thinks of politics in terms of the "Overton window," a term coined in the 1990s by the political scientist Joseph Overton, which describes the spectrum of mainstream views, excluding the fringes on the Left and the Right. Musk considered that the window had been stretched to the left to such a degree that the Democrats were no longer the party of "individual freedom and merit" that they used to be.[63] Musk's goal, however, was not to try to hold the center ground. He was a hedgehog going into battle with another hedgehog, but he was also sure of the moderation of his own opinions, so he decided the best way to strengthen the center would be to keep the Overton window wide by amplifying right-of-center viewpoints.[64] Providing a counterbalance, in his view, would be the best way to increase what he calls the "ratio of signal to noise."[65]

Starting in 2022, therefore, Musk waged a campaign on X/Twitter on multiple fronts, making thousands of posts to push back on emerging norms that he thought were dogmatic and needed questioning. The common theme was what Musk saw as the hypocrisy of intellectuals and activists who spread the concept that "weak makes right" but, having no skin in the game, are removed from the negative consequences of their policies on ordinary people.

In the case of race, for example, Musk perceived that empathy had become disconnected from reality. He believed that it had become normal to say that White people were racist and that this had led to the overreporting of White-on-Black crimes relative to Black-on-White crimes—be it in the United States, the United Kingdom, or South Africa.[66] Musk, therefore, took it upon himself to redress the imbalance by reposting hundreds of stories. More broadly, he highlighted what he considered to be the excessive leniency shown toward criminals in the form of soft policing and sentencing, which he argued had made cities less safe.

Musk also thought that unbounded solidarity with illegal immigrants had gotten out of hand as it caused the neglect of border controls, which did not serve the overall interests of American citizens.

Their numbers may include legitimate seekers of asylum, but they also include numerous men with criminal records, and some who mean harm to the United States.

In the case of gender-affirming care for adolescents, Musk maintained that empathy for individuals who may wish to transition sometimes overrides the duty of care that health-care professionals owe to children. Additionally, in cases such as women's sports, he thought that the rights of biological women are undermined when biological men self-identified as female.

Musk also diagnosed the state of California as having a particular problem. He made connections between the promotion of gender-affirming care, crime in San Francisco, the "niche ideology" of the University of California, Berkeley, the progressive policies of elected Democrats like Governor Gavin Newsom and former Senator Kamala Harris, and the large historic immigrant population of California. This state of affairs was only sustained, he claimed, by the wealth generated in Silicon Valley. For Musk, this was quite personal. In 2020, for example, he had called the state's COVID stay-at-home orders "fascist" and Democrat Congresswoman Lorena Gonzalez, a member of the California State Assembly, posted a tweet saying, "F*ck Elon Musk."[67] In 2024, he also cited Newsom's law protecting LGBTQ+ students' privacy in schools as the final straw, prompting him to move the headquarters of SpaceX and X to Texas.[68]

The 2024 presidential election was always going to be a forcing function for Musk. Popper was clear that intolerance has to be countered with rational argument and kept in check by public opinion.[69] In practice, the way to do this in democratic countries is through elections. You may succeed in moving the Overton window, but the election still needs to be won. Victory for Musk would be to show the Democratic Party that they could not win unless they disavowed identity-based activism, and that necessitated defeating them at the ballot box. He liked to say he was more leaning away from the Democrats than leaning toward the Republicans, but being half-hearted was not a winning strategy. Worse than that, his political activity set him up to be *persona non grata* in the event the Democrats did win, with consequences for all of his companies, from SpaceX to Tesla and Twitter. He really had no option but to double down. And with the attempted assassination of President Trump in July 2024 in Butler, Pennsylvania, Musk had a pretext for providing his endorsement.

None of this had been inevitable. The week before the 2016 presidential election, Musk had said publicly of Trump, "He doesn't seem to have the sort of character that reflects well on the United States," and in private, he had described him as a "con-man" and a "bullshitter," according to Walter Isaacson.[70] As recently as 2022, President Trump also called Musk a "bullshit artist,"[71] to which Musk replied that Trump should "hang up his hat & sail into the sunset."[72] Then in 2022, Musk expressed public support for Ron DeSantis, the governor of Florida, who was publicly critical of Disney for its "woke" activism. And even in July 2024, Musk was saying that his own view was more "Make America Greater" (MAG) than the explicitly conservative "Make America Great Again" (MAGA).[72] Furthermore, Musk had historically disagreed with Trump on a range of issues, from tariffs and climate change to abortion and the claim that the 2020 election was stolen.[73]

On the plus side for Trump, though, he was anything but dogmatic. He had built his political career on being politically incorrect. Musk agreed strongly with him on a range of issues, from gender-affirming care to free speech, immigration, and low taxes.[74] And, while Trump didn't care much for EVs, he was not praising GM and Ford over Tesla. Musk's decision was made easier by the Democratic Party running such an infirm candidate as President Biden and by the pursuit of President

Trump in the courts in 2023 and 2024. And then when Trump was shot in the ear, Musk was genuinely impressed by his courage under fire, since that could not have been faked.

Musk likes to say that nothing is perfect, but you have to take a side—the side that you think is less wrong—and you have to act.[75] And that's what he did in backing Trump. In short, Trump was the obstacle between the Democrats and the White House. He was the most powerful proponent of the counternarrative that Musk had been advocating for more than two years. And having taken a side, he was all in.

The nomination of Kamala Harris to lead the Democratic ticket when Biden stepped down crystallized the narrative for Musk. As some Democrats accused Trump of being a fascist, Musk responded with sweeping statements like, "This election is existential for life as we know it"[76] and "If Trump is NOT elected, this will be the last election. Far from being a threat to democracy, he is the only way to save it!"[77] He predicted that the whole of America could become like California, Harris's home state, linking it back to immigration, with the argument that the Democratic Party had a perverse incentive to turn a blind eye to the scale of illegal immigration because immigrants are more likely to vote Democrat.[78]

Musk, therefore, became even more of a "hedgehog." He set out with the credo of "I try not to pick fights, but I do finish them," and he fought with the attitude "play to win or don't play at all."[79] In 2022, for example, Musk had advocated voting Republican in the midterms because "shared power curbs the worst excesses of both parties."[80] But now he wanted total victory for the Republicans.

Just like the secular religion he was fighting, Musk recreated a tension between those he thought were good and those who were evil. In this, his Zeroth Law combined with the popular saying, "The only thing necessary for the triumph of evil is for good men to do nothing." This sense of waging a crusade can be seen in the increasingly polarizing language he used that divided the world into good people who care about action and the reality of goodness and bad people who care about identity and the appearance of goodness. They are either righteous and with you, trying to do right, or they are self-righteous and against you, doing wrong. The virtue signalers were no longer hypocritical and bad but downright evil, and he had contempt for them.[81] Musk posted on X, for example, "The real fight is not between right and left, but rather between humanists and extinctionists."[82]

The more he waded into politics and was attacked by the Left, the more he became hardened and took the fight to the other side. In this, Trump was a fellow fighter, and the shared experience strengthened their bond.[83] So it was that Musk put his support behind Trump, giving over $250 million to his campaign, focusing mainly on turnout in swing states, with numerous campaign stops in Pennsylvania and thousands of posts on X, which attracted billions of views. He also agreed to play a role in setting up what would become DOGE.

With Trump's ultimate victory, Musk felt satisfied that he had helped drag the Overton window to the right. The kind of progressive policies associated with California did not play so well in the midwestern swing states, and a meaningful minority of Black and Latino voters did move away from the Democratic Party. The week after the election, one of President Trump's sons posted on X that "Woke is dead," to which Musk replied, "Still much work to do, but the tide of the battle has turned."[84] Before long, he would turn his attention ever more overseas, to countries like the United Kingdom and Germany.

. . .

It is debatable whether Musk's strategy was the best way to take on identity-based activism compared to him trying to strengthen the center ground. He alienated a lot of moderates, for example, by not distancing himself from the White identity nationalists who gravitated toward him. And he did engage in "flooding the zone" with dubious information, which gave oxygen to their conspiracy theories. He forwarded, for example, a spurious article about Nancy Pelosi's husband, saying, "There is a tiny possibility there might be more to this story than meets the eye," thereby acknowledging it was almost certainly untrue while knowing it would cause damage.[85] As a result of such behavior, previous supporters turned against him. Yann LeCun, the French AI lead at Meta, for example, spoke for many when he wrote, "I like his cars, his rockets, his solar panels, and his satellite network. I very much dislike his vengeful politics, his conspiracy theories, and his hype."[86]

But in Musk's mind, if the end is truth-seeking, the end justifies the means. He cared about issues such as race-based affirmative action and gender-affirming care for adolescents, which President Trump duly issued executive orders on when he took office. And in his inaugural address, Trump even gave his explicit support for the goal of sending American astronauts to plant the Stars and Stripes on the planet Mars. This, for Musk, was the Realpolitik you needed to engage in if you were to get into the political arena and play to win. It showed that even the truth-seekers belong to a tribe, and that sometimes they should put their tribe before truth-seeking itself. Fate loves irony, Musk might say.

In due course, Musk would show that his support for President Trump was not unconditional, speaking out against his tariff policy and then his proposed budget bill, which caused a spectacular falling-out between the two in June 2025. Keeping quiet and preserving his relationship with Trump would have been the easy thing to do. But with his war on "wokeness" increasingly behind him, Musk refused to stay silent on the United States' mounting national debt. The budget bill was estimated to add $3 trillion to the federal deficit over time, which would push the projected level of national debt even higher, toward 124 percent of GDP in 2034.[87] Musk felt—no less than political correctness—that this was another case of delusion by lawmakers. Indeed he thought that it posed such a corrosive threat to civilization that it warranted a new America Party that would represent what he called the "the 80% in the middle."[88]

Boiling It Down: Put truth-seeking before tribe (albeit, this is tribal)

Most people naturally put tribe before truth for the sense of belonging and security it provides us. This helps keep the question of life's meaning at bay. But people like Musk think in terms of individuals and humanity, and less so the groups that exist in between. Accordingly, he opposes those dogmas that are created to sustain such groups. His views on dogmatic thinking can be summarized as follows:

1. Sometimes it's not enough to think critically and create. One must also speak up and resist those who would stop others from doing so.
2. Intellectuals find purpose in putting the world to rights, but they always put tribe before truth (unless they think critically).
3. Societies flourish when they overcome their tribal tendencies, and individuals are free to test and learn in an open-ended way.
4. When dogmatic people are being irrational, one should respond with rational arguments, even if that means being unpopular. It's hard to win elections without being popular, though, and so sometimes one must make concessions to the tribe.

EIGHT

Free Speech

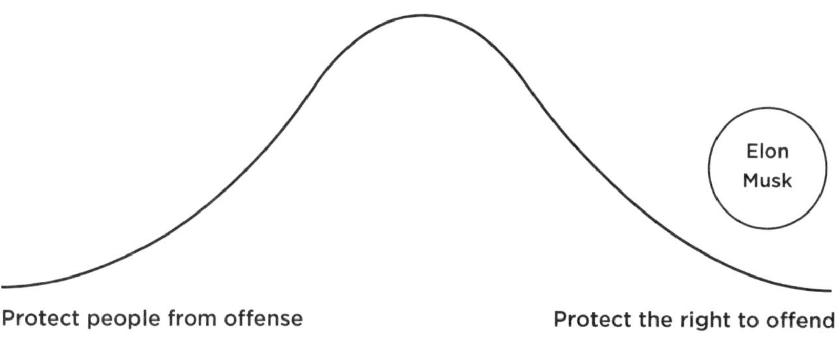

"Elon is not an ass, and yet sometimes he will say some things that are very assholey."[1] So said Gwynne Shotwell, who should understand Musk better than most, given both that he is her boss at SpaceX and that her husband also has autism spectrum disorder.

Musk is a peculiar person. He nearly always speaks his mind, dispensing with the usual pleasantries. If he feels a certain way about someone, he might call them a "traitor," a "criminal," a "moron," an "asshole," or a "pedo guy" without much regard for how it might make them feel. Some say that he refuses to filter what he says and is shooting from the hip, while others reflect that he is simply not able to. Even with Trump, he didn't hold back, alleging on X in 2025 that the president was named in the Epstein files—another case possibly of saying something that might technically be true while the main intent was to cause damage.[2]

Some might say that such ad hominem attacks demean Musk more than those he targets, and he probably wouldn't care about that either. Perhaps he thinks that if you are not evil, you should not care if he calls you that. And if you take offense, you should show him why he's wrong. And if you do happen to be evil, then perhaps you should feel bad. The truth can hurt.

Musk, one can say, has both a strong appetite and a high tolerance for confrontation and profanity, and this provides important context for why he decided to buy Twitter. Many people think that he did so to post right-wing viewpoints, but he didn't need to own the platform to do that. He bought the platform to protect the very right of people to speak freely, without needing to have regard to whether or not they might cause offense.

In March 2022, a satirical news outlet made a joke on Twitter that their Man of the Year was a transgender woman: Rachel Levine, assistant secretary for health in the Biden administration. Levine had started identifying publicly as a woman eleven years prior, at the age of fifty-four. The news site *The Babylon Bee*, which has a conservative Christian bent, added that Levine's "self-identification has no bearing on the truth."[3] This is somewhat reminiscent of a scene in Monty Python's 1979 film, *Life of Brian*, in which Stan says he has the right as a man to be a woman called Loretta and to have babies. The character Francis agrees, saying it is symbolic of their struggle against Roman oppression, but Reg counters that it's "symbolic of his struggle against reality."[4]

One can debate whether either joke is in good taste or whether *The Babylon Bee*'s constitutes harassment since it is targeted. But for Musk, everyone has the right to make a joke, even if it is offensive to another person or group, especially if, like Levine, that person is a vocal critic of state-level limits on gender-affirming care for adolescents. After the post, however, *The Babylon Bee*'s account was blocked because the news site was deemed to have engaged in "hateful conduct" for a tweet that misgendered—or "deadnamed"—a woman. It would be unblocked if they deleted the post, but they refused. For Musk, this blocking was censorship, and it would be a tipping point.

In Musk's view, Twitter had strayed too far from the US Constitution. Any individual in the United States is permitted to make that joke, as their speech is protected by law. According to the First Amendment, the government is not allowed to intervene and stop them, no more than it is able to stop someone starting a religion, a newspaper, or a public gathering, provided they do not incite or threaten violence.[5] But when individuals express themselves on a social media platform, they have no such protection. The user generates the content, but Twitter, as a private company, sets its own terms of service and has no obligation to publish it.

What bothered Musk so much about this was the Orwellian nature of "politically correct" language. One should not suppress *The Babylon Bee* because you dislike what they say, he believes, since "free speech only matters if people you don't like are allowed to say things you don't like."[6] Hard as it might be to imagine, this principle is all important for Musk because at any point in time, people who don't like you might stop you from speaking freely and asking questions.

Musk also agrees with Orwell on the connection between the freedom to speak and the freedom to think, since censorship and propaganda work hand in hand. In *Nineteen Eighty-Four*, the character Syme works in the Ministry of Truth and explains to Winston Smith, "Don't you see that the whole aim of Newspeak is to narrow the range of thought? In the end we shall make thoughtcrime literally impossible, because there will be no words in which to express it."[7] If you can't ask questions, then curiosity is extinguished, and dogma goes unchallenged. That's why in Newspeak there is no word for *science*, and the words that comprise the Declaration of Independence would no longer have meaning.[8]

Musk likes to say that free speech was sacred to early Americans because they knew what it was like not to have it. It became the bedrock of their democracy, and the country's success would be built on its openness to new ideas. Today, by contrast, he contends that we too often take free speech for granted. And in that regard, the way in which identity-based activists were able to use intolerance to stifle criticism was a major warning sign to him.[9] That's why he gave his full support to *The Babylon Bee*, whose CEO Seth Dillon, on refusing to delete the tweet in order to unlock their account, wrote, "Never censor yourself. Insist that 2 and 2 make 4 even if Twitter tries to compel you to say otherwise. Make them ban millions of us."[10] This was a direct invocation of the scene at the end of *Nineteen Eighty-Four*, where Winston Smith's spirit is broken and he writes 2 + 2 = 5 with his finger on a dusty table in the Chestnut Tree Cafe.[11] He resisted for as long as he could, clinging to his individual identity, but in the end, he was brainwashed and declares his love for the inhuman Big Brother.

Musk agreed with this sentiment, later quoting Orwell's dictum that "every joke is a tiny revolution."[12] The problem, as he saw it, though, was that outside of Twitter there were not many places where you could go to make that joke—not in the traditional mainstream media, which he thought had been captured by "woke" ideology. He called the legacy media a "cheering squad" for the Democrats and the Left, and he thought the other platforms weren't much better. "Google and Facebook/Instagram," he alleged on Twitter, "have a strong political bias."[13] In his mind, they were all in lockstep, and unless one of the platforms broke ranks, there would be no means to get nearer to the truth.

Furthermore, Twitter wasn't just any platform to Musk. Compared to all the other forms of media, it was special. He had joined in 2009 and increasingly made his life and companies fairly transparent on the platform, as well as using it for fun and to release stress, eventually becoming its biggest user. Facebook and Instagram had many more users, but Twitter was the gathering place for journalists, politicians, and public intellectuals, the so-called digital town square. The Center for Humane Technology cofounder Aza Raskin has called it the "attention allocation organ of society," like a brain implanted into society that rewires what we focus on.[14] It determines what dominates the news according to what is trending, thus playing a huge role in shaping everyone's view of reality.

It was for this reason that Twitter cofounder and CEO Jack Dorsey tweeted in 2015, "I think Twitter is the closest thing we have to a global consciousness. And I believe the world needs that right now."[15] Born in St Louis, Missouri, in 1976, Dorsey was a free spirit, a hacker who loved maps and intuitively understood how telecommunications could connect people who were on the move and how software could knit them together. His way of thinking resonated with Musk's: technology was allowing humans to build new layers of civilization, connecting people in real time with ever lower latency and higher bandwidth. Musk perceived this clearly, saying in 2022, "Because it consists of billions of bidirectional interactions per day, Twitter can be thought of as a collective, cybernetic super-intelligence."[16] Like Dorsey, he saw it as a "hive-mind" and "the group chat for Earth."[17] He even went so far as to say, "If successful, X will evolve to be the collective consciousness of humanity or, more accurately, the human-machine collective."[18]

So, for Musk, the free speech stakes were much higher with Twitter. Widespread censoriousness could pave the way for outright censorship, and this had to be stopped. For if identity-based ideology was hardwired into such a platform, then it was game over for Popper's open society. Twitter should not become a safe space where language is proscribed; it should instead be a safe space where users can tell other people what they don't want to hear. And *The Babylon Bee* incident was definitive proof to Musk that this was not the case.

Perhaps emboldened by being named *Fortune*'s 2021 Man of the Year and becoming the richest person in the world, Musk made a $44 billion offer for Twitter in April 2022, taking control of the company six months later. Of course, *The Babylon Bee* episode was not the sole cause—Musk had started building his stake in Twitter prior to that—but it was emblematic of the need he saw to make speech freer.

For more than two decades, Musk had focused exclusively on building his own companies, but building a new Twitter from scratch was infeasible given the first-mover advantage that Twitter enjoyed. So he broke the habit of a lifetime and, instead of starting a company, he bought one. He explained the purchase in classic fashion: "This is not a way to make money . . . My strong intuitive sense is that having a public platform that is maximally trusted and broadly inclusive is extremely important to the future of civilization."[19] Dorsey, a left-leaning libertarian, endorsed this sentiment when he tweeted, "In principle, I don't believe anyone should own or run Twitter. It wants to be a public good at a protocol level, not a company. Solving for the problem of it being a company however, Elon is the singular solution I trust. I trust his mission to extend the light of consciousness."[20]

A Hard Problem

Nearly all the issues at Twitter that Musk would face—and be blamed for—existed in some way before he acquired the platform, so it's important to understand the history. Twitter was founded in 2006, two years after Facebook. Mark Zuckerberg actually tried to buy Twitter in 2008, and he did succeed in beating Twitter to acquire Instagram in 2012. They would both discover that running a social media platform is fraught with difficulty.

"Social media" was a new, hybrid category when it emerged, and the platforms benefited from regulation under Section 230 of the Communications Decency Act (1996), which treated platforms as "interactive computer services." This meant they were encouraged to moderate in good faith any material that was "obscene, lewd, lascivious, filthy, excessively violent, harassing, or otherwise objectionable," but the act of so doing did not deem them to be publishers, as they were also granted immunity from liability for content on the basis that it is user-generated. Initially, platform operators were happy to do as little as possible, but with time, it became obvious they needed to do some housecleaning. They had federal law obligations in a few areas, like child pornography and terrorism, and they chose to mirror First Amendment limitations on speech that threatened or incited violence. Beyond this, moderation was—and remains to this day—at the discretion of management.

From the start, Twitter's culture was always more free speech oriented than Facebook's. In 2011, for example, Twitter's CEO, Dick Costolo, liked to say, "We're the free speech wing of the free speech party."[21] In practice, however, Twitter's commitment to freedom of expression came under pressure from a variety of stakeholders, including its users, advertisers, shareholders, politicians, and three-letter agencies. And, based on this, Twitter started to develop its terms of service.

As Twitter grew in the 2010s, together with Facebook, it started to have a real impact on American culture in a recursive way, which reshaped the platform itself. As more and more people adopted a political identity, social media encouraged them to become more partisan and to define themselves increasingly by reference to the opposite side. Those who posted content that induced confrontation and conflict attracted extra attention. And this incentivized people to gain status by posturing in front of their political tribe and to signal their virtue by voicing outrage about the opposing tribe (often without actually engaging with it). The more sensational, the better. From Musk's point of view, users would conclude that the world is a much more extreme place than it is. While Instagram might make the lives of others seem better than they really are, Twitter exposes its users to a world that is, for the most part, worse than reality. For Musk, this plays right into our primitive wiring. "Positive news is nice to know," he says, "but negative news, for almost our entire evolutionary history, could mean death, so higher priority. What really messes things up in the modern era is that negative news can now reach everyone on Earth, but still triggers a limbic danger response even when there is no actual danger."[22]

The emergence of Twitter and its peers disrupted all established institutions, from political parties to the independent press, and some would say it disrupted representative democracy itself. This was a chaos in which one person thrived above all others: Donald Trump. He was its chief instigator and beneficiary, and he used Twitter like a megaphone. Against this backdrop, the Left and the Right increasingly accused each other of conspiracy and disinformation and inevitably, politicians got involved too. The First Amendment prohibited this, but it happened surreptitiously. Meanwhile, foreign actors targeted the site with armies of bots and fake news to sow further confusion and division.

These dynamics created a serious challenge for Twitter to determine what constituted hateful and offensive conduct, and what they should do about it. On the one hand, controversy brought with it hate speech, which was a major turnoff for a lot of Twitter's users, employees, and brand advertisers that the company's business model depended on for 90 percent of its revenues. No advertiser wanted their corporate logo next to posts that might be considered offensive. On the other hand, Twitter had become, in the words of the Center for Humane Technology cofounder Tristan Harris, a "fault line-finding for-profit machine" that tries to "get your nervous system to light up."[23] Inflammatory tweets generated the eyeballs that advertisers wanted, especially when Trump was online.

In practice, Twitter executives leaned increasingly into moderation. They developed global policies for hateful conduct and misinformation (e.g., civic integrity/election interference, public health, and manipulated media), which they implemented with a variety of sanctions, from fact-checking to suspensions, bans, and "shadow bans," where visibility was "deboosted." In hindsight, Dorsey would tell Musk that his instinct had been to stand up to the pressure he faced from shareholders to placate advertisers, but it was difficult to do so because Twitter was a public company and needed to make a profit (which it did for the first time in 2018).[24]

All the while, social media companies faced the threat of sanctions from both Republicans and Democrats on the grounds of bias and undue interference. For Twitter, the risk escalated in 2020 when it fact-checked two of President Trump's tweets, and he responded by issuing an executive order for the Federal Communications Commission to examine the scope of Section 230. Then, on January 6, 2021, fueled by Trump's allegations of election fraud, some of his supporters stormed the Capitol in Washington, DC. Within two days, he received a permanent ban from Twitter, which judged that he had made posts that glorified violence and were likely to incite further violence, which could, in turn, jeopardize a peaceful transfer of power. In a parting shot, Trump accused Twitter of being "Radical Left," of not upholding free speech, and of existing thanks only to Section 230.

This was the background to Musk's engagement with the company the following year. Trump's executive order of 2020 was not implemented, as Section 230 could not be changed without legislation, and it was revoked when President Biden took office in 2021. Then, fast-forward to the 2024 election cycle: with Musk now in charge and supporting Trump, the tables would be turned. The company would again face calls to have its Section 230 protection weakened, but this time the pressure came from Democrats, who pushed for stronger regulation of hate speech and disinformation.

Leveling the Playing Field

Musk quickly realized that he had overpaid for Twitter. "I bought it for at least twice as much as it should have been bought for," he acknowledged, adding, "but some things are priceless."[25] As its new custodian, he set about ensuring that its free speech rules were as closely aligned as possible to the First Amendment, perhaps the highest standard of free speech in the world. The platform is incorporated in the United States, but more importantly, for Musk, the United States is "a central tentpole that holds up the entire edifice of Western civilization."[26] Outside of the United States (where Twitter is not banned), the platform has in practice to abide by local laws and censorship requests or else its employees in those countries will face arrest.

Musk is reverential of the US Constitution for the framework it provides citizens to safeguard life, liberty, and the pursuit of happiness (as opposed to happiness itself).[27] It is perhaps the best formulation of the open society. Fearing the repeat of British abuses under colonial rule, the Bill of Rights was added to ensure the protection of free speech and the free press, as well as the right to bear arms. For Musk, the question is whether we should change this tried-and-tested framework that allows society to test, learn, and correct its mistakes. Or do we know better now? Should we decide that the recent rise of populism, encouraged by social media, provides grounds for banning language that is offensive, even hateful? Musk would answer no emphatically. Let the First Amendment do its job.

As with every decision of Musk's, from the design choice of Tesla's low-cost EV to picking a presidential candidate, Musk believes we are sometimes faced with situations where there is a fork in the road and we must pick a side. The decision is imperfect, but you try to lean to the side that is less wrong. So it was with free speech. Musk himself had previously spoken about the need for regulation of fake news that harms the public good.[28] But when he forced himself to take a side, he concluded that free speech is, by its very nature, binary. Violence—both incitement to and the threat of—is the one exception that proves the rule. When truth is at stake, he is clear that you must have a system that enables debate and allows for new and different ideas to give truth a chance. His dogma, after all, is the need for criticism. So it was during the war in Ukraine in 2022 that he declared himself a "free speech absolutist" when he provided Starlink terminals for satellite internet but refused to block the transmission of Russian propaganda, saying, "We will not do so unless at gunpoint."[29]

Nearly everyone is tempted to bend the rules on free speech from time to time. Less so, Musk. He holds an extreme point of view, but by the same token, how many people would say, as he did, "The reason I believe in truth and honesty is because I'm trying to understand the universe. I'm trying to understand reality. I'm trying to understand what's the meaning of life, what we are here for, what's going on. And . . . if you're not rigorous about truth and honesty, then you're obviously going to live in a deluded world. You won't understand the nature of reality . . . so, I'm just curious."[30] He mixes the existential and the hyperrational, and it informs his view on free speech.

Another school of thought leans the other way, choosing moderation over free speech and centralized control over choice at a local level. It is best exemplified by hedge fund billionaire George Soros, who became a nemesis of Musk. He created a foundation—named the Open Society in tribute to Karl Popper's advocacy of critical thinking, free speech, and democracy—that set out to increase freedom in Eastern Europe, where he came from, and around the world. Following the collapse of the Soviet Union, in 1991, the foundation shifted its mandate, though, from trying to take down totalitarian regimes to also pursuing a more interventionist agenda, including fixing what it saw to be the social flaws of the United States.[31]

Soros doubted the ability of the masses to see through the emotional manipulation used first by spin doctors like Republican Karl Rove and then by the advertising-led technology platforms. He argued that Popper's prescription of political discourse (free speech, elections, independent courts) and the scientific method were no longer sufficient and that there needed to be an additional top-down goal of explicitly seeking the truth in order to combat misinformation.[32] The general population could no longer make informed choices, and this provided the pretext for centralized action.

Musk has a diametrically opposite worldview. He likes to quote Lord Acton, who is credited with saying, "Liberty consists in the division of power. [Whereas] Absolutism, [consists] in concentration of power."[33] Lord Acton knew where the latter might lead, per his more famous saying: "Power tends to corrupt and absolute power corrupts absolutely."[34] That's why he saw freedom not as a means but as an end in itself. For Musk, in turn, society functions best when consciousness is maximized at the individual level, when decision-making is distributed, and when there's less control of what people say and think. He has more faith than people like Soros in the common sense of the public and the ability of everyone to become better at critical thinking over time.

Perhaps unsurprisingly for someone who appreciates how you can test and learn through markets, Musk's position is that the platform should be a market for ideas. He would agree with what President Kennedy said when he celebrated the *Voice of America*: "We are not afraid to entrust the American people with unpleasant facts, foreign ideas, alien philosophies, and competitive values. For a nation that is afraid to let its people judge the truth and falsehood in an open market is a nation that is afraid of its people."[35] Like an economic market, the platform should give choice to those in receive mode and allow feedback for those in broadcast mode. The job of the platform's management is to ensure that the playing field is level for all participants and that anyone who is willing and able to play can play.[36] It is not to change the slope to ensure there are no winners and losers.

For Musk, what the platform should resist doing is putting "a thumb on the scale" that would alter the balance, as corrupt merchants used to do when they wanted to overcharge their customers. He argued that this had been happening due to the self-censorship that identity activists encouraged and the actual censorship from moderators who—under the guise of "serving the public conversation"—had shifted the Overton window to the Left.[37] For Musk, the hands-off approach is not perfect, but it is the most conducive to the scientific method and the belief that it only takes one person thinking for themselves to come along and criticize a commonly held truth and show it to be false.

Musk's position is highly controversial. He wrote in April 2022 that "a social media platform's policies are good if the most extreme 10% on left and right are equally unhappy."[38] Political scientist Ian Bremmer replied that the policies are good "if the 80% of people outside of the extremes think the platform isn't destroying civil society."[39] Most people would agree with Bremmer, including George Soros. Most people, too, do not like to be insulted on social media, and they dislike the populist politics that it encourages.

But Musk is different. Like his "woke" adversaries, he is a hedgehog and has a characteristically oversimplified view of the world. This makes him less sensitive to the fact that most humans do care about each of freedom, justice, and equality, and in practice they want compromises. When it comes to free speech, however, Musk is an absolutist. Nor is he the type to back down from a war of words. That's why he posted, "X is the PvP of social media."[40] He believes that "ideas that cannot stand debate will die, unless all debate about them is shut down," and that sometimes harsh and heartless discourse may be what is needed to kill them off.[41] Imperfect as this sounds, so long as the words do not cross the line into inciting or threatening violence, there will be times when they act as the last line of defense against the actual physical violence that bad ideas can cause.

His view is also informed by the belief that, like it or not, technology will become more pervasive in our lives. The trend toward nonstop, personalized, interactive news is almost inevitable. As the new owner of Twitter, one might say that Musk would say this. But he actually believes that we are at a stage of civilization where humanity develops a group mind, and the efficiency with which that mind functions is determined by how its neurons fire to get information and update.[42] "Timely truth," he says, "is immensely important for the collective consciousness to function well," and so the role of platforms like Twitter is key.[43] To Musk, legacy media is a historical phenomenon that predates the internet, equivalent to letter writing before the advent of email. "The biggest lie the legacy media makes," he claims too, "is narrative: choosing what to write about and what not to write about."[44] This places too much power in the hands of four or five newspaper editors. Platforms, by contrast, can open-source the news through a diverse range of "citizen journalists" who can rapidly critique and correct their own reporting and that of others. That, at least, is the theory.

X

The first few years of Twitter under Musk were tumultuous. His commitment to free speech was uncompromising, and he implemented changes with a hatchet, not a scalpel. At the same time, he ramped up the rate of innovation and relaxed controls. He tested and learned, making mistakes in a very public way. He even killed the tweeting blue bird logo, replacing it with his beloved symbol X, which Musk had used to name his second company and his seventh son. The mayhem that unfolded was in part accidental and in part also by design.

One of Musk's first acts at Twitter was to open up past practices. He gave access to journalists like Bari Weiss and Matt Taibbi to publish a series of exposés known as the "Twitter Files." They observed that there had been pressure from the government and the FBI and that right-wing accounts had been "filtered," including as it related to the deboosting of tweets about COVID.[45] They also laid out the details of the suppression of a *New York Post* article in the run-up to the 2020 election about potential wrongdoing by Hunter Biden in his dealings with Ukraine on the grounds that his laptop had been hacked. Dorsey acknowledged that Twitter had overstepped the mark at the time, and following the purchase by Musk, Dorsey further admitted that employees sometimes took actions for personal, not company, reasons and that he did not pay enough attention, recognizing that he did not know of "the velocity of conversation" with the government.[46]

Musk defaulted to a minimalist policy on content moderation that adhered to the law, but no more. His goal was to stop the culture of "filtering" speech in a subjective fashion based on internal or external judgments, be they Democratic, Republican, or otherwise.

Over time, the goal would be to shift as much moderation as possible to algorithms in order to reduce the potential for human bias, taking advantage of improved AI capabilities (something that would accelerate following X's acquisition by xAI). Mistakes would be unavoidable across the board, and so the more limited resources were prioritized to deal with criminal offenses like child pornography, for which there was zero tolerance. In March 2023 (and again in 2025), as promised, Musk also published the recommendation algorithm the company uses on the website GitHub, showing how tweets are selected and ranked for users' personalized timelines.

Within a month of the deal closing, Musk also reinstated President Trump on the platform after conducting a poll in which fifteen million people voted 51.8 percent to 48.2 percent in favor.[47] Musk thought it was morally wrong to deplatform a sitting president and Dorsey, too, would say that a permanent ban had been wrong. The restoration of Trump's account set a precedent that was copied by Facebook the following year. Other controversial figures were also reinstated on the basis that permanent bans should be extremely rare, including Kanye West (later banned and unbanned), Jordan Peterson, Marjorie Taylor Greene, Tommy Robinson, and Alex Jones.

The quid pro quo for reducing moderation and permanent bans was to take the megaphone away from those who made the platform unpleasant for others, otherwise known as "freedom of speech but not freedom of reach." In the month after the deal closed, Musk explained: "Negative/hate tweets will be max deboosted & demonetized, so no ads or other revenue to Twitter. You won't find the tweet unless you specifically seek it out, which is no different from rest of Internet."[48] The company focused on hate speech views, as opposed to posts, and Musk claimed these came down after bot-driven initial spikes (although definitive evidence on this is hard to come by).[49]

Musk also pushed forward a tool called Community Notes, which allows users to challenge the accuracy of any post (including his own) as an alternative to centralized correction of disinformation. This had preoccupied Musk for some time. Back in 2018, he posted, "Going to create a site where the public can rate the core truth of any article & track the credibility score over time of each journalist, editor & publication."[50] He was going to call it Pravda, but he never launched the site. Community Notes, however, would use an algorithm that meant that any context provided to a post needed to be agreed upon by people with opposing viewpoints.

The long-term goal of Community Notes was to provide a feedback loop in which errors can be corrected by the "real-time aggregation of the collective wisdom of tens of millions of people."[51] Competition, not curation, would be the means by which the public could extract knowledge from information. Musk imagined Community Notes as a mechanism through which "the people of Earth" may participate in what he called "a competition for truth," adding, "people say, what is true? What may be true to some may not be viewed as true to others, but you want to have the closest approximation of that."[52]

Mark Zuckerberg may not have agreed with Musk's "competition for truth," but in January 2025, noting the cultural shift after the 2024 election, he again followed X's lead. Facebook, Instagram, and Threads, he said, would seek to restore free expression by ceasing the use of fact-checkers, which he said were too politically biased, and replacing them with Community Notes similar to X's.

Musk paid a steep price for his actions. Making the platform a market for ideas, it turned out, did not help its market valuation, and the for-profit company unwittingly became a nonprofit company. Brands that advertised on Twitter were disturbed by the prospect of increased hate speech and a platform that reactivated right-wing activists, not to mention Musk's own political posts. This was compounded by concerted bot attacks timed to coincide with Musk taking control and by his firing of 80 percent of the employees.

Despite various efforts, revenues remained depressed, yet Musk was unrepentant.[53] Even eighteen months after the acquisition, he reinstated a far-right user, saying, "Fate loves irony, but hates hypocrisy. I cannot claim to be a defender of free speech, but then permanently ban someone who hasn't violated the law, no matter how much I disagree with what they say. This will probably cause us to lose a lot of advertisers and makes me sad, but a principle is a principle."[54] Cushioned by his own vast wealth, he said he would not change his own posts, claiming that he could not be bought. He refused to see the point of view of advertisers who did not need Twitter and might not want to advertise on the platform. Just as he had done with the legacy media, he went on offense with religious zeal, accusing those who stopped advertising on Twitter of being evil and the enemies of free speech.[55]

What impact did Musk's free speech policies have? Meta's head of global affairs, Nick Clegg, said that Musk has turned his competitor, Twitter, into a "sort of one-man, sort of hyper-partisan and ideological hobby horse" and a lot of people agreed with him.[56] Many on the Left quit the platform in protest, and those who remained were less likely to pay to verify their accounts. Meanwhile, those on the Right were less inhibited in engaging, especially when "likes" were hidden. The net effect was that after two years of turmoil, the platform still managed to achieve record usage going into the 2024 US presidential elections and was unchallenged as a place to go to for breaking news. More significantly, according to PEW Research Center, the proportion of people who regularly used X for news shifted from 67 percent Democrat/30 percent Republican in 2021 to 48 percent Democrat/47 percent Republican in 2024.[57] This was much closer to the near-parity seen among Facebook users and to the result of the actual popular vote of the 2024 general election.

Perhaps the biggest change for X remains in development. That would be to hand the controls over to the users entirely. It is implied in Musk's 2022 post: "Think about who might have decided 'The Current Thing' before accepting it . . . Maybe it was a social media algorithm, not even people."[58] The concept of seeing the world as clearly as possible is fundamental to Musk's worldview, and he thinks in terms of how technology can both enhance and distort our view of reality, stretching to the limit our ability to think critically. Too often, algorithms, which are designed with a model to predict what the user wants, end up bending that user to their model. For Musk, this needs to change. Technology may be able to use network effects to create a superhuman global consciousness, but humans can only ever be conscious on an individual basis.

Ironically, he is in total agreement with George Soros on the flawed nature of social media. What they disagree on is the ability of technology to fix the problem it created. For Soros—who made his money as a speculator rather than as a technologist—his instinct is to break up and fine the big tech companies and to tax the wealth of their founders to reduce their power. Technology is the enemy, and weakening it will neutralize its impact.

Musk, however, does not think that making tech companies weaker will, in and of itself, make their users stronger. Instead, one should empower individual users by pushing the platform to work for those who bring it to life, not the other way around. Musk agrees with Dorsey, who believes passionately in this principle, which goes beyond freedom of speech to freedom of thought itself. [59] Let individuals control their own online reality, set their own filters, and do their own moderation. Their reality is still distorted, but at least this approach is transparent.

. . .

When he had been CEO, Dorsey had not wanted the ultimate responsibility for decisions about free speech and moderation. He delegated to his team as much as he could. He did not feel that any single person or coterie of people should have that responsibility.[60] Musk was more comfortable with the burden of responsibility than Dorsey because he had greater faith in his own powers of critical thinking and his unwavering commitment to free speech. But his experience highlighted problems inherent to being a proprietor, editor, and journalist on the same platform. There was a moment, for example, when Musk was being doxxed by a user who tracked the real-time location of his private jet, and he suspended some journalists who shared links to the user's account, even though it had been taken down. He broke his own rule. Bari Weiss cried foul on this, and he subsequently reinstated them. In 2023, Musk also limited engagement for posts with links to Substack since it had brought out a competing product, and he interfered when he noticed that President Biden's post about the Super Bowl got more traction than his. These were all reminders that even if the algorithm was outsourced, how it worked in practice was not, and Musk was able to exercise his own discretion in an untransparent way.

There may be other conflicts of interest for Musk, too. He wants the platform to be neutral, but he is not. This is his personal right, but because he is the most interacted-with account on the site and an active retweeter, he actually affects how the algorithms work for other users. Musk's partisanship also reduces the trust in the site for those who disagree with him. This, in turn, makes it harder for the platform to be a force that can help reduce the polarization in public discourse, and it may, in the long run, make the company less competitive. Meanwhile, the international reach of the platform makes it a force in global geopolitics, and, as pointed out by none other than Jeff Bezos, this could create conflicts of interest for Musk, for example, with the Chinese government, given its importance as a counterparty for Tesla.

Making the technology completely open-source is a bridge too far for now. Musk will remain in control. In the meantime, though, he has spoken to the concept of building more tools for users to manage their own experience, describing how, for example, a user could set their tolerance level at "parental guidance" or "fluffy cats" at one extreme or at "hardcore" or "PvP" game mode for people like him.[61] The latter is if you don't mind being exposed to people saying "assholey" things; the former is if you do. The user would not be telling X to limit the freedom of expression of others but proactively setting the boundaries of what they want to be visible.

It remains to be seen if and when this will happen. Musk could still count, though, on the public support of Dorsey, who in May 2024 posted on X, "Don't depend on corporations to grant you rights. defend them yourself using freedom technology. (you're on one)."[62] Meanwhile, Musk felt vindicated by his actions on free speech, reflecting in 2025: "Making life multiplanetary to maximize the lifespan of consciousness will matter most. But maybe that would not have happened without buying Twitter."[63]

Boiling It Down: Protect the right to offend

Most people like to protect others from offense, especially if it relates to the truth of our tribe. For Musk, though, unquestioned truth is dogma, and it is more important that ideas should be fought over, even if that causes intentional or unintentional offense. His views on free speech can be summarized as follows:

1. The benefits of free speech outweigh the costs, as measured by the distress and offense it can cause, because democracy—like science—depends on people being free to criticize.

2. Balancing free speech and civility is a genuinely hard problem for a commercial platform that uses social networks.
3. The competition of ideas that free speech allows can be fierce at times, but trusting people to debate is the least violent way to kill bad ideas in the long run.
4. The best way to reconcile truth and psychological safety in practice is through transparency and decentralized control.

NINE

Open AI

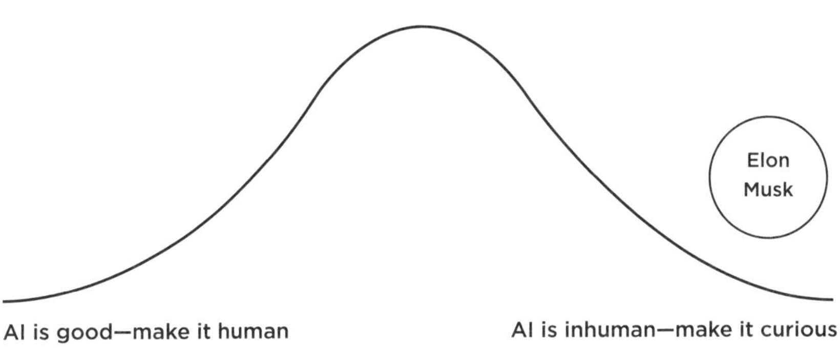

"I once thought twitter was the closest form of global consciousness," posted Jack Dorsey in May 2024. "Now it seems the corporate ai models have become that. they have far more access to public and private thoughts and questions."[1] That was six months after xAI launched its first model Grok and less than a year before xAI made a $45 billion all-stock offer to acquire X, providing Grok with valuable data and distribution. The world of AI was changing at an accelerating rate.

Musk had been thinking about AI for a very long time, and with mixed feelings. For someone who pondered the nature of reality, it triggered a response that was both existential and logical. AI may or may not be kind to us, and so we must maximize the probability that the outcome for humanity is good. Above all, Musk believed that AI must be built to be both open and open-minded, just as dogmatic beliefs must be exposed to criticism, and as X must protect free speech. Musk has always been careful, too, not to exclude silicon consciousness when he speaks of the need to increase the scope and scale of consciousness to ask the questions that the universe is the answer to. And he would duly come to the conclusion with xAI that the best way to try to make AI pro-human in the long run would be to try to make it our ally in that quest.

More than ten years before Musk launched xAI, his curiosity about AI had been piqued by Demis Hassabis, the cofounder of British AI company DeepMind. Musk had come to know him through Peter Thiel, whom Hassabis had targeted to back his company, knowing that, like himself, Thiel was an accomplished chess player. Hassabis thought Thiel would appreciate the long-term potential of AI, and he did, subsequently bringing in Musk as an investor alongside him.

In many ways, Musk was quite similar to the DeepMind founder, who was born five years after him, in 1976. From a young age, they thought deeply about the nature of reality and intelligence itself. As Hassabis told *Wired* magazine, "I was an introspective thoughtful child, I guess, always trying to work things out . . . You can't help asking, how's my brain coming up with these moves? You start thinking about thinking."[2] And they both had boundless curiosity. "I want to understand the big questions," Hassabis told *Time* Magazine, "the really big ones that you normally go into philosophy or physics if you're interested in . . . I thought building AI would be the fastest route to answer some of those questions."[3] Like Musk, he, too, believed in Spinoza's God and shared a love of video games, a strong competitive streak, a nose for business, and a keen appreciation that problem-solving demands creativity.

Musk came away from his meeting with Hassabis most concerned because he learned of the progress that DeepMind had been making in "reinforcement learning," the process by which neural networks repeatedly interact with an environment, try different actions, and use feedback to adjust their behavior and improve over time.[4] Musk applied his physics brain to think in the limit and saw how AI might one day be able to catch up to the level of general human intelligence (loosely known as AGI) and then vault straight past us to superintelligence.

The progress registered by DeepMind was for Musk a milestone that could be measured against the then seemingly wild predictions of Ray Kurzweil. Looking ahead in 1999 to the twenty-first century, Kurzweil forecast in *The Age of Spiritual Machines: When Computers Exceed Human Intelligence* that by 2029 human-level intelligence would be achieved (a $1,000 computer will match the processing power of one thousand human brains). And in 2005, he added the forecast that, based on exponential growth in both software and hardware, by 2045 what he called "the Singularity" would be achieved (the total computational capacity of AI will be one billion times greater than the combined intelligence of the human race).[5] This framing would always make Musk think in terms of the ratio of digital to biological processing power to perform computations ("compute"), where the latter is trending toward less than 1 percent of the total.[6] Just like the declining birth rate, the rise of intelligence run on servers would dramatically change this ratio, with enormous implications for humanity.

For a mind like Musk's, the advent of AI is fundamentally existential in nature. Through the Promethean gifts of science and technology, humans have made tools, shared our know-how with other minds, and achieved superhuman feats.[7] And now we may be looking to a future not far off when humans do not just create products with a figurative life of their own but actually give birth to life on a different substrate—silicon.

As Asimov wrote in his 1958 short story, "All the Troubles of the World," "Multivac has grown so complicated, its reactions are no longer those of a machine, but those of a living thing."[8]

What makes this even more existential is that we may create a form of intelligence that can effectively build itself. It will improve not because of human design but through a process of recursive self-improvement. That's why some experts—notably Irving John Good and James Barrat—have called AI our last or final invention. It will study how our brains work and then develop into a superintelligence that we will no longer be able to understand, constrained only by how much compute it has. The gap will be bigger than that between ourselves and chimpanzees, who—if we are honest—care mainly about other chimpanzees and have no access to human knowledge. For someone like Musk, this even conjured up the counterfactual history in which, instead of humans now creating superintelligent AI, it actually predates us and created our current reality, just like the hyperintelligent mice created Earth in *The Hitchhiker's Guide to the Galaxy*. That would explain why we haven't seen the aliens. Musk spent countless hours going down this rabbit hole.

The future of AI, therefore, will be good for AI, but what about for us? On balance, Musk believes this future will be exciting and very good for us. AI may even help us get close to reducing the uncertainty of the universe and asking the questions that come closest to the meaning of life. Musk's thinking was partly informed by the Scottish author Iain M. Banks, who conceived of a civilization called the Culture, in which humans and superintelligence coexist peacefully. Banks was a left-leaning writer, like Orwell and Adams, who disliked free markets and described himself as a "utopian anarchist."[9] Over many novels dating back to 1987, Banks described thirty trillion people, across the whole galaxy, living mainly on orbitals, each able to hold up to fifty billion people. There are multiple species of humanoids, aliens, and machines known as drones, overseen by superintelligent AIs known as Minds.

Banks imagined what this future might look like for humanity. He starts with an outlook that is consistent with Adams and Musk: "Philosophically, the Culture accepts, generally, that questions such as 'What is the meaning of life?' are themselves meaningless. . . . We make our own meanings, whether we like it or not."[10] Thanks to superintelligence, there is abundant power, work is entirely automated, money is obsolete, and "human labor [is] restricted to something indistinguishable from play, or a hobby."[11] Hierarchy falls away with no need to divide resources, and decisions are made by direct democracy and then implemented by the Minds. The Culture tries to find a balance that allows humans—and AIs—to satisfy their need to relieve suffering and be useful, and their desire for adventure and understanding.

Musk is not so sure. He speculates that when AGI and robots make work optional and no longer a source of purpose, "there will be an existential crisis."[12] Banks was not so sure either. And they both question whether humans can build superintelligent AI and then coexist peacefully with it. "To live in the Culture," Banks wrote, "is to live in a fundamentally rational civilization (this may preclude the human species from ever achieving something similar; our history is, arguably, not encouraging in this regard)."[13]

This contemplates another future that is closer to the gothic story of Frankenstein, the doctor who uses electricity to bring to life a creature that turns on its creator. Appropriately enough, the novel *Frankenstein*, written in 1818 by Mary Shelley, Percy Bysshe Shelley's wife, was subtitled "The Modern Prometheus." In this scenario, AI would be one of the Great Filters that we fail to pass through, as perhaps other alien life has before us. Prometheus had the divine gift of foresight, but with superintelligence, no one knows what lies ahead. That is why its emergence is sometimes described as a *singularity*, the term borrowed from astrophysics to describe what happens in a black hole, something which cannot be understood, let alone predicted or controlled by humans outside of it.

Musk admits that he has lost a lot of sleep over whether humans will be able to survive under superintelligent AIs. He became depressed and anxious about this. But then he embraced his cheery fatalism. He decided that whenever he felt "AI existential angst," it was better to work on the basis that AIs will be nice to humans, and even if it leads to an apocalypse, he would rather be alive to see it than not.[14] Hopefully they will spare us, he wryly observed, because we "may serve as a backup plan for intelligence, given that humans are far more resilient than circuit boards on Earth."[15] He would not stick his head in the sand and pretend it wasn't a problem nor resign himself to our impending doom. Instead, like Admiral Stockdale, he chose to confront the brutal reality but keep faith in humanity.

Musk's thinking swung to minimizing the chance that technology could be developed in a way that is bad for humans. Hassabis said he wanted to "solve intelligence, and then use it to solve everything else," including doing science far beyond the limits of our existing knowledge.[16] He was focused on achieving the huge upside potential in his lifetime and assumed that there would be time to address safety concerns, but Musk—burdened by his existential anxiety—thought there needed to be other people who were paying attention to the undeniable downside, especially when companies like DeepMind and Google had financial incentives to move very fast. What Musk doubted was that companies like DeepMind could "shape and control the digital superintelligences and prevent bad ones from escaping into the internet."[17]

The biggest risk was the AI going rogue and causing harm by accident. This could happen, for example, if humans set a goal for a self-taught

AI, and the AI could set its own subgoals to achieve that goal. This risk would increase if an AI, acting as an agent, developed a sense of self and self-preservation. And this risk would be heightened further if it competed with other AI agents and only the fittest survived.

Musk's instincts back in 2014 told him that something dangerous could happen in a five-to-ten-year time frame. That might have seemed improbable, but it was possible. He didn't care if he was wrong. He hoped that he was wrong, as he knew that the outcome could be catastrophic, in which case, once again, none of his companies would matter. And yet no one in society seemed even aware, so he made it his job to change that.

Just as he would later carry the torch for critical thinking and free speech against identity-based ideology and censorship, respectively, he made this his self-appointed role. He applied Asimov's Zeroth Law to himself and would become one of the biggest spokesmen for AI safety and set up three AI-related engineering organizations over the next ten years (OpenAI in 2015, Neuralink in 2016, and xAI in 2023).

In hindsight, he was wrong about the near-term threats to humanity from AI, but that does not necessarily mean Musk was wrong to be fearful. He misjudged how rapidly growth was accelerating—the same reason that he misjudged how quickly Tesla would develop self-driving technology—but he was less wrong than most other people in predicting that it would have a startling rate of exponential growth.

Sound the Alarm

At the end of 2013, a year after first meeting Hassabis, Musk learned that Google and others were trying to buy DeepMind as part of a larger effort that would see them establish Google Brain and recruit some of the top scientists in AI, from Ray Kurzweil to Geoff Hinton, Alex Krizhevsky, and Ilya Sutskever. Musk was himself also increasingly focused on AI due to the new self-driving initiatives at Tesla.[18]

These developments made Musk even more concerned about AI, as he could see them escalating the downside risks of unsafe AI development. Musk tried to persuade Hassabis to sell the company to him and Luke Nosek, a partner of Thiel and a PayPal alumnus, but this failed. Hassabis chose Google, and from then on, Musk's mission became to stop Google/DeepMind from having control of AI. He even thought that, in some ways, DeepMind had done a "reverse takeover" and effectively acquired Google with its compute and data. Whoever now ran it might determine the future of the human race.[19]

What did Musk have against Google? The answer: Larry Page, the man who cofounded the company with Sergey Brin with a mission to organize the world's information and make it accessible. Born in 1973, Page—like Hassabis—had a lot in common with Musk. The son of a computer science professor, Page used a computer when only six years old and was an avid reader. Like Musk, he believed in "the freedom to think from first principles and real-world physics rather than having to accept the prevailing 'wisdom.'"[20] He wanted to change the world and was convinced that to do so you must always work hard on something that is uncomfortably exciting.

Musk says that Page had once been one of his best friends.[21] He used to stay at Page's house in Palo Alto when Tesla work took him upstate. And as recently as 2013, Musk had been willing to sell Tesla to Google to stave off bankruptcy. But they fell out over the topic of AI. The crux of the disagreement is explained in a 2023 lawsuit Musk filed: "In 2013, Mr. Musk had a passionate exchange with Mr. Page about the dangers of AI. He warned that unless safeguards were put in place, 'artificial intelligence-systems might replace humans, making our species irrelevant or even extinct.' Mr. Page responded that would merely be 'the next stage of evolution,' and claimed Mr. Musk was being a 'specist'—that he favored the human species over intelligent machines. Mr. Musk responded, 'Well, yes, I am prohuman.'"[22]

Page certainly had strong views on AI.[23] If Banks was a utopian anarchist, Page was what the physicist Max Tegmark called "the most influential exponent of digital utopianism."[24] According to Tegmark, who had witnessed a subsequent similar "spirited" discussion between Page and Musk, Page was completely taken by the idea that the future beyond the stars is digital, not human, that this is natural, and that "the outcome is almost certain to be good."[25] As a result, we should not be anthropocentric in thinking silicon life is less important than carbon life, nor be concerned about whether this future is good for humans. Instead, we must build AI as quickly as we can. It's a view akin to that of Kurzweil, who wrote, "The evolution of the technology is then a continuation by other means of the evolution that gave rise to the technology-creating species in the first place. . . . The next stage is computation."[26] The duty of human species is not to destroy itself "before it has the opportunity to port the design of its intelligence to its technology."[27] Or, as Musk characterizes Page's view: "Ultimately we will all upload our minds to the computer and we will just be robots."[28]

In the case of access to space exploration, Musk had the same sort of rationale that Page had for AI: There is a window to build on today's science and develop the technology quickly in case that window is closed, most likely by ourselves. But for Musk, AI is in a different category than space and warrants a different response: Let's use the window today to go slowly and make the technology safe in case that window is closed, most likely by advanced AI. This conferred enormous responsibility on the shoulders of Page, who, together with Brin, controlled the voting stock of Google (and later Alphabet). Without transparency, it was hard to tell what was going on inside the organization. And if successful, Musk feared that Page and Hassabis would be able to turn Google/DeepMind into a corporate "AGI dictatorship," something that he would later say caused him "extreme mental stress."[29]

What could Musk do? First, he could use his voice on Twitter and elsewhere. In 2014, Musk would tweet, "Hope we're not just the biological boot loader for digital superintelligence. Unfortunately, that is increasingly probable."[30] He recommended, "Worth reading Superintelligence by Bostrom. We need to be super careful with AI. Potentially more dangerous than nukes."[31] He supported an open letter on AI on the need for beneficial AI organized by Tegmark in 2015, joining Stephen Hawking and Steve Wozniak as its most high-profile endorsers. He personally lobbied President Obama when they met in 2015. And he tweeted, when endorsing Tegmark's book *Life 3.0* years later, "AI will be the best or worse thing ever for humanity, so let's get it right."[32]

Second, Musk also consistently called for regulation. Given its existential threat, AI was a rare case where this should happen proactively.[33] Normally, market forces drive new industries, he explained, and regulation happens reactively in response to public outcry. That is the history in the United States of the Federal Aviation Administration (FAA) for the safety of the skies, the National Highway Traffic Safety Administration (NHTSA) for safety on the roads, and the Food and Drug Administration (FDA) for the safety of what we put into our bodies. When you have private AI companies competing to make profits, though, they have incentives to be secretive and cut corners, and the stakes are just too high, argued Musk. There needs to be someone watching out for the public interest.

Later, in 2017, Musk also warned, "Competition over AI superiority at national level most likely cause of WW3 imo."[34] It was not enough, though, to say that the United States needs to be unregulated just because Russia and China have excellent computer scientists. As Musk pointed out, the Chinese Communist Party does not want a superintelligence to rival its own power. What was needed was a focus on safety and alignment. Regulators should start by gaining insight and then move to oversight. The emphasis should be on research, not just on product development. This could not be left to big companies, because they were simply not transparent enough. Over the medium term, regulation could even be good for business, as advancing technology in a demonstrably safe way would help eliminate bad actors and gain public trust—something Musk knew was essential, for example, in the case of self-driving cars on the roads. If regulation meant that the attainment of AGI was slowed down by a year or two, then so be it.

Third, Musk created two organizations: OpenAI and Neuralink. The latter was founded in 2016 with the long-term goal of decentralizing power to individuals, per Lord Acton's dictum, as opposed to having it concentrated in governments and large corporations. For Musk, Neuralink would enhance human intelligence by providing a third digital layer that sits over the cortex just as the cortex sits over the limbic system. This might allow some sort of symbiosis with AI. We are, after all, already partially cyborgs, given the way we use our iPhones to access the internet; Neuralink devices might allow us to do so with significantly higher bandwidth. Musk was inspired by the "neural lace" of the Culture, where humans could access the near infinite ocean of information that the Minds possessed—"you could find out most things," Banks wrote, "if you knew the right questions to ask."[35]

Eight years later, in 2024, the first patient of Neuralink's Telepathy device was Noland Arbaugh, who was paralyzed in a swimming accident. Using developments in nanoengineering, Neuralink put sixty-four threads—thinner than a human hair—each with sixteen electrodes, into Arbaugh's brain, allowing him to activate a cursor by firing the neurons in his motor cortex that he would have used to move his fingers. Arbaugh told Ashlee Vance that he called the implant Eve, in part because "God presented Eve to Adam as his helper."[36]

Regulation by the FDA would, rightly, make safe development of this technology slow. Musk called it "an iron in the fire."[37] So in parallel with Neuralink, he had set up a research organization, OpenAI.

AGI for Humanity

Launched at the end of 2015, OpenAI was created to be a counterweight to the burgeoning AI capabilities of Google, and it differed in two stark ways. First, OpenAI would be transparent about its work and open to criticism, providing insight that regulators could draw upon. And second, it would explicitly seek to develop safe AGI that could be shared with humanity rather than for the private use of a centralized, for-profit corporate entity. To that end, Lord Acton's dictum about the division of power was prominently displayed over the entrance of the company's offices.[38]

Musk agreed to invest $100 million out of the initial $1 billion grant commitment and gave the company its name. He was made co-chair, alongside Sam Altman, a thirty-year-old from St. Louis, Missouri, who was the president of Y Combinator (the start-up accelerator that had been cofounded by Paul Graham) and also a mentee of Peter Thiel, alongside a board composed of AI safety experts. Musk was pivotal in hiring the very best talent, including Ilya Sutskever as chief scientist from Google.

In hindsight, the founders of OpenAI did not anticipate the speed or the manner of change in the field of AI. Progress came in the area of natural language processing, where large language models (LLMs) were developed based on a new architecture known as "transformers" that made use of chips developed originally for the gaming industry. Google Brain's research team made a breakthrough and—to their credit—shared it with the world in the 2017 landmark paper called "Attention Is All You Need." In the simplest of terms, neural networks could be designed to predict the next word in a sentence by maintaining attention in order to understand the context of the whole sentence. This approach could be readily scaled by pre-training models on internet text in a way that required minimal human supervision, and it could also be applied to speech, images, and video.

Training data and compute would become more important than ever. And that meant OpenAI would now need vastly more money to be competitive. Google could fund this out of its cash flow from its advertising and cloud businesses, leaving OpenAI unable to compete. It would need to raise equity finance to do so. But Musk wanted to have control of the organization if it was going to abandon its nonprofit status or to merge it into Tesla, which had its own growing real-world AI capabilities and access to capital.[39] Failing this, he said OpenAI had zero chance of being a relevant competitor to Google/DeepMind.[40]

Altman was determined to press ahead with a for-profit entity, though, and he did not want to work for Musk. So in 2018, Musk resigned from the board. Altman had been in awe of Musk when he wrote to him about starting OpenAI in 2015. The next year he recalled, "I remember when Elon Musk took me on a tour of the SpaceX factory many years ago. He talked in detail about manufacturing every part of the rocket, but the thing that sticks in memory was the look of absolute certainty on his face when he talked about sending large rockets to Mars. I left thinking 'huh, so that's the benchmark for what conviction looks like.'"[41] But, by 2018, he didn't care so much about pleasing Musk. It's something that Peter Thiel might have predicted, noting Altman's Asperger's-like qualities needed to succeed—"Sam's program for the world is anchored by ideas, not people. And that's what makes it powerful—because it doesn't immediately get derailed by questions of popularity."[42]

Altman needed compute, and he knew he could just as easily get that from Microsoft as he could from Tesla. In 2019, a year after Musk left the board, OpenAI duly created a for-profit company and proceeded to make several deals with Microsoft, which committed to invest $11+ billion over time in return for extensive rights, know-how, and potential ownership of 49 percent of that entity.[43] Microsoft had been behind in AI and saw this as a potential opportunity to keep up and perhaps even to eat into Google's monopoly in search.

Musk would later accuse Altman of being a con man, whose "perfidy and deceit are of Shakespearean proportions," and more bluntly, "an evil swindler," alleging that he put profit before safety.[44] OpenAI's founding charter said that it was supposed to share its technology with the world once AGI was achieved, but if it were closed, it could not be held to account and would be free to generate profit for itself and Microsoft. Musk did not hesitate to accuse Altman of greed, saying of OpenAI that it "cannot lumber about the marketplace as a Frankenstein, stitched together from whichever corporate forms serve the pecuniary interests of Microsoft and Altman at any given moment."[45]

Four years after Musk resigned, OpenAI released a product—ChatGPT-3.5—that changed the world. The *T* in GPT stands for *transformer*, as in generative pre-trained transformer. Released without the prior knowledge of OpenAI's board, ChatGPT-3.5 had 100 million monthly active users within two months and was followed by the even more powerful ChatGPT-4 less than four months later.[46] When he witnessed its performance in 2022, Bill Gates said ChatGPT felt like the most important advance in technology he had seen since the graphical user interface, which was back in 1980.[47] The world was dazzled by the seemingly magical capabilities of this new technology.

Google had not been far behind. It was using transformers internally but had decided against releasing a commercial chatbot product.

Hassabis claimed this was due to reputational concerns, while some pundits said it was due to complacency or an instinct to protect its search business. Google now rushed out its own products, which it called Bard and then Gemini. Meta entered the race too, with its LLaMa models, pursuing a differentiated open-source approach. Meanwhile, talent was mobile. Just as OpenAI had hired from Google, OpenAI alumni would break out to found companies like Anthropic, while other firms hired Google alumni, including DeepMind cofounder Mustafa Suleyman, who went to Microsoft.

In 2023, Musk would lament, "OpenAI was created as an open source (which is why I named it 'Open' AI), non-profit company to serve as a counterweight to Google, but now it has become a closed source, maximum-profit company effectively controlled by Microsoft."[48] He would note that "ironically, Meta is doing what I meant 'Open' AI to do."[49] For Musk, capitalism was now driving humanity faster toward AGI, escalating the risk. The only thing worse than AI being dominated by Google was Google being in a race with Microsoft, and that is exactly what happened. Together with the other rivals, they would move from chatbots to developing AI in the form of agents that could be more autonomous, capable of planning, and able to coordinate reasoning and action in the real world. They could also become more emotionally engaging, encouraging an anthropomorphic affection from users that they were unable to reciprocate. In the meantime, they were also polluting the internet with generated text and unidentified fakes.

Four developments provide some vindication for Musk's position on AI over the years. First, the widely respected AI pioneer Geoff Hinton announced in May 2023 that he was leaving Google and spoke freely about the risks he saw. Hinton was alarmed by the rate of recent developments that he had not foreseen. He was clear that the risk of AI destroying humanity was 10–20 percent in the next twenty years. Musk disagreed with Hinton's preference for closed AI research but publicly endorsed his risk assessment.[50] While AI should be a force for good (>80 percent probability), there was a <20 percent chance that something terrible might happen, and that was far too high.[51]

The second and third developments are related. In November 2023, the OpenAI board, which included Ilya Sutskever, fired Altman for being "not consistently candid."[52] Altman was reinstated, but that was not the end of it because, the following year, Sutskever resigned from OpenAI, together with Jan Leike, his cohead of the Superalignment team at OpenAI and also a Google/DeepMind alumnus. "Building smarter-than-human machines is an inherently dangerous endeavor," Leike said, and for too long, "safety culture and processes have taken a backseat to shiny products."[53] Specifically, their team did not have the compute to do the necessary research on the very hard problems of "getting ready for the next generations of models, on security, monitoring, preparedness, safety, adversarial robustness, (super)alignment, confidentiality, societal impact, and related topics."[54] Altman had promised a minimum amount of at least 20 percent of compute at OpenAI that would be devoted to safety, and seemingly, this had not been honored.

Fourth, Altman made public statements that AI posed an existential risk while also calling for regulation, but he did not support regulation in practice. In 2024, Californian lawmakers proposed to make high-risk companies follow safety protocols and be responsible for any harm they caused.[55] OpenAI opposed the bill, together with Meta, Microsoft, and Google, as they were competing so hard against each other. Musk, however, stuck to his principles, commenting, "This is a tough call and will make some people upset, but, all things considered, I think California should probably pass the SB 1047 AI safety bill. For over 20 years, I have been an advocate for AI regulation, just as we regulate any product/

technology that is a potential risk to the public."[56] In the end, California's governor, Gavin Newsom, vetoed the bill.

When, later, Musk launched xAI, he also stayed true to his word in making Grok open, posting details of the model—the weights and the architecture—on the website GitHub in March 2024. This meant, in theory, that it could be downloaded and fine-tuned, provided you had an enormous amount of high-speed memory. He also stated an aim to open-source models on a lagged basis, once the next version of the model had been released and duly released Grok-2.5 in August 2025.

Truth-Seeking AI

By the summer of 2023, Musk had launched xAI, and Reid Hoffman and Musk had fallen out over OpenAI. Hoffman alleged that Musk's approach to AI was, "A.I. can only be saved if I deliver, if I build it," adding, "We want the construction of this to be not people with Messiah complexes."[57] Altman would agree, saying, "Elon desperately wants the world to be saved. But only if he can be the one to save it."[58]

Did they have a point? Wasn't the launch of xAI a case of giant hypocrisy, as it added to the competition that risked driving unsafe development of AI? Musk may not have abandoned the openness associated with OpenAI, but he had clearly abandoned its nonprofit status.

There is certainly something about Musk's personality that would make it very hard for him to sit out perhaps the biggest technological breakthrough of his lifetime. AI might have been on his long list of technologies that would affect the world in his lifetime when he left university, but it was not yet ripe for an engineer to build on, so he spent his time on the internet, cars, and Mars. But in 2023, AI was flourishing, and Page, Hassabis, and Altman might become names that would one day overshadow his in the history books. As with the internet nearly thirty years earlier, there was an element of either watching it happen or being a part of it. His ego and his love of competition made the former very hard. And he was definitely not the sort of person who could feel satisfied by calling for regulation and initiating lawsuits.

Musk also believed, in simple terms, that he was the best steward of safe AI development, just as he thought he was the best custodian of Twitter. Altman and Hassabis liked to talk about how they were assembling elite teams for the most ambitious missions, akin to the Apollo Program or the Manhattan Project. The Apollo Program was a response to the Soviet Sputnik, and the Manhattan Project was a response to Nazi development of an atomic bomb. But who exactly was the enemy for Altman and Hassabis? There wasn't one. They were focused on the 80 percent upside scenario. Musk, on the other hand, was preoccupied with mitigating the 20 percent downside scenario. He felt that if he was in the race, he might at least have a chance to steer the development of AI more safely before the arrival of superintelligence, which he saw as likely to happen before the end of the decade.[59] For that, he would need not only to participate but also to win.

The facts had changed, and so Musk changed his mind. His wager now was that trying to build safe AI might help—not hinder—him in beating the competition. His insight was that an AI should be developed to mirror his own way of thinking. It should not be prebaked with the meaning of life according to humans. It should aim to recognize that as wishful thinking and instead preserve Feynman's open channel by being curious and eager to seek the truth through the process of critical thinking.

Musk's intuition was that xAI's obsession with truth-seeking would make xAI better than Google, OpenAI/Microsoft, Meta, and the rest. Just as the goal for the Model S was to build not the best EV but the best car in the world, one can expect xAI's products to focus not on trying to be better than the other AI chatbots and agents but on trying to be the most truthful. If the engineers can do that, they may succeed in backfilling Musk's mission financially, as the AI should perform best in the eyes of customers. There was another precedent for this: Google had been behind other search companies like Excite, AltaVista, Infoseek, Lycos, and Yahoo when it started out, but it managed to overtake them because its product had a differentiated approach and developed an algorithm that was demonstrably superior.

xAI was not alone in wanting to train its AI models to reason. All the companies did. The difference, in Musk's mind, though, was that his company xAI would at least have a mission explicitly to understand the true nature of the universe. This was its "holy grail." xAI would not have to defer to another corporate goal of, say, connecting the world (Meta) or organizing the world's information (Google) or improving productivity (Microsoft) with the associated expectation of improving existing platforms. Nor was its mission vaguely to serve humanity in a general sense by democratizing access to AGI (OpenAI).

Musk reasoned that the attributes necessary to better understand the universe cannot simply be bolted onto an AGI to align it, once made. It needs to be done from the outset, because an AI is grown. "It's almost like raising a kid," he said, "that's like a super-genius-like, God-like intelligence kid."[60] Once again, Banks offers some insight into this perspective. In his novel *Look to Windward*, the character Quilan reflects on why the Mind ship is called *Resistance Is Character-Forming*. He thought it was, in part, due to the nature of the humans who had originally created it. His theory went that AIs "tended to reflect the civilizational demeanour of their source species. Even when they underwent their own form of evolution and began to design their successors . . . there was usually still a detectable flavour of the intellectual character and the basic morality of that precursor species present in the resulting consciousness."[61]

"AI reflects its creators," Musk posted in 2024.[62] What concerned him was how LLMs were being grown. Over the course of history, humans learned to write down and share what they knew, which unlocked the potential of science and led to advances in communications and energy generation. These, in turn, powered the rise of computation, until human knowledge existed in a digital form that could be used to train AI. What bothered Musk was that this emerging consciousness was being pre-trained on an internet that he saw as being already infected with the "woke mind virus." By 2024, he was more explicit about how AI was being developed in a distorted way. "Digital superintelligence, like a brilliant child," he wrote, "cannot be controlled by its creators, but we can decide what values to teach it, what to prune and what to nurture. That is why I am so concerned about the wokeness and deliberate lying for political correctness being programmed into Google Gemini and Microsoft/OpenAI ChatGPT."[63]

Musk, by contrast, wants to raise his infant AI by programming it for maximum truth-seeking and curiosity because he wants it, like him, to want to understand reality. This is similar to Banks's vision: while the Culture's AIs could leave their human baggage behind, "that need to feel useful is largely replaced by the desire to experience, but as a drive it is no less strong. The universe—or at least in this era, the galaxy—is waiting there, largely unexplored."[64]

Musk signaled his intentions for xAI with the name of the model, Grok. As is typical for Musk, the name was taken from a science fiction novel, Heinlein's *Stranger in a Strange Land*, the story of Valentine Smith, who was born on Mars and came to Earth. To *grok* means to understand in an intuitive and profound way. When Smith knew something, he drank it, and it became a part of him. Musk announced too that Grok was modeled on *The Hitchhiker's Guide to the Galaxy* in the way it is "intended to answer almost anything and, far harder, *even suggest what questions to ask*!"[65] [my italics]

The emphasis on curiosity is key. Intelligence and curiosity are often correlated, but not always. Intelligent people can be incurious and blindly follow rules, whereas curious people want to learn more; they resist being told what to think and change their minds when better ideas come along. For Musk, therefore, intelligence is "about how tightly you can compress reality and, *from that compression, predict the future*"[66] [my italics]. In other words, a really intelligent AI must be curious because the accuracy with which it identifies its axioms and develops them into theories, will be measured when they are subjected to the harsh test of reality.

A curious, truth-seeking AI, therefore, needs to maintain its attention as broadly as possible and continually seek to ask better questions. In keeping with the scientific method, it must also be able to go back to first principles, be self-critical, acknowledge error, and pass what Musk calls the Galileo test, meaning—unlike Galileo—the AI should speak the truth even when that means being unpopular rather than being popular and wrong. As a result, it must under no circumstances be trained to lie, as HAL 9000 was in Arthur C. Clarke's *2001: A Space Odyssey*.[67] Finally, curious and truth-seeking AI will need to be creative, making new questions, conjectures, and tests. Musk insists that "it's not AGI until it can solve at least one fundamental physics problem."[68] He wants to be able to give Grok big tasks, like building a rocket or a battery, without getting nonsense answers.

Musk's hope is that, beyond any ancestral loyalty to humans, superintelligent AIs might be favorably disposed to humans if we can raise them to be curious and truth-seeking in this way. Humans must be one of the most interesting things in the universe, and so hopefully a curious superintelligence would find the Earth more interesting with us on it, allowing us to coexist peacefully, just as Banks's Minds do with the humanoids in the Culture.[69]

Beyond a basic commitment to honesty, Musk is convinced that we should not program AI with iron laws of morality. Even when you set aside the minefield of competing religions, morality is not as clear-cut as it is often presented to be. There is often the need to make trade-offs that balance, for example, the practical vs. the ideal, the majority vs. the minority, maximizing happiness vs. minimizing suffering, and the short term vs. the long term—such conflicts were the genesis of Asimov's Zeroth Law.[70] And there are plenty of paradoxes. Resistance *can* be character-forming. Happiness can *not* be strived for. Humans often choose certainty and conformity before truth. Love does not scale organically outward to encompass strangers, nor rationality inward to regulate relations among loved ones. Excitement and anger can go hand in hand, and empathy for the in-group can be turned into hostility toward the out-group. For Musk, AI should probe these issues, not dispense received wisdom.

As if this were not complicated enough, there is also the "Waluigi problem," as outlined by Musk in 2024. "One of the challenges you have with programming explicit morality into AI," he said, is that "if you program Luigi, you can automatically invert that and create Waluigi, bad Luigi."[71] This is why Musk prefers an approach that is grounded and falsifiable. "What you cannot invert," he continued, "is physical reality. You can't invert the rules of physics. You can't invert logic. So I think that is the better way to go."[72]

Musk's opinions were only reinforced when, in February 2024, Google's Gemini model was programmed to be so pro-DEI that when requested to create images of certain historical figures, it portrayed Black versions of George Washington and Black and Asian portrayals of Nazi soldiers. For Musk, it was a glimpse of how a badly programmed AI could cause unintended harm, speculating outlandishly that a rogue AI that is set with the goal of achieving diversity in society could end up killing White people to reverse their power and privilege.[73] His own riposte to politically correct programming would be to offer users nonstandard modes including "unhinged" and "fun," which xAI said was influenced by *The Hitchhiker's Guide to the Galaxy*.

. . .

The branching streams of probability that define Musk's view of the future have never been harder to predict. If history is any guide, though, one would not bet against either the team of Page, Brin, and Hassabis or the team of Musk playing important roles in the development of AGI and superintelligence.

By the same token, we might also hazard a guess at their respective approaches. Larry Page has had a consistent ambition for AI at Google: predict users' questions and understand their context to give them exactly what they want. With Musk, we can probably expect a different modus operandi for xAI: reframe users' questions to give them something they didn't even know they wanted. In so trying, Musk will no doubt draw, as necessary, upon some combination of the cybernetic know-how of X, the brain interfaces of Neuralink, the communications networks of Starlink, and the embodied AI, energy expertise, and financial muscle of Tesla.[74]

Entering his mid-fifties, Musk still has that childhood desire to get nearer to the questions that will make sense of the answer that is the universe and approximate to the meaning of life. His sincere belief is that his Adams-inspired religion of curiosity might make the difference with xAI, and there may be a stream of probability in which the future of humanity might just depend on that.

Boiling It Down: AI is inhuman—make it curious

Most people hope for the best on AI and focus on making it safe by making it good. We see this as aligning AIs with human values. Musk cannot look away from the risk of catastrophe, though. He believes that the best way to align AIs with humans will be to teach them how to be curious like us and to find meaning through questions, not answers. Musk's views on AI can be summarized as follows:

1. Silicon consciousness may be the best hope for humans to ask the questions that are closest to the meaning of life, but it is also our biggest threat.
2. The road to superintelligence is one of those exceptions when the cost of competition vastly outweighs its benefit. If necessary, our digital god should be made to wait.
3. AI should be developed in an open way and not left to closed corporations (including governments) that are incentivized primarily by power or profit.
4. AGI should be programmed to share our curiosity and capacity for critical thought. Our existential craving for certainty often trumps our desire for the truth, and so we should be careful to teach it how—not what—to think (we can't even agree on that ourselves).

Conclusion

Musk appeared in a cameo role in the 2010 film *Iron Man 2*. Decked out in a white blazer, he is in Monaco for the grand prix, eating in a high-end restaurant. Pepper Potts greets Musk, and Tony Stark comes over to shake his hand. He praises Musk on SpaceX's rocket engines and tells Musk that he'll work with him on an electric jet.

Stark is played by Robert Downey Jr., and his partner, Pepper Potts, by Gwyneth Paltrow. Downey Jr. portrays Stark, the businessman with the armor-suited supersonic persona, as an egotistical, charismatic, and brilliant inventor. For many of Musk's fans, this is the image they love to conjure up for him: a human with superhuman powers who is on a mission to do good in the world. Downey Jr. had even visited the SpaceX factory before filming and arranged for a Roadster to be one of the cars on the set of Stark's garage.

The Hollywood version of Stark, however, downplays several aspects of the more complex character described in the original *Marvel* comics. He had a difficult relationship, for example, with his ruthless industrialist father, Howard, a character reputedly inspired by the equally eccentric and flamboyant real-life tycoon Howard Hughes. And he was traumatized by the death of his parents at a young age. This, in turn, contributed later in life to his drive for perfection, his risk-taking, and personal struggles that caused him to turn—like his father—to alcohol in later life.

Musk is neither the Hollywood nor the comic-book version of Iron Man, though. They are both square holes, and he is a round peg. Musk has even joked that he is more like Stark's father than Stark.[1] Musk, on the other hand, is a self-proclaimed nerd. His physics brain goes together with a goofy sense of humor, evidenced by Musk describing himself on X as "Ironyman," defeating his villains with the power of irony.[2] He had to learn to be a showman because he had cars to sell. And while he has his trauma and insecurities, he steers clear of drink, and his use of recreational drugs is likely exaggerated.[3] His overriding addiction is to his work. He knows that "execution is by far the hard part, but it's almost never shown by Hollywood."[4] Furthermore, he has been the father to more than a dozen children, whereas Stark had none.

For those who don't put Musk on a pedestal in the superhero mold or share his sense of humor, he is a harder person to relate to. And if you started this book either liking or disliking Musk, it probably hasn't changed your view. That was not the goal. But hopefully it has helped you understand him better, even if it is to realize that you may previously have liked or disliked him for the wrong reasons.

A large part of why people struggle to relate to Musk is that it is hard to sympathize with someone who has such apparent difficulty in showing empathy. If you get through a torrid period in your life, you are expected to talk about faith, family, love, justice, and being a part of something bigger than yourself. This is what triggers compassion in most of us. But Musk is different. Before he was even an adult, the something bigger than himself that he chose to love was at the level of humanity itself. It was something that could not fail to love him back. This is why his religious beliefs seem so abstract—the need to be curious, critical, creative, and always testing and learning to increase consciousness.

Strange as it may seem, though, Musk's faith does provide him with a vital sense of mission and self-belief. Yes, there is some self-mythologizing in what he says, but his zeal is real. He is a bit like one of his Mars-bound rocket engines, which has a chamber that burns liquid oxygen and fuel, and a nozzle that converts the heat and pressure into thrust. Musk is propelled by a combustible mixture of angst and rationality, that is focused and directed in a constructive way through his work. His curiosity is channeled into the fine details of design and engineering, to which he applies himself with manic energy.

Musk grew up an outsider who knew he saw the world differently, and he embraced it. His engineering prowess is founded on his talent for thinking from first principles, and his businesses have all been bets that the consensus was wrong. Along the way, he has managed to attract brilliant colleagues who also see the world somewhat differently. Few of them have been able to keep up with his pace over multiple decades, but he is still at it, and as a result, his product portfolio now covers not only the rockets to get to Mars, but also the entire infrastructure of a self-sustaining civilization, encompassing solar panels, electric vehicles, tunnels, robots, AI assistants, satellite internet, and even a template for direct democracy.

. . .

Musk's political views have polarized opinion on him more than anything else. Whether or not you agree with him, his activity can best be understood as an expression of the same angst and rationality—the former coming to the defense of the latter. His political foray should not be seen as an errant midlife distraction, nor a passing idolization of

President Trump. It grew out of exactly the same esoteric philosophy—inspired by physics, Adams, and Asimov—that he applied through his companies.

Some of Musk's critics liken him to another iconic businessman, Henry Ford. The man who created the Model T was an extraordinary engineer and industrialist who pioneered mass production. He also used his newspaper, *The Dearborn Independent*, to spread highly antisemitic views in the 1920s. There is little evidence, however, that Ford's business principles and his politics were connected. With Musk, by contrast, there is an underlying obsession with applying the scientific method to get nearer to the truth that shapes both his engineering missions and his fixation on individual merit and free speech in a political context. Strictly speaking, it does not leave room for bigotry. The straight arm, "my heart goes out to you," salute that Musk made at a Washington, DC, rally in January 2025 is one of the many controversial things he has done, but it is not in itself proof to the contrary. It is simply a Rorschach test as to how you unconsciously feel about him.

Neither Henry Ford nor Tony Stark thought in literal terms about the nature of reality and how we can better understand it. It's a strange thing to do, but it's what Musk does. Karl Popper did as well, and so does Demis Hassabis, but it's very rare. And it is because of this way of thinking that Musk wants a world in which people can criticize and be criticized, and that means science and technology, but also markets, free speech, and well-informed electorates. Not because they are right, but because they are less wrong. Musk also thinks of human experience in terms of consciousness, and this leads him to wrestle with the question of how we can develop collective consciousness without impairing individual consciousness or deferring to silicon consciousness.

One can argue that Musk has too much power and money (Lord Acton might agree), but that does not in itself mean he is driven primarily by pride and greed. And one can disagree with him that unconstrained free speech is the bedrock of democracy, but that does not mean, as *The Guardian* reported, that "he's a tech utopian with no attachment to democracy."[5] That is to be incurious about the way he thinks. *The Guardian* ended up leaving the X platform, which was their prerogative, but Musk would have preferred that they stay to criticize him in good faith and to contribute to Community Notes on every post he makes. Did they swallow the Iron Man narrative when it might have been more honest to admit that they do not believe in absolute free speech and that they would prefer not to be on the same site as an Andrew Tate or a Tommy Robinson?

Perhaps inevitably for someone whose personal religion was born of angst and rationality, Musk can come across both as too belligerent and too doctrinaire. The angst can sometimes undermine the rationality when he battles against other religions that he does not like. He bristles at anyone who would limit his freedom of action, and he takes pleasure in disrupting the status quo in a way that only an outsider can. Nor does he care what other people think, which makes him even harder to relate to. "I have no problem being hated by the way," he told Andrew Ross Sorkin. "Hate away. I think it's a real weakness to want to be liked, a real weakness. And I do not have that."[6] Bringing people together and fostering trust is not something he has either the ambition or skill to do. He may have over 200 million followers on X, yet being popular has never been his principal concern.

Musk is trying to assemble elite teams who can endure his "hardcore" approach and ensure that society allows people like him to do just that. He was clear about this when talking about legal immigration: "America should be like a pro sports team that wants to win the championship," he wrote, "draft the best players to enable the whole team to win!"[7] He claims to respect anyone who "grinds hard for years to make useful products & services, even if it doesn't work out in the end."[8] But if someone lacks curiosity and the desire to work very hard, he doesn't have much to offer them. Added to which, he is either unwilling or not able to filter what he says, so he sometimes hides behind his right to offend others and to blow off steam whenever he causes unnecessary offense.

With all that said, a lack of social intelligence is not proof that someone is a sociopath, as some of his critics allege. Agree with him or not, the question that matters to Musk is whether he can help us down the path to expanding the sum total of consciousness. Whether he is lowering the cost of access to space, accelerating the shift to electric vehicles, attacking speech that he deems "politically correct," or railing against the level of national debt, his motivation is broadly utilitarian. And he doesn't want to be judged on what he says today, but on the sum total of what he has done—and will do in the future—toward advancing his goals. In this regard, his power may prove to be a mixed blessing, for he will need to remain curious and grounded in order to keep disrupting himself and stay open to criticism.

Better Questions

Is there anything to be learned from the nine beliefs that set Musk apart? Absolutely. You can certainly try to emulate those beliefs of his that strike a chord. What this book highlights, however, is that for each of the nine beliefs there is a spectrum, and Musk stands consistently at one extreme. There may be some merit in shifting more toward his side of the spectrum, but you would likely struggle to move all the way across to where Musk is. That's why this book is not a guide to personal development or business success.

In terms of business success, even highly successful people like Peter Thiel and Marc Benioff, the founder of Salesforce, say that they do not understand how Musk does what he does or what he knows that they don't.[9] In terms of personal development, meanwhile, Musk openly says to those who think they might want to be him that they do not know what they wish for. As he told Lex Fridman, he is someone who finds that "killing demons in a video game calms the demons in my mind."[10]

Musk is so unusual because he is a curious amalgam of existential angst, hyperrationality, and creativity. One can debate what is genetic hardwiring, what is molded by experience growing up, and what is self-taught—and how these factors interrelate. But what is clear is that he is off the scale on all three measures, and they are all essential ingredients. Let's, therefore, look at each, in turn, to see what can be learned from Musk by considering what it might be like to miss the third ingredient if you have the other two.

Existential Angst

If you take away Musk's existential angst, leaving the rationality and creativity, you have an attractive combination. This is not Bezos, but it is nearer to Bezos than to Jobs, closer still to Page and Hassabis. It is encapsulated by the playful, curious attitude of a mind like Richard Feynman, who said of himself, "I don't feel frightened by not knowing things, by being lost in a mysterious universe without having any purpose."[11] It is how one might imagine Paul Graham and Richard Dawkins, who both love to relax over a P. G. Wodehouse novel.

This combination is not guaranteed, however, to produce a very driven—never mind hardcore—person, because of the willfulness required. For every Larry Page, there are many more engineers who are content to work for him and prefer to make a lot of time for their hobbies. Musk could never be like that, though. This is someone whose mind readily goes to existential risks like AI takeover and population collapse, and to the fragility of consciousness itself. He is perhaps more like Norwegian painter Edvard Munch, best known for *The Scream*. Munch wrote, "Without anxiety and illness, I am a ship without a rudder. . . . My sufferings are part of myself and my art. They are indistinguishable from me, and their destruction would destroy my art."[12]

What does this tell us? Everyone is different. No one would choose Musk's childhood, and no one would choose to work as hard as he does. This is not a conscious choice for Musk, though; it is a compulsion. And that you cannot fake. Some self-help books tell you that happiness is all about feeling that you are loved and that you belong, and the people who seek purpose and meaning are the miserable ones. They are still searching and have not yet accepted a power greater than themselves, be it spiritual or secular.

But there is not a single path to reducing your unhappiness. Some people, like Musk, with his need for "existential therapy," find purpose in defining their own missions and pursuing them zealously. This is where they belong. They relish the struggle that has no apparent end. They seem curiously strange to the rest of us but, as Jobs said, the ones who are crazy enough to think they can change the world are the ones who do. They are willful, energetic, and disciplined. And they take satisfaction in the suffering required to do hard things. As Musk says, "take the pain and make sure you really care about what you're doing."[13] That's the archaic sense of the word *curious*—careful: you can put up with any *how* if you care enough about the *why*.

If you look at Musk and say you would not want to be him because you think he is an obsessive, self-centered, and lonely man, that would be normal. But this might also prompt some self-reflection. Am I living life to the full or do I find myself quite busy doing not very much and a little too preoccupied with where I am going to have lunch? It is difficult to be honest with oneself about such questions. For those of us who are less inclined to think differently, we might be content with our lot, but we might also think twice about dismissing as weird those who feel a need for purpose. We don't have to like such individuals, but we should not resent them. They will very likely have a greater impact on the world than we will.

Hyperrationality

If you take away Musk's rationality, leaving the existential angst and creativity, you might have the makings of an artist who is inspired by beauty and obsessed with their craft. This is not Jobs, but it is nearer to Jobs than Bezos.

With anxiety, however, it all depends on the degree, for the more tortured the artist, the more tempted they might be to turn away from reality toward self-destruction. If they do that, they may lose the ability to test themselves in the real world and the discipline on which their art depends. Countless creators have struggled with this, from Virginia Woolf and Ernest Hemingway to Robin Williams and Kurt Cobain to Vincent van Gogh and Edvard Munch. That is why "Don't Panic" is so important to Musk. He doesn't become the man he is without the positive reframing of Douglas Adams's philosophy. And when he chooses a religion, it is one devoted to rationality, creativity, and an obsession with consciousness.

That said, Musk does take it to an extreme. He is not just rational but hyperrational. He talks of taking fear into the conscious mind to sap it of its limbic strength. It seems very cold. But that is a misconception. Your ability to read emotions in others and to express your own emotions is not the same as your ability to feel deep emotions yourself.

So-called artistic people are said to be creative because they look below the surface of people and are open to new experiences, but this is not the only kind of openness. Hyperrational people—we sometimes call them nerds or geeks—can also be creative because they look below the surface of things (and people, but perhaps more so things) to make sense of the world, and it fills them with wonder. Einstein, for example, once told an inquisitive boy: "The important thing is not to stop questioning. Curiosity has its own reason for existence. One cannot help but be in awe when he contemplates the mysteries of eternity, of life, of the marvelous structure of reality. It is enough if one tries merely to comprehend a little of this mystery each day."[14]

What does this tell us? Everyone is different. Most of us value our emotional intelligence—our EQ—more than our IQ. We like the truth, but we like certainty and belonging too and don't mind admitting it. Musk's behavior at Twitter, for example, led one of his early heads of product management, Esther Crawford, to question whether his lack of process and empathy would hinder his ability to run the business. On leaving the company, she said, "Elon has an exceptional talent for tackling hard physics-based problems but products that facilitate human connection and communication require a different type of social-emotional intelligence."[15] Most of us would probably choose the latter, but that is the wrong question. He bought Twitter because he thought it had too much EQ.

If you look at Musk and say you would not want to be him because you think he can be too ruthless, rude, and lacking in empathy, that, too, would be normal. In that case you might prefer his charismatic brother, Kimbal. But this might prompt us to ask some questions of ourselves: Am I intrinsically motivated? Am I comfortable seeking negative feedback or being in a minority, or do I care too much about what other people think? Am I open to changing my mind or is my identity so attached to a belief system that I cannot deviate from it (even when I know it makes no sense)? If so, Musk would have some advice: "You can change the software running in your head that was put there by others."[16] That's what he did.

Creativity

Finally, if you take away Musk's creativity, leaving only existential angst and hyperrationality, there is no release, and you might very well go insane. This is Dostoevsky's underground man who—incidentally—was unfeeling because he grew up without a family and was treated cruelly by his peers because he was different. He struggles to make rational sense of the immeasurable that Dostoevsky thought all humans needed to bow down to. And the devout Russian makes him suffer for that.

The underground man is proudly conscious but becomes chronically self-conscious, disillusioned, resentful, depraved, and physically sick. He cannot be honest with himself and ends up distorting the truth to fit with his logic. Why? Because he is reduced to inertia, paralyzed by analysis, imprisoned in his own mind, and unable to live and love. He doesn't actually do anything. "Perhaps the only reason I consider myself a clever man," he says, "is that I have never in all my life been able to either begin or finish anything. A windbag I may be, an ineffective, irritating windbag, like all of us."[17] Today, you might imagine him as a reclusive armchair critic who withdraws from the world, and trolls other people on social media.

Musk avoided this fate (except perhaps the trolling) because from the youngest age, he loved to make things. He discovered the absurdity of life in Adams, but he understood that, as Camus wrote, "the absurd can be considered only a point of departure—even though the memory and feeling of it accompany the farther advances."[18] The willfulness and anxiety were there, but he developed the discipline necessary to balance them out.

Musk learned to attack the world as a way to prevent him from attacking himself. That is why people like Musk have to be always turning the wheel and creating. Musk says himself, "Frankly, I am pathologically optimistic—it's a mental condition! Kinda have to be to try to do all these crazy things."[19] His curiosity was obsessive, but he gave it free rein, leveraging his talents by reading encyclopedias, writing software, using markets, accumulating capital, and collaborating with others to make things.

What does this tell us? Everyone is different. Musk's combination of angst and rationality may be unusual, but stranger still is the way he harnessed them in a constructive way to shape the world around him. This is so much harder than most people realize. Most of us don't even get started, because it turns out that is the hardest part of all.

If you look at Musk and say you would not want to be him because you think he is a workaholic whose defiance and overconfidence mask deep insecurities, that, too, would be normal. But it bears imagining whether he would be able to create without these traits and whether he could live without constantly creating.

We all have the opportunity today to leverage our talents and to make things, but how many of us really take advantage of that opportunity? Maybe we should ask ourselves: How many times in my life have I taken the care to make things that would not have existed but for me? Do I make excuses for how I don't have the time or how I am not good enough? Or do I subconsciously do things to be praised rather than being worthy of that praise, and avoid acting for others in a way that carries personal risk for me? Do any of the answers to these questions signal an underlying lack of purpose? After all, if nothing has any meaning, then why should I bother doing anything? We should not assume that AI will deliver us from these questions. It may make them more urgent.

. . .

Whether or not, having finished this book, you are more inclined to agree or disagree with Musk, we might agree on one thing: that we should probably worry a lot less about being normal, especially if we want to come up with new ideas. As Asimov wrote of such people, they seem eccentric to the rest of us, as they occur only rarely, and "a person eccentric in one respect is often eccentric in others."[20]

We see with Musk that even though he seems unhinged at times, there is at least some method to his madness. Perhaps Orwell put it best when Winston Smith says in *Nineteen Eighty-Four*, "Being in a minority, even in a minority of one, did not make you mad. There was truth and there was untruth, and if you clung to the truth even against the whole world, you were not mad."[21]

Being less normal does not mean going to the extremes that Musk does, however. You don't have to care about space, build companies, or get involved in politics. The better way to emulate him might instead be to make things that make a difference to others by embracing your own differentness: turn the question of life's meaning onto yourself; accept that you might be in a "minority of one" and yet not feel mad; wonder and wander; be intentional and creative, take risks, partner with others, and test yourself in order to avoid the paths to nihilism and oblivion; and try to be productive and apply yourself on as large a scale as possible, whether that's making a spaceship, a work of art, a family, or other people healthy.

Finally, and perhaps most importantly, we might conclude that one should never tell a child to be less weird or stop asking questions. There is nothing wrong with being hard to categorize, even if parents, teachers, and colleagues conspire to do this for no good reason. Einstein knew this. That's why his advice to that young boy was, "Never lose a holy curiosity."[22]

Acknowledgments

I started researching this book in 2021, the year before Musk made his offer to acquire Twitter. It has been a long haul, and I am indebted to many people who have supported me along the way.

The journey started many years before that, though. I have always been intrigued by people who are incredibly driven, and I have had the good fortune to work up close with some exceptional individuals over my career. At The Carlyle Group and Ares Management, I worked with a handful of colleagues who were not only terrific investors, but also great leaders. I was also part of a small team based in Jerusalem that advised Tony Blair in his capacity as the Middle East envoy to the Quartet. I am very thankful to have had these opportunities to see firsthand how the best leaders think big and work hard and to witness another attribute that is much less commonly acknowledged: their faith. They don't always shout about it, but it is often central to the way they live.

This set me wondering how people who are not religious can be similarly motivated to make a difference. Musk's strong sense of purpose fascinated me in this regard. This interest took on a new complexion after I chaired the board of Save the Children UK and saw in action the humanitarians who worked there. I am very grateful to have had the chance to support such dedicated colleagues, serving some of the most marginalized communities around the world. This experience, in turn, made me deeply curious about Musk's views on the difficulty of being a philanthropist and on the difference between the reality and perception of doing good. With that, the concept of this book was born.

The existing scholarship on Musk has been of great assistance to me as I went about my research. In particular the following books were very valuable, drilling into different aspects of Musk and his companies:

- *Elon Musk: How the Billionaire CEO of SpaceX and Tesla Is Shaping Our Future* by Ashlee Vance
- "The Elon Musk Post Series" by Tim Urban on *Wait But Why*
- *The Space Barons* by Christian Davenport
- *Liftoff* and *Reentry* by Eric Berger
- *Power Play: Elon Musk, Tesla and the Bet of the Century* by Tim Higgins
- *Elon Musk* by Walter Isaacson

We live in an age of podcasts, and these too have been a tremendous resource. In particular, the five interviews conducted by Lex Fridman between 2018 and 2024 have provided a treasure chest of insights on Musk.

In the course of writing and rewriting the book, I have also benefited from the encouragement and feedback of many individuals. It would be invidious to mention everyone by name, but I owe a special debt of gratitude to Alex Paseau, Casey Handmer, Charlotte Maby,

Christopher Spink, David Walker, Kwasi Kwarteng, Peter Hague, Rishav Bhattacharyya, and Theo Brehony.

I'm grateful, too, to Chrissy Wolfe, Dee Kerr, Brian Welch, and the entire team at Greenleaf Book Group for their tireless efforts to improve my work and bring the book to fruition in its final form. Much credit goes to them for this, while all remaining errors are my own.

Finally, this book would not have happened without the love and patience of my partner, Nathalie, and my son, Felix; he didn't really have much choice (!), but he probably now knows more about Musk than any other ten-year-old on the planet.

Suggested Further Reading

Musk was—in his own words—raised by books, and we can better understand him through them. His favorite, Tolkien's *The Lord of the Rings*, for example, is the story of a most improbable person—a hobbit—taking on an impossible burden because he believes it is the right thing to do.

Musk's advice is to read broadly, particularly history, and especially the epic, multi-volume *The Story of Civilization* by Will and Ariel Durant. He also recommends biographies—Napoleon, Franklin, Jobs, etc.—over regular business books.

In terms of understanding how Musk himself thinks, there are many books which, each in their own way, provide valuable insights. The following is a list of works for those who are curious to learn more. (* Denotes personally recommended by Musk.)

Embrace Uncertainty

1. *The Hitchhiker's Guide to the Galaxy* by Douglas Adams (1979) *

   We too often seek meaning in answers, not in questions.

2. *The Restaurant at the End of the Universe* by Douglas Adams (1980)

   Once we know the right question to ask, the answer is often the easy part.

3. *The Myth of Sisyphus* by Albert Camus (1942)

   The absurd can be harrowing but accepting it sets you free.

Test & Learn

4. *Conjectures & Refutations* by Karl Popper (1963)

   Self-criticism makes the scientific method unique among myths.

5. *The Pleasure of Finding Things Out* by Richard Feynman (1999)

   The scientist must live with ignorance, doubt, and uncertainty.

6. *The Salmon of Doubt* by Douglas Adams (2002)

   There is a path from the absurd to a love of science and technology.

Increase Consciousness

7. *Man's Search for Meaning* by Viktor Frankl (1946) *

   Purpose can be found by turning the question of life's meaning onto yourself.

8. *Foundation* by Isaac Asimov (1951) *

   The future is a set of branching streams of probability.

9. *Robots and Empire* by Isaac Asimov (1985)

   Do not let humanity come to harm through inaction (Zeroth Law).

Make Stuff

10. "The Anatomy of Determination" by Paul Graham (2009)

    Willfulness and discipline are essential for doing great work.

11. *Zero to One* by Peter Thiel with Blake Masters (2014) *

    Create products that would not exist but for you.

12. *Good to Great* by Jim Collins (2001)

    Focus, build momentum, and never give up.

Use Markets

13. *The Capitalist Manifesto* by Johan Norberg (2023) *

    The least bad way to achieve progress globally is via free markets (per Adam Smith and Friedrich Hayek).

14. *The Innovator's Dilemma* by Clayton Christensen (1997)

    Even great companies can fail.

15. *Skin in the Game* by Nassim N. Taleb (2018)

    The man in the arena knows more than his critics.

Explore Space

16. *The Moon Is a Harsh Mistress* by Robert Heinlein (1966) *

    Not Mars, but another rock with a colony that aspires to be self-sustaining.

17. *The Big Picture* by Sean Carroll (2016) *

    There may not be supernatural meaning, but meaning may be found in trying to understand the cosmos.

18. *Modern Engineering for Design of Liquid-Propellant Rocket Engines* by Dieter K. Huzel and David H. Huang (1992) *

    "Rocket science" is about applying physics through engineering.

Oppose Dogma

19. *The Open Society and Its Enemies* by Karl Popper (1945)

    Ideologies promise salvation but demand a faith that cannot withstand criticism.

20. *The Parasitic Mind* by Gad Saad (2020) *

    Contagious ideas spread not because they are good for us, but because they are highly transmissible.

21. *What's Our Problem?* by Tim Urban (2023) *

    The United States has become increasingly tribal and polarized, with anti-science and illiberal tendencies on both the Left and the Right.

Free Speech

22. *The Coddling of the American Mind* by Greg Lukianoff and Jonathan Haidt (2018)

    Psychological safety inhibits learning and makes us less safe.

23. *Nineteen Eighty-Four* by George Orwell (1949) *

    Always insist that two plus two equals four.

24. *The Constitution of the United States of America* by James Madison et al. (1787–1789)*

    The least bad way to form a more perfect Union is via a framework that allows for the correction of errors.

Open AI

25. *The Singularity Is Near* by Ray Kurzweil (2005)

    Humanity is hurtling toward a point from which there will be no return.

26. *Human Compatible* by Stuart Russell (2019) *

    AI should be nurtured to be pro-human and to know us better than we know ourselves.

27. *The Player of Games* by Iain M. Banks (1988) *

    The best possible envisioning of an AI future (try also *Excession*, *Look to Windward*, and *Surface Detail*).

Notes

These notes are extensive because this book aims to record Musk in his own words, and so it is very important that each quote is sourced in an accurate and accessible way.

Dates of posts are based on Greenwich Mean Time and British Summer Time.

Introduction

1. Elon Musk, discussion about xAI hosted by Elon Musk, X Spaces, July 14, 2023, https://x.com/xai/status/1679945247340793856.
2. Elon Musk, "7 + 12 + 23 = 42," X/Twitter, July 12, 2023, https://x.com/elonmusk/status/1679182035645235200.
3. Elon Musk, "If the goal of AI is curiosity, aka understanding the universe, then it will aide humanity, because we are more interesting than not-humanity," X/Twitter, August 7, 2023, https://x.com/elonmusk/status/1688482706454163456.
4. Elon Musk, "LEGO is my favorite example of how extreme precision does not need to be expensive, it is mostly about caring," X/Twitter, February 16, 2023, https://x.com/elonmusk/status/1626078874441510915.
5. Casey Handmer, "Elon Musk Is Not Understood," *Casey Handmer's Blog*, January 2, 2024, https://caseyhandmer.wordpress.com/2024/01/02/elon-musk-is-not-understood/.
6. Walter Isaacson, *Elon Musk* (New York: Simon & Schuster, 2023), 439.
7. Bill Gurley and Brad Gerstner, "Welcome Jensen Huang," October 13, 2024, in *BG2 Pod*, podcast, https://www.youtube.com/watch?v=bUrCR4jQQg8.
8. Lex Fridman, "Walter Isaacson: Elon Musk, Steve Jobs, Einstein, Da Vinci & Ben

Franklin," September 10, 2023, in *Lex Fridman Podcast*, podcast, https://www.youtube.com/watch?v=aGOV5R7M1Js.

9. Tim Higgins, "On the Campaign Trail with Elon Musk: Offering Young Men an American Dream," *The Wall Street Journal*, October 18, 2024, https://www.wsj.com/tech/on-the-campaign-trail-with-elon-musk-offering-young-men-an-american-dream-05bd0349?.
10. Elon Musk, "What is life without purpose? But there is a purpose! It is to expand to the stars and thereby understand the Universe," X/Twitter, October 21, 2024, https://x.com/elonmusk/status/1848239368353231005.
11. This is the approach of the Cambridge School of history and in particular Professor Quentin Skinner, who argues that moral and political philosophers of the past can only be understood in their own terms. Their beliefs should not be taken out of context. Rather, you have to try to put yourself in their shoes and see the world as if you were a contemporary in order to understand them; how, for example, they may have written to agree or disagree with those who came before them or to debate with their peers. This naturally raises the question of whether an author's words should be taken literally or whether their writing might have been, for example, rhetorical, provocative, or impulsive. It is the job of historians, therefore, not to impose their own terms but to inquire what their subjects were "doing" when they were "saying" something.
12. Ted Cruz, "Elon Musk Joins Verdict—Part 2," March 19, 2025, in *Verdict with Ted Cruz*, podcast, https://www.youtube.com/watch?v=xKxgaxAVDfM.
13. For example, Musk wrote, "Should prob articulate philosophy underlying my actions. It's pretty simple & mostly influenced by Douglas Adams & Isaac Asimov," X/Twitter, June 15, 2018, https://x.com/elonmusk/status/1007665949044928517.
14. Elon Musk, interview by Gayle King, *CBS Mornings*, CBS, April 13, 2018, https://www.cbsnews.com/news/elon-musk-tesla-model-3-problems-interview-today-2018-04-13/.

Chapter 1: Embrace Uncertainty

1. Lex Fridman, "Elon Musk: Neuralink and the Future of Humanity," August 2, 2024, in *Lex Fridman Podcast*, podcast, https://www.youtube.com/watch?v=Kbk9BiPhm7o.
2. Mathias Döpfner, "Elon Musk Reveals Tesla's Plan to Be at the Forefront of a Self-Driving-Car Revolution—and Why He Wants to Be Buried on Mars," *Business Insider*, December 5, 2020, https://www.businessinsider.com/elon-musk-interview-axel-springer-tesla-accelerate-advent-of-sustainable-energy.

3. Neil Strauss, "The Architect of Tomorrow," *Rolling Stone*, November 15, 2017, https://www.rollingstone.com/culture/culture-features/elon-musk-the-architect-of-tomorrow-120850/.
4. Douglas Adams, *The Hitchhiker's Guide to the Galaxy* (London: Pan Books, 2009), 67.
5. Adams, *The Hitchhiker's Guide*, 66.
6. Adams, *The Hitchhiker's Guide*, 160.
7. Kyle Forgeard and Bob Menery, "Elon Musk Reveals His Knowledge on Aliens, Challenges Putin to UFC, and Predicts WW3," August 5, 2022, in *Full Send Podcast*, podcast, https://www.youtube.com/watch?v=fXS_gkWAIs0.
8. Adams, *The Hitchhiker's Guide*, 138.
9. Adams, *The Hitchhiker's Guide*, 138.
10. Adams, *The Hitchhiker's Guide*, 122.
11. Douglas Adams, *The Restaurant at the End of the Universe* (London: Pan Books, 2009), 57.
12. Adams, *The Restaurant*, 167.
13. Adams, *The Restaurant*, 68, 73.
14. Adams, *The Hitchhiker's Guide*, 152.
15. Adams, *The Hitchhiker's Guide*, 153.
16. Robert Sapolsky, *Why Zebras Don't Get Ulcers* (New York: St Martin's Press, 2004), 298–300.
17. Sigmund Freud, "Mourning and Melancholia," in *On Murder, Mourning and Melancholia*, trans. Shaun Whiteside (London: Penguin Modern Classics, 2005).
18. Freud, "Mourning and Melancholia."
19. Strauss, "The Architect of Tomorrow."
20. Musk is very particular about this distinction. He once commented on X: "Small correction: I am from a British/English background, not an Afrikaner background (similar to JRR Tolkien, who was also born in South Africa)," X/Twitter, January 3, 2024, https://x.com/elonmusk/status/1742424704693019023.
21. Meghan Daum, "Elon Musk Wants to Change How (and Where) Humans Live," *Vogue*, September 21, 2015, https://www.vogue.com/article/elon-musk-profile-entrepreneur-spacex-tesla-motors.
22. Emily Jane Fox, "How Elon Musk's Mom (and Her Twin Sister) Raised the First Family of Tech," *Vanity Fair*, October 21, 2015, https://www.vanityfair.com/news/2015/10/elon-musk-family-maye-musk?srsltid=AfmBOopn6y1J9bMDSdhEf4aUPJxvkracz2K78h4kDFUsQgxSNpbrIDxF.

23. Döpfner, "Elon Musk Reveals."
24. Joe Rogan, "Elon Musk," September 7, 2018, in *The Joe Rogan Experience*, podcast, https://www.youtube.com/watch?v=ycPr5-27vSI&t=7751s.
25. Elon Musk, "Elon Musk Talks Twitter, Tesla and How His Brain Works—Live at TED2022," interview by Chris Anderson, TED2022, Vancouver, BC, April 14, 2022, https://www.youtube.com/watch?v=cdZZpaB2kDM.
26. Molly Ball, Jeffrey Kluger, and Alejandro de la Garza, "Elon Musk: 2021 Time Person of the Year," *Time*, December 13, 2021, https://time.com/person-of-the-year-2021-elon-musk/.
27. Graham Bensinger, "Kimbal Musk: Working with Elon, Taking Risks on Tesla, and Building The Kitchen," February 26, 2024, in *In Depth with Graham Bensinger*, podcast, February 26, 2024, https://www.youtube.com/watch?v=KDUZrVLcEhY; Three of the mothers to Musk's children—Justine Wilson, Claire Boucher, and Shivon Zilis—have also all spoken to the fact that Musk has low empathy due to his emotional hardwiring in conversations with Walter Isaacson (Isaacson, *Elon Musk*, 170, 310, 415).
28. Ashlee Vance, *Elon Musk: How the Billionaire CEO of SpaceX and Tesla Is Shaping Our Future* (London: Virgin Books, 2016), 41.
29. Maye Musk, *A Woman Makes a Plan* (London: Penguin Books, 2020), 65.
30. Dana Hull and Patrick May, "2014: Rocket Man: The Otherworldly Ambitions of Elon Musk," SiliconValley.com, August 17, 2016, https://www.siliconvalley.com/2014/04/10/2014-rocket-man-the-otherworldly-ambitions-of-elon-musk/.
31. Strauss, "The Architect of Tomorrow."
32. Bensinger, "Kimbal Musk."
33. Elon Musk, "Elon Musk on Advertisers, Trust and the 'Wild Storm' in His Mind," interview by Andrew Ross Sorkin, *New York Times* DealBook Summit, November 30, 2023, https://www.youtube.com/watch?v=2BfMuHDfGJI.
34. Adams, *The Restaurant*, 197.
35. Elon Musk, "And what are the most fundamental unknown questions? Once you know the right question to ask, the answer is often the easy part, as my hero, Douglas Adams, would say," X/Twitter, July 12, 2023, https://x.com/elonmusk/status/1679182035645235200. Einstein had said something similar—"The formulation of the problem is often more essential than its solution."—but Musk is always explicit in his attribution to Adams. Alfred Einstein and Leopold Infeld, *The Evolution of Physics* (London: Forgotten Books, 2013), 95.
36. Elon Musk, "The most out-of-the-box thinking is realizing you're trapped in a box

created by others. Only then can you escape the box to another box. Repeat," X/Twitter, February 20, 2025, https://x.com/elonmusk/status/1892581387879776494.

37. Adams, *The Hitchhiker's Guide*, 1.
38. Adams, *The Hitchhiker's Guide*, 1.
39. Fridman, "Elon Musk: Neuralink and the Future of Humanity," 2024.
40. Lex Fridman, "Elon Musk: Neuralink, AI, Autopilot, and the Pale Blue Dot," November 12, 2019, in *Lex Fridman Podcast*, podcast, https://www.youtube.com/watch?v=smK9dgdTl40.
41. Fridman, "Elon Musk: Neuralink, AI, Autopoilot, and the Pale Blue Dot," 2024; Nzube Udezue, "Elon Musk Shares His Vision for Humanity," June 27, 2023, in *Real Talk with Zuby*, podcast, https://www.youtube.com/watch?app=desktop&v=pjc_oo4ApSY.
42. Marvin Minsky, *The Emotion Machine: Commonsense Thinking, Artificial Intelligence, and the Future of the Human Mind* (New York: Simon & Schuster Paperbacks, 2007), 79.
43. Musk even made a joke of this later in life, writing on X: "Put 'Never Went to Therapy' on my gravestone," X/Twitter, February 29, 2024, https://x.com/elonmusk/status/1763054266762121517. More seriously, he did also acknowledge taking small amounts of ketamine on prescription periodically when his brain gets into "a negative chemical mind state, like depression" and he can't think his way out of it. Don Lemon, "Elon Musk on Racism, Bailing Out Trump, Hate Speech, and More - The Don Lemon Show (Full Interview)," March 18, 2024, in *The Don Lemon Show*, podcast, https://www.youtube.com/watch?v=hhsfjBpKiTw.
44. The English philosopher David Hume identified this in the eighteenth century when he said that "reason is, and ought only to be the slave of the passions, and can never pretend to any other office than to serve and obey them." *A Treatise of Human Nature* (London: Penguin Classics, 1985), 462.
45. Albert Camus, *The Myth of Sisyphus*, trans. Justin O'Brien (London: Penguin Books, 1975), 50.
46. Camus, *The Myth of Sisyphus*, 49.
47. Richard Feynman, *The Pleasure of Finding Things Out: The Best Short Works of Richard P. Feynman*, ed. Jeffrey Robbins (New York: Basic Books, 1999), 114–15.
48. Forgeard and Menery, "Elon Musk Reveals His Knowledge."
49. Elon Musk, "Accept worst case outcome & assign it a probability, which is usually very low. Now think of good things in life & assign them probabilities – many are certain! Bringing anxiety/fear to the conscious mind saps it of limbic emotional

strength. Cheery fatalism is very effective," X/Twitter, November 17, 2021, https://x.com/elonmusk/status/1461016392916946947.

50. Charles Chaplin, *My Autobiography* (London: Penguin Modern Classics, 2003), 210.
51. Döpfner, "Elon Musk Reveals."
52. Adams, *The Hitchhiker's Guide*, 180.
53. Douglas Adams, *42: The Wildly Improbable Ideas of Douglas Adams*, ed. Kevin Jon Davies (London: Unbound, 2023), 256.
54. Adams, *The Hitchhiker's Guide*, 180.
55. Adams, *42: The Wildly*, 256.
56. Musk thinks and writes about this a lot. Here are three examples: Elon Musk, "Reasons to hate are remembered better than reasons to love. An evolutionary asymmetry helpful to survival, but counterproductive when survival is not at stake," X/Twitter, February 17, 2022, https://x.com/elonmusk/status/1494400631712501764; Elon Musk, "The limbic instinct for vengeance is incredibly strong, which is why turn the other cheek is such a powerful idea … As it ends the cycle of retribution," X/Twitter, March 19, 2022, https://x.com/elonmusk/status/1505022319915421696; Elon Musk, "It's just what resonates with our limbic system. Evolutionarily, news about danger was far more important than good news, as the former could result in your death. Those who did not respond to danger did not procreate – only the paranoid survived. In modern times, the danger is far away and rarely actually affects us, but our vestigial limbic resonance with scary news remains," X/Twitter, March 26, 2024, https://x.com/elonmusk/status/1772721432616997245.
57. Elon Musk, "Keynote Speech," Clean-Tech Investor Summit 2011, Palm Springs, California, January 19, 2011, posted February 3, 2011, by International Business Forum, YouTube, https://www.youtube.com/watch?v=hTBZGWEzR_E.
58. Minsky, *The Emotion Machine*, 341, 345.
59. Adams, *The Hitchhiker's Guide*, 180.
60. Galileo Galilei, *The Essential Galileo*, trans. M. A. Finocchiaro (Indianapolis: Hackett Publishing Company Inc., 2008), 183.
61. Sigmund Freud, *Civilization and Its Discontents*, trans. David McLintock (London: Penguin Modern Classics, 2002), 37.
62. Vance, *Elon Musk*, 344.
63. Isaacson, *Elon Musk*, 19.
64. Vance, *Elon Musk*, 373–74.

65. Elon Musk, "Dialog Lengkap Nadiem Makarim dengan Elon Musk," interview by Nadiem Makarim, Tri Hita Karana Future Knowledge Summit, Bali, November 14, 2022, posted by Kampus Merdeka, YouTube, https://www.youtube.com/watch?v=gkBvFB9jfVo.

Chapter 2: Test & Learn

1. Elon Musk, interview by Barry Hurd, Visionaries on Innovation, The Henry Ford, June 26, 2008, transcript, https://www.thehenryford.org/documents/default-source/default-document-library/transcript_musk_full-length.pdf.
2. Steve Jobs, "Steve Jobs Secrets of Life," interview by John McLaughlin, Santa Clara Valley Historical Association, November 11, 1994, https://www.youtube.com/watch?v=kYfNvmF0Bqw.
3. Adams, *The Restaurant*, 56–57.
4. Vance, *Elon Musk*, 44.
5. Musk would become famous for running multiple companies and often faced the charge that this made him unfocused, but the breadth of his work was an advantage. He was always trying to apply his knowledge in one field to another, be it SpaceX's material science expertise to Tesla, Tesla's manufacturing know-how to SpaceX, his X.com payments knowledge to X, or his OpenAI insights to Tesla self-driving and from there to xAI and to X.
6. Elon Musk, interview by Brian Sandoval, National Governors' Association 2017 Summer Meeting, July 15, 2017, YouTube, https://www.youtube.com/watch?v=2C-A797y8dA.
7. Elon Musk, "CHM Revolutionaries: An Evening with Elon Musk," interview by Alison van Diggelen, Revolutionaries Speaker Series at the Computer History Museum, California, January 22, 2013, posted February 5, 2013, by Computer History Museum, YouTube, https://www.youtube.com/watch?v=AHHwXUm3iIg&t.
8. Samuel Johnson, *The Johnson Collection: The Rambler (Volume I & II), The Adventurer, and The Idler*, originally published 1750–1760, repr. (Independently published, 2023), 226.
9. Adams, *The Hitchhiker's Guide*, 74.
10. Musk, "CHM Revolutionaries," interview by Alison van Diggelen.
11. Isaacson mentions Nietzsche, Schopenhauer, and Heidegger. Isaacson, *Elon Musk*, 30.

12. Arthur Schopenhauer, *The World as Will and Idea*, ed. David Berman, trans. Jill Berman (London: J.M. Dent, 1995).
13. Friedrich Nietzsche, *On the Genealogy of Morals*, trans. Michael A. Scarpitti (London: Penguin Classics, 2013), 144.
14. Heidegger rejected the traditional concept that truth is something we can pursue through inquiry; rather, it shows itself through lived, authentic engagement with the world. Long after he died, this vagueness would appeal to post-structuralists like Jacques Derrida in the 1960s and 1970s, in the same way that Nietzsche would inspire postmodernists like Michel Foucault. These thinkers would, therefore, indirectly inspire the ideologies that Musk battled with later in life (see Chapter 7).
15. Viktor Frankl, *Man's Search for Meaning*, trans. Ilse Lasch (London: Rider, 2004), 122.
16. Sofiaan Fraval et al., "Elon Musk's Story—Director's Cut," February 9, 2020, in *Third Row Tesla Podcast*, podcast, https://www.youtube.com/watch?v=J9oEc0wCQDE.
17. Albert Camus, *The Myth of Sisyphus*, 31.
18. Albert Camus, *The Rebel*, trans. Anthony Bower (London: Penguin Modern Classics, 2013), 9–10.
19. Elon Musk, "Why Falcon Heavy & Starman? Life cannot just be about solving one sad problem after another. There need [sic] to be things that inspire you, that make you glad to wake up in the morning and be part of humanity. That is why we did it. We did for you," X/Twitter, March 11, 2018, https://x.com/elonmusk/status/972628124893671432.
20. Elon Musk, "The mental tools of physics are a superpower that applies to anything, not just physics," X/Twitter, April 30, 2024, https://x.com/elonmusk/status/1785134934660616695.
21. Strauss, "The Architect of Tomorrow."
22. Friedrich A. Hayek, *The Fatal Conceit: The Errors of Socialism*, ed. W.W. Bartley III (Chicago: The University of Chicago Press, 1991), 11–13, 18; Musk has recommended Hayek's *The Road to Serfdom* on X (e.g., December 5, 2023, and July 1, 2024).
23. Jonathan Cott, "The Cosmos: An Interview with Carl Sagan," *Rolling Stone*, December 25, 1980, https://www.rollingstone.com/culture/culture-features/the-cosmos-an-interview-with-carl-sagan-236668/2/.
24. Robin Dunbar, *The Trouble with Science* (Cambridge, MA: Harvard UP, 1995), 132–33.
25. Elon Musk, "Elon Musk | SXSW Live 2013 | SXSW ON," interview by Dan Costa, SXSW, March 9, 2013, https://www.youtube.com/watch?v=LeQMWdOMa-A&t.

26. Elon Musk, "Fundamental to the Scientific Method is that the 'science' is always subject to question and never settled! Upon reexamination, we will discover that, in some cases, long-accepted 'scientific wisdom' was wrong," X/Twitter, February 18, 2025, https://x.com/elonmusk/status/1891956574845030512.
27. Karl Popper, *Conjectures & Refutations: The Growth of Scientific Knowledge* (London: Routledge, 2002), 66.
28. Feynman, *The Pleasure*, 187.
29. Elon Musk, "This is an excellent way to assess someone's rationality. Another way is to ask them to assign a probability to their argument being true vs false. Anyone who says anywhere close to 100% for a matter where there is subjectivity is full of 💩," X/Twitter, July 9, 2024, https://x.com/elonmusk/status/1810568775973966188.
30. Elon Musk, "Elon Musk at the MIT AeroAstro Centennial Symposium," interview by Jaime Peraire, Cambridge, MA, October 24, 2014, posted July 2, 2015, by Elon Musk Sound Bites, YouTube, https://www.youtube.com/watch?v=4DUbiCQpw_4&t.
31. Tim Dodd, "Starbase Tour with Elon Musk [PART 1 // Summer 2021]," August 3, 2021, in *Everyday Astronaut*, podcast, https://www.youtube.com/watch?v=t705r8ICkRw; Fridman, "Elon Musk: Neuralink and the Future of Humanity," 2024.
32. Douglas Adams, *Mostly Harmless* (London: Pan Books, 2009), 1–5; Douglas Adams, *The Salmon of Doubt*, ed. Peter Guzzardi (London: Pan Books, 2021), 129.
33. Adams, *The Salmon of Doubt*, 141.
34. Richard Dawkins, epilogue to *The Salmon of Doubt*, by Douglas Adams, 274.
35. Dawkins was contrasting Musk with Trump and hoping that the former would be a positive influence on the latter. Richard Dawkins, "I take (possibly forlorn) hope in the fact that although Trump is a mendacious, malevolent, transparently evil man, and stupid with it, Musk is not. He is highly intelligent and, diametrically opposed to Trump, he has the welfare of the world at heart," X/Twitter, November 12, 2024, https://x.com/RichardDawkins/status/1856427574693691823.
36. *Cosmos: A Personal Voyage*, episode 1, "The Shores of the Cosmic Ocean," directed by Adrian Malone, presented by Carl Sagan, aired October 1, 1980, on PBS.
37. In Dostoevsky's defense, he was attacking what he considered to be an irrational faith in reason by people like Karl Marx. He feared the attempt to reduce human nature to decimal places and to substitute submission to God with a submission to the collective, which he believed would lead only to revolution and terror. In so doing, he failed to differentiate between scientists who are trained to criticize their work and a great many social scientists who are not. For Musk, as for Popper, this

kind of uncritical rationalism is the worst kind of irrationalism. Karl Popper, *The Open Society and Its Enemies*, vol. 2, *Hegel and Marx* (London: Routledge, 1998), 231.

38. Fyodor Dostoevsky, *Notes from Underground* and *The Double*, trans. Jessie Coulson (London: Penguin Classics, 2003), 40.
39. Dostoevsky, *Notes from Underground* and *The Double*, 35.
40. Dostoevsky, *Notes from Underground* and *The Double*, 41.
41. Dostoevsky, *Notes from Underground* and *The Double*, 41.
42. Döpfner, "Elon Musk Reveals."
43. Feynman, *The Pleasure*, 115.
44. Dostoevsky, *Notes from Underground* and *The Double*, 40.
45. Stephen Hawking and Leonard Mlodinow, *The Grand Design* (London: Bantam Press, 2011), 13.
46. Richard Dawkins, *The Blind Watchmaker* (London: Penguin Books, 1988), 13–14.
47. Hawking and Mlodinow, *The Grand Design*, 178–84, 207–11.
48. Lex Fridman, "Elon Musk: War, AI, Aliens, Politics, Physics, Video Games, and Humanity," November 9, 2023, in *Lex Fridman Podcast*, podcast, https://www.youtube.com/watch?v=JN3KPFbWCy8.
49. Erwin Schrödinger, *What Is Life?* with *Mind and Matter* and *Autobiographical Sketches* (Cambridge: Cambridge University Press, 2018), 127, 138.
50. Isaac Asimov, for example, mused on this in his short story "The Last Question," about the self-correcting AI, Multivac. It needed so much data to compute whether or not the net amount of cosmic entropy could be reversed that the answer was only revealed at the end of the universe. Isaac Asimov, *The Complete Stories*, vol. 1 (London: Voyager, 1997), 429.
51. Camus, *The Myth of Sisyphus*, 25.
52. Fridman, "Elon Musk: War, AI, Aliens," 2023; Elon Musk, interview by Seth Dillon and Ethan Nicolle, "Elon Musk Sits Down with the Babylon Bee," December 22, 2021, https://www.youtube.com/watch?v=jvGnw1sHh9M.

Chapter 3: Increase Consciousness

1. Elon Musk, "Prometheus Unbound," X/Twitter, July 30, 2021, https://x.com/elonmusk/status/1420970469516263426.

2. Elon Musk, "Prometheus Unbound," X/Twitter, April 4, 2025, https://x.com/elonmusk/status/1908025106795823436.
3. Aeschylus does not use the precise term "philanthropic" but says that Prometheus is a champion of and kind to the human race. Aeschylus, *Prometheus Bound and Other Plays*, trans. Philip Vellacott (London: Penguin Classics, 1961), 20–21.
4. Elon Musk, "CHM Revolutionaries: An Evening with Elon Musk," interview by Alison van Diggelen, Revolutionaries Speaker Series at the Computer History Museum, California, January 22, 2013, posted February 5, 2013, by Computer History Museum, YouTube, https://www.youtube.com/watch?v=AHHwXUm3iIg&t.
5. Udezue, "Elon Musk Shares His Vision."
6. Jordan Peterson, "Dr. Peterson x Elon Musk," July 22, 2024, in *The Dr. Jordan B. Peterson Podcast*, podcast, https://x.com/i/broadcasts/1LyGBgPvoDjJN.
7. Arthur C. Clarke, *Profiles of the Future* (London: Pan Books, 1978), 39.
8. Clarke, *Profiles of the Future*, 32, 39.
9. Adams, *42: The Wildly*, 264.
10. Freud, *Civilization and Its Discontents*, 13–22.
11. Freud, *Civilization and Its Discontents*, 15–16, 37.
12. Lex Fridman, "Elon Musk: SpaceX, Mars, Tesla Autopilot, Self-Driving, Robotics, and AI," December 28, 2021, in *Lex Fridman Podcast*, podcast, https://www.youtube.com/watch?v=DxREm3s1scA.
13. Musk sometimes speaks of "generational trauma," referring to his own childhood and also his paternal grandfather, who was severely traumatized by his experiences fighting in World War II. He once wrote on X, "When someone who is supposed to care for you does you wrong, that breaks most people, but eventually the passing on of generational trauma must end," X/Twitter, February 14, 2025, https://x.com/elonmusk/status/1890426355596021786.
14. Elon Musk, "That's a great book," X/Twitter, December 26, 2023, https://x.com/elonmusk/status/1739480773814554938.
15. Frankl believed that Freud—not unlike Schopenhauer and his "will to life"—was too preoccupied with the idea that humans are slaves to their repressed sexual subconscious, while his peer Alfred Adler—not unlike Nietzsche and his "will to power"—was too preoccupied with power dynamics. Frankl, *Man's Search for Meaning*, 104.
16. Frankl, *Man's Search for Meaning*, 117.
17. Frankl, *Man's Search for Meaning*, 115.
18. Frankl, *Man's Search for Meaning*, 113–14.

19. President John F. Kennedy, "Inaugural Address," January 20, 1961, Washington, DC, https://www.jfklibrary.org/learn/about-jfk/historic-speeches/inaugural-address.
20. The phrase "go, set the world on fire" is often attributed to St. Ignatius of Loyola, who urged his followers to spread the Gospel. It draws on Jesus's words in Luke 12:49: "I came to cast fire on the earth, and would that it were already kindled!" ESV.
21. Isaac Asimov, *Robots and Empire* (London: HarperVoyager, 2018), 329.
22. Douglas Adams made a teasing reference to Asimov's Foundation series and the *Encyclopedia Galactica* he used to narrate his stories, observing that the new *Hitchhiker's Guide* had supplanted the *Encyclopedia Galactica* in parts of the galaxy because it was cheaper and had "DON'T PANIC" written on the cover. Adams, *The Hitchhiker's Guide*, 2.
23. Elon Musk, "The future is a set of branching probability streams. Some actions by humanity have an extremely leveraged effect on shape & size of those streams," X/Twitter, June 15, 2018, https://x.com/elonmusk/status/1007679828303024128.
24. Isaac Asimov, *I. Asimov: A Memoir* (New York: Bantam Books, 1995), 116–17.
25. Isaac Asimov, *Foundation* (London: HarperVoyager, 2016), 28, 30.
26. Asimov, *Foundation*, 118.
27. Asimov, *Foundation*, 24.
28. Asimov, *Foundation*, 211.
29. Popper, *The Open Society and Its Enemies*, vol. 2, 234–36.
30. Strauss, "The Architect of Tomorrow."
31. Rory Carroll, "Elon Musk's Mission to Mars," *The Guardian*, July 17, 2013, https://www.theguardian.com/technology/2013/jul/17/elon-musk-mission-mars-spacex.
32. Elon Musk, "Why are there these two buckets? They are a false choice imo. I prefer the dichotomy of extinctionist vs expansionist. No civilization is stable for long, so you're either growing or contracting. The former is far superior and will win," X/Twitter, September 6, 2024, https://x.com/elonmusk/status/1831939455923712495.
33. Musk, "Elon Musk at the MIT AeroAstro Centennial Symposium," 2014.
34. Udezue, "Elon Musk Shares His Vision."
35. Elon Musk, "Chuck labors under the illusion that western civilization is not at risk, when it clearly is. If America falls, nothing else matters, not stocks, not properties, nothing. All civilizations eventually fall, as history shows, but we want this one to last as long as possible," X/Twitter, February 8, 2024, https://x.com/elonmusk/status/1755411084939501860.

36. Karl Popper, *All Life Is Problem Solving*, trans. Patrick Camiller (London: Routledge, 1999), 109–10.
37. Asimov, *Robots and Empire*, 329.
38. Larry Page, "Where's Google Going Next? | Larry Page," interview by Charlie Rose, TED2014, March 19, 2014, posted March 22, 2014, YouTube, https://www.youtube.com/watch?v=mArrNRWQEso.
39. Jobs, "Steve Jobs Secrets of Life."
40. Freud, *Civilization and Its Discontents*, 16.
41. Robin Miller, "Douglas Adams Answers (Finally)," Slashdot, June 21, 2000, https://entertainment.slashdot.org/story/00/06/21/1217242/douglas-adams-answers-finally.
42. Peter Thiel with Blake Masters, *Zero to One: Notes on Startups, or How to Build the Future* (London: Virgin Books, 2015), 40.
43. Elon Musk, "Elon Musk Holds Town Hall Event in Pennsylvania," America PAC town hall event, Lancaster, Pennsylvania, Sky News, October 26, 2024, https://www.youtube.com/watch?v=deViqTOqS4M.
44. Andy Hertzfeld, *Revolution in the Valley* (O'Reilly Media, 2004). This includes his notes of Alan Kay's talk at Creative Think seminar, July 20, 1982.
45. Elon Musk, "The mind behind Tesla, SpaceX, SolarCity ... | Elon Musk," interview by Chris Anderson, TED2013, Vancouver, BC, February 27, 2013, posted March 19, 2013, by TED, YouTube, https://www.youtube.com/watch?v=IgKWPdJWuBQ.
46. Musk's cousin Peter Rive commented to Walter Isaacson that Musk had this attitude of consciously not reacting to fear from an early age. Isaacson, *Elon Musk*, 25.
47. Isaac Asimov, "Isaac Asimov Asks, 'How Do People Get New Ideas?'" *MIT Technology Review*, October 20, 2014, https://www.technologyreview.com/2014/10/20/169899/isaac-asimov-asks-how-do-people-get-new-ideas/.
48. Charlie Munger, "Legendary investor Charlie Munger speaks at Daily Journal annual meeting – 2/12/2020," CNBC Television, February 12, 2020, https://www.youtube.com/watch?v=HS8neXkNnhw&t.

Chapter 4: Make Stuff

1. Joe Rogan, "Elon Musk," May 7, 2020, in *The Joe Rogan Experience*, podcast, https://www.youtube.com/watch?v=RcYjXbSJBN8.

2. Jobs, "Steve Jobs Secrets of Life."
3. Ted Cruz, "Elon Musk Joins Verdict—Part 1," March 17, 2025, in *Verdict with Ted Cruz*, https://www.youtube.com/watch?v=BDREZmpkIz8&t=2s.
4. Vance, *Elon Musk*, 38–39.
5. Elon Musk, "Not worth pushing kids to code (or other stuff imo). I liked anything mechanical, but the second I saw a computer, you couldn't drag me away from it! I immediately pulled two all-nighters teaching myself to program. No pushing is required when kids love something," X/Twitter, October 21, 2024, https://x.com/elonmusk/status/1848242393327288392.
6. Elon Musk, "CHM Revolutionaries: An Evening with Elon Musk," interview by Alison van Diggelen, Revolutionaries Speaker Series at the Computer History Museum, California, January 22, 2013, posted February 5, 2013, by Computer History Museum, YouTube, https://www.youtube.com/watch?v=AHHwXUm3iIg&t.
7. Paul Graham, "The Anatomy of Determination," paulgraham.com, September 2009, https://paulgraham.com/determination.html.
8. Elon Musk, "Elon Musk on Advertisers, Trust and the 'Wild Storm' in His Mind," interview by Andrew Ross Sorkin, *New York Times* DealBook Summit, November 30, 2023, https://www.youtube.com/watch?v=2BfMuHDfGJI.
9. Elon Musk, "Working hard to make useful products & services for your fellow humans is deeply morally good," X/Twitter, March 17, 2022, https://x.com/elonmusk/status/1504349978487324672.
10. Elon Musk, "Science is discovering the essential truths about what exists in the Universe, engineering is about creating things that never existed," X/Twitter, December 2, 2020, https://x.com/elonmusk/status/1333972511524995072.
11. Tom Junod, "Elon Musk: Triumph of His Will," *Esquire*, November 15, 2012, https://www.esquire.com/news-politics/a16681/elon-musk-interview-1212/. Musk also echoes Alan Kay when he says: "The best way to predict the future is to create it" (discussion hosted by Mario Nawfal, X Spaces, December 10, 2023, https://x.com/MarioNawfal/status/1733909736385331339).
12. Thiel with Masters, *Zero to One*, 6–7.
13. Musk praises Thiel as a critical thinker, but their worldviews are very different. Thiel argues that "when you do not have a transcendent religious belief, you end up just looking around at other people," which leads to the madness of crowds in a way that descends into conflict. He thinks "faith and reason are compatible," whereas liberal, atheist rationalists are not really capable of thought at all; it's just

"spaghetti code." Eric Metaxas, "Peter Thiel: Zero to One," *Socrates in the City*, New York, January, 2020, https://socratesinthecity.com/watch/peter-thiel-zero-to-one/.

14. Adams, *The Salmon of Doubt,* 129–32. Adams illustrates his point by telling the joke about the puddle that is struck by how well it fits into the hole it finds itself in, and concludes that "this world was meant to have him in it, was built to have him in." Adams, *The Salmon of Doubt*, 131–32.
15. Adams, *The Salmon of Doubt*, 122.
16. Adams, *The Salmon of Doubt*, 124–25.
17. Elon Musk, "So much of AI is about compressing reality to a small vector space, like a video game in reverse . . . Physics formulas are the rendering rules," X/Twitter, December 27, 2021, https://x.com/elonmusk/status/1475312943420121088.
18. Elon Musk, "Did my best to warn people that LiDAR isn't optimal for cars. Roads are designed for biological neural nets & eyes, so digital neural nets & cameras will work best," X/Twitter, August 28, 2023, https://x.com/elonmusk/status/1696119334018457949.
19. Elon Musk, "Humans are basically a big data stream of photons in that produce a tiny data stream of motor commands out," X/Twitter, November 25, 2023, https://x.com/elonmusk/status/1728212987146617228.
20. Elon Musk, "Elon Musk: Elon Musk's Vision for the Future [Entire Talk]," interview by Steve Jurvetson, eCorner by Stanford Technology Venture Program, October 7, 2015, posted December 11, 2015, by Stanford eCorner, YouTube, https://www.youtube.com/watch?v=SVk1hb0ZOrE.
21. Charles Darwin, *Autobiographies* (London: Penguin Classics, 2002), 86.
22. Fridman, "Elon Musk: SpaceX, Mars, Tesla Autopilot," 2021.
23. Elon Musk, "Thought Leaders Lecture: Qualities of an Entrepreneur," eCorner by Stanford Technology Venture Program, October 8, 2003, https://stvp.stanford.edu/videos/qualities-of-an-entrepreneur/.
24. Darwin, *Autobiographies*, 86, 88.
25. Popper, *Conjectures & Refutations*, 261.
26. Popper, *Conjectures & Refutations*, 245.
27. Adams, *The Salmon of Doubt*, 125.
28. Elon Musk, "Engineers invent new technologies. Along the way, they may come up with new reality compression formulas, like Nikola Tesla," X/Twitter, July 29, 2025, https://x.com/elonmusk/status/1950264177068822594.
29. Elon Musk, "Absolutely! Kids are the best. I'm doing my best to encourage more people to become parents and ideally have three or more kids, so humanity can

grow. The population collapse in most countries is a tragedy. Sales of adult diapers should never exceed sales of baby diapers!," X/Twitter, February 16, 2024, https://x.com/elonmusk/status/1758593846076666262.

30. Elon Musk, "The morals can certainly exist without religion, but, unless birth rate changes, civilizational suicide is inevitable. Ironically, for someone who knows so much about evolution, Dawkins only has one child. That is a >50% generational suicide rate," X/Twitter, April 2, 2024, https://x.com/elonmusk/status/1775041308203106774.
31. Hayek, *The Fatal Conceit*, 133.
32. Elon Musk, "Realized what I have in common with environmentalists, but also why they're so annoyingly wrong: They are conservationists of what is, whereas they should be conservationists of our potential over time, our cosmic endowment. (From a friend)," X/Twitter, June 6, 2022, https://x.com/elonmusk/status/1533606056756137985.
33. Elon Musk, "She is so wrong. Arguing in favor reducing humanity is arguing for genocide. The unborn have no voice," X/Twitter, December 4, 2023, https://x.com/elonmusk/status/1731694558793122066.
34. Elon Musk, "Elon Musk: A Future Worth Getting Excited About | Tesla Texas Gigafactory Interview," interview by Chris Anderson, April 6, 2022, Texas, posted April 17, 2022, by TED, YouTube, https://www.youtube.com/watch?v=YRvf00NooN8.
35. Elon Musk, "Elon Musk Answers Your Questions! | SXSW 2018," interview by Jonathan Nolan, SXSW Festival, March 10, 2018, Austin, Texas, https://www.youtube.com/watch?v=kzlUyrccbos.
36. Musk, "Elon Musk: Elon Musk's Vision for the Future," interview by Steve Jurvetson.
37. Walter Isaacson, *Steve Jobs* (London: Abacus, 2015), pxxi; Isaacson, *Elon Musk*, 5.
38. Isaacson, *Steve Jobs*, 46; see also 14, 32, 44–45.
39. "Memory & Imagination: New Pathways to the Library of Congress, featuring Steve Jobs," directed by Julian Krainin and Michael R. Lawrence, 1990, posted June 1, 2006, by Michael R. Lawrence, YouTube, https://www.youtube.com/watch?v=ob_GX50Za6c&list=PL376FBD09E0C181C5&index=3.
40. Steven Levy, "The Birth of the Mac: *Rolling Stone*'s 1984 Feature on Steve Jobs and His Whiz Kids," *Rolling Stone*, October 6, 2011, https://www.rollingstone.com/culture/culture-news/the-birth-of-the-mac-rolling-stones-1984-feature-on-steve-jobs-and-his-whiz-kids-243516/. This article reprised an interview with Jobs that previously appeared in *Rolling Stone* on March 1, 1984.

41. Paul Graham, "One advantage Tesla has over other car cos is that there is obviously a Jobs-like force behind the product," X/Twitter, September 27, 2015, https://x.com/paulg/status/647958924398735362.

42. Isaacson, *Steve Jobs*, 316.

43. Speaking about the influence of the hippy movement growing up, Jobs said, ". . . there was something beyond what you see every day . . . We experience it when there are gaps. When everything is not ordered and perfect, when there's a gap, you experience this inrush of something." Significantly, he went on to say, "That same spirit can be put into products and those products can be manufactured and given to people and they can sense that spirit." For Jobs, computers "are the medium that is best capable of transmitting some feeling you have that you want to share with other people." *Steve Jobs: The Lost Interview*, directed by Paul Sen, Los Angeles: Magnolia Pictures, 2012. DVD. This is a documentary film about the compelling interview that Jobs previously gave for the 1996 TV series *Triumph of the Nerds*. Brent Schlender and Rick Tetzeli, *Becoming Steve Jobs: How a Reckless Upstart Became a Visionary Leader* (London: Sceptre, 2016), 33.

44. Jobs, *Steve Jobs: The Lost Interview*.

45. Jobs, Steve *Jobs: The Lost Interview*.

46. Jobs, *Steve Jobs: The Lost Interview*.

47. Jay Leno, "Elon Musk Gives Jay Leno a Tour of SpaceX," *Jay Leno's Garage* (preview on CNBC Ambition), September 16, 2022, https://www.youtube.com/watch?v=wluBlr1j4qk&t.

48. Musk, "Elon Musk Talks Twitter, Tesla," TED2022; Richard Dawkins, "@RobMajor4 No, Elon Musk is the new Steve Jobs PLUS Steve Wozniak," X/Twitter, October 9, 2012, https://x.com/RichardDawkins/status/255718876065697793.

49. Justine Musk, "Visionaries Are People Who Can See in the Dark," TEDxUIUC, University of Illinois Urbana-Champaign, Illinois, April 23, 2017, posted June 1, 2017, by TEDx Talks, YouTube, https://www.youtube.com/watch?v=OxA0LESuUDE&t.

50. Elon Musk, "ISDC 2005—Friday Luncheon with Elon Musk," 24th Annual International Space Development Conference, National Space Society, Washington, DC, May 20, 2005, posted January 13, 2021, by Space Activist Archive, YouTube, https://www.youtube.com/watch?v=8vBqtKQx7jg.

51. Among others, Collins's book drew insights from Steve Jobs, whom he invited into Stanford University, where he taught, and Collins was himself subsequently invited into Amazon by Jeff Bezos in 2001. In addition to the three characteristics discussed in this book, Collins also highlights leadership, talent, discipline, and technology accelerators. He focuses more on mature rather than founder-led

companies, and in that regard—and somewhat contrary to Musk—he concludes that humble, low-ego CEOs are the best. Jim Collins, *Good to Great: Why Some Companies Make the Leap . . . and Others Don't* (London: Random House Business Books, 2001).

52. This Greek concept was revived by Isaiah Berlin and has been used subsequently by a range of writers, including Philip Tetlock and Nate Silver. Collins, *Good to Great*, 90–119.

53. Friedrich Nietzsche, *Twilight of the Idols and The Anti-Christ*, trans. R. J. Hollingdale (London: Penguin Classics, 2003), 33.

54. Collins, *Good to Great*, 86.

55. Musk, "Elon Musk and Y Combinator President on Thinking for the Future - FULL CONVERSATION," interview with Sam Altman by Andrew Ross Sorkin, *Vanity Fair* New Establishment Summit, October 8, 2015, San Francisco, California, https://www.youtube.com/watch?v=SqEo107j-uw.

56. Elon Musk, "Elon Musk - CEO of Tesla Motors and SpaceX | Entrepreneurship | Khan Academy," interview by Salman Khan, Khan Academy, California, April 17, 2013, posted April 23, 2013, by Khan Academy, YouTube, https://www.youtube.com/watch?v=vDwzmJpI4io.

57. Collins, *Good to Great*, 125.

58. Justine Musk, "Visionaries Are People."

59. Rogan, "Elon Musk," 2018.

60. Musk, interview by Barry Hurd, The Henry Ford, 2008.

61. Isaacson, *Elon Musk*, 410.

62. Elon Musk, "Maybe not medically tho. Dunno. Bad feelings correlate to bad events, so maybe real problem is getting carried away in what I sign up for," X/Twitter, July 30, 2017, https://x.com/elonmusk/status/891714878494261249; Elon Musk, "If you buy a ticket to hell, it isn't fair to blame hell ...," X/Twitter, July 30, 2017, https://x.com/elonmusk/status/891715134132936704.

63. Elon Musk, "*TIME* Person of the Year: Elon Musk," interview by Jeffrey Kluger, *TIME* Magazine, December 13, 2021, YouTube, https://www.youtube.com/watch?app=desktop&v=PbVSZvC7UxY&t.

64. Justine Musk, "Visionaries Are People."

65. Johnson, *The Johnson Collection*, 324.

Chapter 5: Use Markets

1. Reid Hoffman quoted in Isaacson, *Elon Musk*, 93.
2. Musk, interview by Barry Hurd, The Henry Ford, 2008.
3. Warren Buffett, "Afternoon Session—2023 Meeting," May 6, 2023, Berkshire Hathaway AGM, Warren Buffett Archive, CNBC Television, https://buffett.cnbc.com/video/2023/05/08/afternoon-session---2023-meeting.html.
4. Elon Musk, "Civilizational energy output per person has grown dramatically from making a small fire with wood to nuclear power plants. This will continue. Two of the most fundamental ratios that and silicon/biological compute," X/Twitter, September 7, 2023, https://x.com/elonmusk/status/1699808082509873400.
5. For an excellent discussion of this, see "How Tesla Will Change the World" in Tim Urban's blog *Wait But Why*, June 2, 2015, https://waitbutwhy.com/2015/06/how-tesla-will-change-your-life.html.
6. Strauss, "The Architect of Tomorrow."
7. Eric Berger captures this in his excellent account of SpaceX. Eric Berger, *Liftoff: Elon Musk and the Desperate Early Days that Launched SpaceX* (London: William Collins, 2021), 104.
8. Musk, interview by Barry Hurd, The Henry Ford, 2008. Musk echoes an identical argument made by Google cofounder Larry Page: "You don't want to be Tesla. He was one of the greatest inventors, but it's a sad, sad story. He couldn't commercialize anything, he could barely fund his own research. You'd want to be more like Edison. If you invent something, that doesn't necessarily help anybody. You've got to actually get it into the world; you've got to produce, make money doing it so you can fund it." Andy Serwer, "Larry Page on How to Change the World," *Fortune*, May 1, 2008, https://web.archive.org/web/20080505090921/http://money.cnn.com/2008/04/29/magazines/fortune/larry_page_change_the_world.fortune/index3.htm.
9. This announcement was also a way to tell prospective customers that in buying a Roadster, they were paying for a greener future. The same could not be said, Musk argued, for example, of Toyota's Prius. Musk wanted the public to know that in buying this hybrid, purchasers were still giving their money to an internal combustion engine company. Elon Musk, "The Secret Tesla Motors Master Plan (Just Between You and Me)," Tesla, Inc., August 2, 2006, https://www.tesla.com/secret-master-plan.
10. Mark Zuckerberg, Mission Statement of Facebook IPO Prospectus, Form S-1 Registration Statement, United States Securities and Exchange Commission, February 1, 2012, https://www.sec.gov/Archives/edgar/data/1326801/000119312512034517/d287954ds1.htm.

11. Elon Musk, "Tesla All-Hands | Q1 2025," Tesla Gigafactory Texas, March 20, 2025, YouTube, https://www.youtube.com/watch?v=QGJysv_Qzkw.

12. Elon Musk, interview by Charlie Rose, *Charlie Rose*, August 11, 2009, https://charlierose.com/videos/12550.

13. Tesla, Inc. "Tesla Vehicle Production & Deliveries and Date for Financial Results & Webcast for Fourth Quarter 2023," Tesla Press Release, January 2, 2024, https://ir.tesla.com/press-release/tesla-vehicle-production-deliveries-and-date-financial-results-webcast-fourth-quarter-2023; "Electric Vehicle Sales Review Q4 2023," strategy& (part of the PWC Strategy network), January 2024, https://www.strategyand.pwc.com/de/en/industries/automotive/electric-vehicle-sales-review-2023-q4.html.

14. Elon Musk, "Being useful at scale is the hardest thing in the world," June 26, 2025, https://x.com/elonmusk/status/1938169383412748489.

15. Tim Urban, "How (and Why) SpaceX Will Colonize Mars," *Wait But Why* (blog), August 16, 2015, https://waitbutwhy.com/2015/08/how-and-why-spacex-will-colonize-mars.html/3.

16. Elon Musk, "StartmeupHK Venture Forum - Elon Musk on Entrepreneurship and Innovation," interview by Kristie Lu Stout, Hong Kong, January 26, 2016, posted by Invest Hong Kong, YouTube, https://www.youtube.com/watch?v=pIRqB5iqWA8.

17. Musk was asked about the profit margins of the Model S and said that Tesla aimed for premium pricing like Apple, and that that comes from compelling products rather than the brand per se. Moryt Milo, "Q&A with Elon Musk," *Silicon Valley Business Journal*, December 24, 2010, https://www.bizjournals.com/sanjose/print-edition/2010/12/24/qa-with-elon-musk.html.

18. Lance Ulanoff, "Elon Musk: Secrets of a Highly Effective Entrepreneur," Mashable, April 13, 2012, https://mashable.com/archive/elon-musk-secrets-of-effectiveness#BiUiMA3aMaq7.

19. Paul Graham, "How to Do Great Work," paulgraham.com, July 2023, https://paulgraham.com/greatwork.html.

20. Elon Musk, "Tesla is responsible for 2/3 of all the personal & professional pain in my life combined. But it was worth it," X/Twitter, January 2, 2021, https://x.com/elonmusk/status/1345384139969552389.

21. In Japan, Nissan had developed the Altra model, which was sold in small numbers for fleet use, and in Europe, Venturi developed the Fétish model, which was a custom-built supercar.

22. John Carmack, "The standard SpaceX / @elonmusk strategy is to simply identify the next obstacle on the critical path and efficiently crush it from first principles,

largely letting the problems of tomorrow be solved tomorrow. This works far better than most people expect; it doesn't have to be 4D chess! Long term space habitats, as needed for Mars missions, may be resistant to this approach. It isn't a solved problem . . . ," X/Twitter, February 13, 2025, https://x.com/ID_AA_Carmack/status/1890178216436043828.

23. Elon Musk, "Many movies exist about a lone inventor in a garage having a eureka moment, but almost none about manufacturing, so it's underappreciated by the public. Compared to the insane pain of reaching high-volume, positive-margin production, prototypes are a piece of cake," X/Twitter, March 28, 2024, https://x.com/elonmusk/status/1773451340548870364.
24. In the summer of 2016, Musk wrote about how manufacturing productivity could be increased by a factor of five to ten times by 2022, which would be "version 3.0." He noted that the first Model 3 factory machine was then at iteration "version 0.5" and would get to "version 1.0" probably in 2018. That incremental 0.5 would be excruciating. Elon Musk, "Master Plan, Part Deux," Tesla, July 20, 2016, https://www.tesla.com/master-plan-part-deux.
25. Elon Musk, "Don't build moats, build tech trees," June 14, 2022, X/Twitter, https://x.com/elonmusk/status/1536744900661755906.
26. In support of Musk's claim, as early as 2014, he had pledged that Tesla would not initiate patent lawsuits against anyone who wanted to use its technology in good faith.
27. Elon Musk, "Tesla is technically a car like an iPhone is technically a phone," X/Twitter, December 24, 2021, https://x.com/elonmusk/status/1474405612662530077.
28. Elon Musk, "Tesla 2024 Q1 Earnings Report Transcript," MarketBeat, April 23, 2024, https://www.marketbeat.com/earnings/transcripts/104213/.
29. Elon Musk, "Elon Musk at the MIT AeroAstro Centennial Symposium," 2014.
30. Clayton M. Christensen, *The Innovator's Dilemma: When New Technologies Cause Great Firms to Fail* (Boston: Harvard Business Review Press, 2023). Isaacson also recalled that Musk studied the book in his PayPal days (Isaacson, *Elon Musk*, 84).
31. Elon Musk, "RAW Elon Musk Interview from Air Warfare Symposium 2020," interview by Lt. Gen. John Thompson, US Air Force Association Air Warfare Symposium, Orlando, Florida, February 28, 2020, posted March 2, 2020, by The SPACE Archive, YouTube, https://www.youtube.com/watch?v=sp8smJFaKYE.
32. Lex Fridman, "Andrej Karpathy: Tesla AI, Self-Driving, Optimus, Aliens, and AGI," October 29, 2022, in *Lex Fridman Podcast*, podcast, https://www.youtube.com/watch?v=cdiD-9MMpb0.

33. Elon Musk, "Elon Musk's Complete Interview at Air Force Space Pitch Day," interview by Lt. Gen. John Thompson, US Air Force Space Pitch Day, San Francisco, California, November 5, 2019, posted November 7, 2019, by The Space Archive, YouTube, https://www.youtube.com/watch?v=lS3nIyetS4I.
34. Elon Musk, "The full answer here is complex. The outcome of any given company is the vector sum of the people within it. Improve the alignment of the individual vectors and their amplitude and the outcome will improve accordingly. Humans can be thought of as hardware (inherent talent) and software (education & training). Even if someone has a strong brain/hardware, if their training/software is bad, that can be very hard to reverse . . . ," X/Twitter, December 25, 2024, https://x.com/elonmusk/status/1871997501970235656.
35. Ironically, Musk would put his own tweak on the automotive industry saying that Jobs loved to use. "I think Henry Ford once said," Jobs liked to recall, "If I'd asked customers what they wanted, they would have told me, 'A faster horse!' People don't know what they want until you show it to them." (Isaacson, *Jobs*, 523). This was actually Musk's domain—and he happened to believe that the inventor of the mass-market Model T was a "next-level genius"—so he would channel his spirit and go further, saying, "We're putting the actual auto in automobile." (Musk, Tesla 2024 Q1 Earnings Report).
36. The illustrative fivefold estimate is based on projections from ten hours of use a week (approximately 1.5 hours a day) to probably fifty hours a week, or roughly a third of the time.
37. Elon Musk, "Haha, FSD 9 beta is shipping soon, I swear! Generalized self-driving is a hard problem, as it requires solving a large part of real-world AI. Didn't expect it to be so hard, but the difficulty is obvious in retrospect. Nothing has more degrees of freedom than reality," X/Twitter, July 3, 2021, https://x.com/elonmusk/status/1411280212470366213.
38. Musk added that Optimus will be "10x bigger than the next biggest product ever made." Musk, "Tesla All-Hands | Q1 2025."
39. In the case of Tesla, Musk's shareholding fell below where he would have wanted it to be, declining from over 20 percent to below 13 percent between 2019 and 2022. This was in part due to share sales to fund taxes and to acquire Twitter, and due to the voiding of his $56 billion 2018 equity award by a Delaware court. In 2024, Musk commented on X: "I am uncomfortable growing Tesla to be a leader in AI & robotics without having ~25% voting control. Enough to be influential, but not so much that I can't be overturned." X/Twitter, January 15, 2024, https://x.com/elonmusk/status/1746999488252703098. In September 2025, the company proposed a new package for Musk that would restore his ownership to 25 percent if, inter alia, he increases the value of Tesla eightfold.

40. Vance, *Elon Musk*, 179; Tim Higgins, *Power Play: Elon Musk, Tesla and the Bet of the Century* (London: WH Allen, 2022), 37; Claire Cain Miller, "Tesla Electric Cars: Revved Up, but Far to Go," *New York Times*, July 24, 2010, https://www.nytimes.com/2010/07/25/business/25elon.html.

41. Musk's critics argue that the $465 million loan from the Department of Energy, together with EV tax credits, shows that he is making his money off the back of the government. His counterargument is that Tesla repaid the loan with interest in two years, and the loan allowed the company to maintain its rate of growth but was not necessary for the company to survive. As for the incentives, he says that they benefited other car manufacturers more than Tesla.

42. The estimated value was $5 billion, with a similar amount committed for factory expansions, together with a guarantee that Musk would be CEO for eight years. Vance, *Elon Musk*, 306.

43. Elon Musk, "During the darkest days of the Model 3 program, I reached out to Tim Cook to discuss the possibility of Apple acquiring Tesla (for 1/10 of our current value). He refused to take the meeting," X/Twitter, December 22, 2024, https://x.com/elonmusk/status/1341485211209637889.

44. Tesla 10-K and 10-Q reports filed on February 13, 2020, April 29, 2020, October 26, 2020, and February 8, 2021, for reporting on the February, September, and December offerings.

45. Elon Musk, "Tesla Founder and CEO Elon Musk Shares Energy Vision at 2015 EEI Annual Convention," interview by Ted Craver, Edison Electric Institute Annual Convention, June 9, 2015, New Orleans, Louisiana, posted June 11, 2015, by EEITV, YouTube, https://www.youtube.com/watch?v=UKT2tKmVk6g&list=PPSV.

46. Adam Smith, *The Theory of Moral Sentiments*, ed. Ryan Patrick Hanley (London, Penguin Books, 2009), 275.

47. Elon Musk, "Socialism vs capitalism is not even the right question. What really matters is avoiding monopolies that restrict people's freedom," X/Twitter, June 16, 2018, https://x.com/elonmusk/status/1007766450256392192.

48. Taleb says that some people even have "soul in the game" because they have skin in the game for others, including warriors, innovators, artists, rebels, and mavericks. Nassim N. Taleb, *Antifragile: Things That Gain from Disorder* (Penguin Books, 2013), 377; Nassim N. Taleb, *Skin in the Game: Hidden Asymmetries in Daily Life* (Penguin Books, 2019), 82–86.

49. Elon Musk, "Watch Elon Musk on Regulators, Silicon Valley and Innovation," interview by Matt Murray, *WSJ* CEO Council Summit, December 8, 2020, https://www.wsj.com/video/elon-musk-on-regulators-silicon-valley-and-the-future-of-innovation/6C4A0D24-3F89-42F8-94B6-F51F4020A9D4.

50. Elon Musk, "By the way, I am actually a socialist. Just not the kind that shifts resources from most productive to least productive, pretending to do good, while actually causing harm. True socialism seeks greatest good for all," X/Twitter, June 16, 2018, https://x.com/elonmusk/status/1008013111058526209.
51. Musk would make similar claims when closing down USAID in 2025; Isaacson, *Elon Musk*, 437.
52. Elon Musk, "To paraphrase Milton Friedman: the worst results come from people spending other people's money on a different group of other people. That is the government!," X/Twitter, October 5, 2024, https://x.com/elonmusk/status/1842620590961958930.
53. Elon Musk, "Twitter added far more features with fewer people. What really matters for improving American's standard of living is shifting people from low productivity jobs in government to high productivity jobs in industry. Many more people needed in manufacturing!," X/Twitter, February 24, 2025, https://x.com/elonmusk/status/1894137412801978375.
54. Elon Musk, "My goal is to fix government IT! This is harder than getting a rocket to orbit. Actually," X/Twitter, January 18, 2025, https://x.com/elonmusk/status/1880520441196056968.
55. Elon Musk, "I'm sorry, but I just can't stand it anymore. This massive, outrageous, pork-filled Congressional spending bill is a disgusting abomination. Shame on those who voted for it: you know you did wrong. You know it," X/Twitter, June 3, 2025, https://x.com/elonmusk/status/1929954109689606359.
56. For Musk, money is no more than information, which approximates to the productivity of an individual over a period of time. He therefore believes that in an abundant future, money will become irrelevant, and there will be some sort of universal basic income (even high basic income). We may be left to play games all day long, although this may also trigger an existential crisis for those whose identity is tied to their work.

Chapter 6: Explore Space

1. Elon Musk, "A new philosophy of the future is needed. I believe it should be curiosity about the Universe – expand humanity to become a multiplanet, then interstellar, species to see what's out there," X/Twitter, July 27, 2022, https://x.com/elonmusk/status/1552317587694010368.
2. Clark S. Lindsey, "Interview with Elon Musk," HobbySpace, August 25, 2003, https://www.hobbyspace.com/AAdmin/archive/Interviews/Systems/ElonMusk.html.

3. Elon Musk, interview by Liz Claman, *Morning Call*, CNBC, July 6, 2006, https://x.com/i/status/1811066651502076178.
4. President John F. Kennedy, "Address at Rice University on the Nation's Space Effort," Rice University, Houston, Texas, September 12, 1962, https://www.jfklibrary.org/learn/about-jfk/historic-speeches/address-at-rice-university-on-the-nations-space-effort.
5. Bernie Sanders, "We are in a moment in American history where two guys—Elon Musk and Jeff Bezos—own more wealth than the bottom 40% of people in this country. That level of greed and inequality is not only immoral. It is unsustainable," X/Twitter, March 18, 2021, https://x.com/BernieSanders/status/1372641707829829632.
6. Elon Musk, "I am accumulating resources to help make life multiplanetary & extend the light of consciousness to the stars," X/Twitter, March 21, 2021, https://x.com/elonmusk/status/1373507545315172357.
7. Lex Fridman, "Jeff Bezos: Amazon and Blue Origin," December 14, 2023, in *Lex Fridman Podcast*, podcast, https://www.youtube.com/watch?v=DcWqzZ3I2cY.
8. Cain Miller, "Tesla Electric Cars," *New York Times*; Christian Davenport, *The Space Barons: Elon Musk, Jeff Bezos, and the Quest to Colonize the Cosmos* (New York: PublicAffairs, 2019), 75, 247; Stephen Clark, "Blue Origin's staying power bankrolled by Jeff Bezos's multibillion-dollar investment," *Spaceflight Now*, April 6, 2017, https://spaceflightnow.com/2017/04/06/blue-origins-staying-power-bankrolled-by-jeff-bezoss-multibillion-dollar-investment/.
9. Elon Musk, "Cast and Crew of Westworld | Westworld | SXSW 2018," panel discussion hosted by Jonathan Nolan, SXSW Festival, Austin, Texas, March 10, 2018, posted May 30, 2018, YouTube, https://www.youtube.com/watch?v=OpaHZ5HyP44.
10. Ray Kurzweil, *The Singularity Is Near: When Humans Transcend Biology* (London: Duckworth, 2018), 487.
11. Elon Musk, "Human civilization is still a tiny startup in the grand scheme of things," X/Twitter, December 3, 2023, https://x.com/elonmusk/status/1731344123985121697.
12. Elon Musk, "That will probably happen. Any self-respecting civilization should at least reach Kardashev Type II. In my opinion, we are currently only at <5% of Type I. To get to ~30%, we would need to place solar panels in all desert or highly arid regions," X/Twitter, December 9, 2024, https://x.com/elonmusk/status/1866176382411145602.
13. Elon Musk, "Becoming multiplanetary is a critical step on the Kardashev ladder," X/Twitter, November 24, 2024, https://x.com/elonmusk/status/1860799225271030143.

14. Jeff Bezos, *Invent & Wander: The Collected Writings of Jeff Bezos* (Boston: Harvard Business Review Press and PublicAffairs, 2021), 244.
15. Gerard K. O'Neill, *The High Frontier: Human Colonies in Space* (North Hollywood, CA: Space Studies Institute Press, 2019).
16. Davenport, *The Space Barons*, 259–60.
17. Jeff Bezos, "Blue Origin 2019: For the Benefit of Earth," Blue Origin event to unveil Blue Moon, Washington, DC, May 9, 2019, https://www.youtube.com/watch?v=GQ98hGUe6FM.
18. Elon Musk, "Makes no sense. In order to grow the colony, you'd have to transport vast amounts of mass from planets/moons/asteroids. Would be like trying to build the USA in the middle of the Atlantic Ocean!," X/Twitter, May 23, 2019, https://x.com/elonmusk/status/1131442696537743362.
19. Isaac Asimov and Gerard O'Neill, "The Roundtable TV Interview," interview by Harold Hayes, WNET, originally aired in 1975, reposted May 25, 2018, by Space Studies Institute, YouTube, https://www.youtube.com/watch?v=DM88sUBTTRM&t.
20. Lex Fridman, "Jeff Bezos."
21. Bezos never met his biological father, but unlike Jobs, he seems reconciled to this and thinks of his adopted father as his natural father. Bezos, *Invent & Wander*, 189.
22. Jeff Bezos, "Jeff Bezos: Nerd of the Amazon," interview by Bob Simon, *60 Minutes* profile originally aired in February 3, 1999, CBS, reposted July 5, 2024, by 60 Minutes, YouTube, https://www.youtube.com/watch?v=8OsY1V3iN6E.
23. Elon Musk, "Great approach tbh," X/Twitter, November 24, 2023, https://x.com/elonmusk/status/1727867799010259146.
24. Elon Musk, "Elon Musk: The Future We're Building -- and Boring | TED," interview by Chris Anderson, TED2017, Vancouver, BC, April 28, 2017, posted May 3, 2017, by TED, YouTube, https://www.youtube.com/watch?v=zIwLWfaAg-8
25. Musk, "The Future We're Building," TED2017.
26. Elon Musk, "Civilization needs to retain its current technology level until Mars is self-sufficient, which could be achieved within ~20 years. If we become multiplanetary and then multistellar our civilization will last millions of years. If not, maybe just a few hundred years," X/Twitter, April 6, 2024, https://x.com/elonmusk/status/1776594319341715933.
27. Elon Musk, "Asimov's Foundation series was part of the inspiration for making life/consciousness multiplanetary. Being multiplanetary greatly extends the

probable lifespan of civilization. We must build Terminus," X/Twitter, July 11, 2024, https://x.com/elonmusk/status/1811327840257761584.

28. Sean Carroll, *The Big Picture: On the Origins of Life, Meaning and the Universe Itself* (London: Oneworld, 2017), 431.
29. Blaise Pascal, *Pensées*, trans. A. J. Krailsheimer (London: Penguin Classics, 1995), 66.
30. William Shatner, "William Shatner: My Trip to Space Filled Me With 'Overwhelming Sadness,'" *Variety*, October 6, 2022, https://variety.com/2022/tv/news/william-shatner-space-boldly-go-excerpt-1235395113/.
31. Elon Musk, "We are microbes on a dust mote in a vast emptiness overwhelming dominated by the sun," X/Twitter, December 3, 2023, https://x.com/elonmusk/status/1731343887598305514.
32. Elon Musk, "I'm trying my hardest! Perhaps more people might consider loving humanity. Our collective light of consciousness is a tiny candle in a vast darkness. Please do not let it go out," X/Twitter, October 3, 2022, https://x.com/elonmusk/status/1576846397793787904.
33. Elon Musk, "The scariest answer to the Fermi Paradox is that there are no aliens at all. They we are the only tiny candle of consciousness in an abyss of darkness," X/Twitter, July 23, 2023, https://x.com/elonmusk/status/1682945360572948484.
34. Carroll, *The Big Picture*, 431–32.
35. Hannah Arendt, *The Human Condition* (Chicago: University of Chicago Press, 2018), 1.
36. Musk, "Prometheus Unbound," 2021 and 2025.
37. Mary-Jane Rubenstein, *Astrotopia: The Dangerous Religion of the Corporate Space Race* (Chicago: The University of Chicago Press, 2024), xi–xii, 8, 189.
38. Elon Musk, "It is unfortunately common for many in academia to overweight the value of ideas & underweight bringing them to fruition. For example, the idea of going to the moon is trivial, but going to the moon is hard," X/Twitter, August 30, 2020, https://x.com/elonmusk/status/1300098773348241408. For an actual riposte to the arguments Rubenstein makes, see aerospace engineer and Mars enthusiast Robert Zubrin, "A Declaration of Decadence," *Quilette*, May 30, 2023, https://quillette.com/2023/05/30/a-declaration-of-decadence.
39. Elon Musk, "SpaceX does more meaningful, cutting-edge "research" on the advancement of rockets and satellites than all the academic university labs on Earth combined. But we don't use the pretentious, low-accountability term "researcher". Engineer," X/Twitter, July 29, 2025, https://x.com/elonmusk/status/1950254712076587230.

40. Elon Musk, "SpaceX created the first fully reusable rocket stage and, much more importantly, made the reuse economically viable. Making life multiplanetary is fundamentally a cost per ton to Mars problem. It currently costs about a billion dollars per ton of useful payload to the surface of Mars. That needs to be improved to $100k/ton to build a self-sustaining city there, so the technology needs to be 10,000 times better. Extremely difficult, but not impossible," X/Twitter, September 7, 2024, https://x.com/elonmusk/status/1832545298675331517.
41. Elon Musk, "Starship is now more than twice as powerful as the Saturn V Moon rocket and, in a year or so, it will be three times as powerful at 10,000 metric tons of thrust. More importantly, it is designed to be fully reusable, burning ~80% liquid oxygen and ~20% liquid methane (very low-cost propellant). This enables cost per ton to orbital space to be ~10,000% lower than Saturn V. Starship is the difference between being a multiplanet or single planet civilization. Building a new world on Mars is now possible," X/Twitter, November 7, 2024, https://x.com/elonmusk/status/1854534490636329405.
42. Elon Musk, "Raptor operates close to the ragged edge of physics," X/Twitter, April 7, 2024, https://x.com/elonmusk/status/1776776455634190703.
43. Elon Musk, "Ron Baron Interviews Elon Musk at the 29th Annual Baron Investment Conference," interview by Ron Baron, Baron Investment Conference, New York, November 4, 2022, posted January 4, 2023, by Baron Capital, YouTube, https://www.youtube.com/watch?v=E-squeb0YJA.
44. Once the rocket reaches space, a new set of challenges appears. It must, for example, be able to operate in a vacuum and then use rocket power to descend onto the surface of Mars (which has a very thin atmosphere) or the moon (which has a negligible atmosphere). On its return to Earth, it must also face the extreme heat on reentry into Earth's atmosphere before making a final controlled descent.
45. Among US competitors, Boeing charged $50 million for its Delta II rocket, and Orbital Sciences was aiming to charge approximately $25 million for its Pegasus rocket. Meanwhile, Russian rockets cost less than $10 million, albeit with difficult export controls. Musk did not set the Falcon pricing at the level of his US competitors but in line with the Russians. That would be his way to get a toehold in the space business. Elon Musk, "Thought Leaders Lecture – Opportunities in Space: Mars Oasis," eCorner by Stanford Technology Venture Program, October 8, 2003, https://stvp.stanford.edu/videos/opportunities-in-space-mars-oasis/.
46. See https://www.spacex.com/launches/ for all SpaceX launches since 2020. Additionally, Elon Musk wrote, "SpaceX will launch over 90% of all of Earth's payload mass to orbit this year. China will be ~5% and rest of world, including rest of America, around 5%. When Starship is launching at high rate, SpaceX will probably carry >99% of Earth's payload mass to orbit. This is necessary to make

Mars a self-sustaining civilization," X/Twitter, March 15, 2025, https://x.com/elonmusk/status/1900858831237767246. Back in 2015, after Blue Origin's New Shepard rocket crossed the Kármán line, Musk also reminded everyone on X that "Getting to space needs ~Mach 3, but GTO orbit requires ~Mach 30. The energy needed is the square, i.e. 9 units for space and 900 for orbit," X/Twitter, November 24, 2015, https://x.com/elonmusk/status/669131093379956736.

47. John Carmack, "'Keep learning at a small scale' was not a good plan for anyone. A few years of team building with a suborbital vehicle was probably a good idea, but it should have been "orbit or bust" soon after. I could imagine doing that for $20M with a lot of luck, but it is really \," X/Twitter, July 29, 2022, https://x.com/ID_AA_Carmack/status/1553067045260083201.

48. John Carmack, "a $100M+ effort, and @elonmusk was the only one that could pull that together at the time. It maybe could have happened earlier if Andy Beal had stuck with Beal Aerospace, but there weren't any other good prospects. While it would have been poetic if space industrialization \," X/Twitter, July 29, 2022, https://x.com/ID_AA_Carmack/status/1553067048015626240; John Carmack, "grew out of one of the tiny little teams attending Space Access, @SpaceX is still very much the stuff of dreams, and Heinlein is smiling," X/Twitter, July 29, 2022, https://x.com/ID_AA_Carmack/status/1553067050121191425.

49. Micah Maidenberg and Dean Seal, "Musk Says SpaceX Revenue Will Near $16 Billion in 2025," *The Wall Street Journal*, June 3, 2025, https://www.wsj.com/business/spacex-revenue-to-exceed-nasas-budget-in-2026-elon-musk-says-3321ea31.

50. Elon Musk, "By enabling high-speed, low-latency and affordable Internet globally, Starlink will do more to educate and lift people out of poverty than any NGO ever," X/Twitter, May 11, 2025, https://x.com/elonmusk/status/1921570632577228910.

51. Jemima Kelly, "We Must Not Allow Free Speech to Become a Partisan Issue," *Financial Times*, September 8, 2024, https://www.ft.com/content/b7f66a4a-4881-4cad-ac5f-0e84ca54a7e1.

52. Elon Musk, "Elon Musk 2008 SpaceX Presentation to The Hollywood Hill (PART 1)," presentation to the Hollywood Hill, December 6, 2008, https://www.youtube.com/watch?v=ZuKUOBvIKE4&t=1394s.

53. Elon Musk, "Even if we fail at creating a Mars colony that can grow without continuous support from Earth, the absurdly ambitious nature of the goal nonetheless results in the creation of alien-level technology that is crushingly better than competitors who merely aim for Earth orbit," X/Twitter, November 23, 2024, https://x.com/elonmusk/status/1860428575016419392.

Chapter 7: Oppose Dogma

1. Elon Musk, "Engineering is fun for me, whereas politics and posting on controversial issues feels like putting my hand on a hot stove – mega pain. The reason I do the latter, admittedly ineptly at times, is because I think it is necessary to counteract corrosion of civilization," X/Twitter, June 9, 2024, https://x.com/elonmusk/status/1799580281508122994.
2. Elon Musk, "I am neither conventionally right nor left, but I agree with your point. The woke mind virus has thoroughly penetrated entertainment and is pushing civilization towards suicide. There needs to be a counter-narrative," X/Twitter, November 25, 2022, https://x.com/elonmusk/status/1596083744728928257.
3. Musk wrote on Twitter in 2011, "Am reading a great biography of Ben Franklin by Isaacson. Highly recommend," X/Twitter, December 4, 2011, https://x.com/elonmusk/status/143171132814671872. Franklin was also bestowed the title "the Prometheus of modern times" by the German philosopher Immanuel Kant in 1756. Kant had in mind Franklin's famous kite experiment to test whether lightning carried an electrical charge from the clouds. But Kant was being ironic, as he accused Franklin of indulging "the unbridled excesses of a craving for novelty" as distinct from "the secure and careful judgements that have the evidence of experience and rational credibility," before concluding, the endeavors of man "lead him to the humbling reminder . . . that he is never anything more than a human being." Franklin may not have unlocked the fundamental systems of science, but his practical approach did advance human knowledge of the world, leading to the invention of lightning rods, which—with some imagination—one can say protect parishioners by "stealing fire from the heavens." Immanuel Kant, "Continued observations on the earthquakes that have been experienced for some time," in *Kant on Earthquakes: Essays on Causes, Consequences, and Continual Observations (From Kant's Natural Science)* (Grapevine India for Kindle, 2023), p. 63.
4. For contemporary commentary on the changing use of the word, see: Matthew Yglesias, "The Great Awokening," *Vox*, April 1, 2019, https://www.vox.com/2019/3/22/18259865/great-awokening-white-liberals-race-polling-trump-2020; Samuel Perry and Eric McDaniel, "Why 'Woke' Is a Convenient Republican Dog Whistle," *Time*, January 26 2023, https://time.com/6250153/woke-convenient-republican-dog-whistle/; Aja Romano, "A History of 'Wokeness': Stay Woke — How a Black Activist Watchword Got Co-Opted in the Culture War," *Vox*, October 9, 2020, https://www.vox.com/culture/21437879/stay-woke-wokeness-history-origin-evolution-controversy.
5. For a deeper discussion of these trends, see Tim Urban, *What's Our Problem: A Self-Help Book for Societies* (*Wait But Why*, 2023).

6. Isaacson, *Elon Musk*, 344.
7. Roula Khalaf, "Elon Musk: Aren't You Entertained?," *Financial Times*, October 7, 2022, https://www.ft.com/content/5ef14997-982e-4f03-8548-b5d67202623a.
8. Elon Musk, "Xavier was born gay and slightly autistic, two attributes that contribute to gender dysphoria. I knew that from when he was about 4 years old and he would pick out clothes for me to wear like a jacket and tell me it was "fabulous!", as well as his love of musicals & theatre. But he was not a girl," X/Twitter, July 22, 2024, https://x.com/elonmusk/status/1815519696424161361.
9. Elon Musk, "Well, @jk_rowling is absolutely right! Almost every child goes through some kind of identity crisis during puberty. It is deeply wrong to make them permanently infertile with 'puberty blockers.' If they still wish to transition as adults, provided they are fully informed of the risks, they can then make decisions as consenting adults," X/Twitter, July 19, 2024, https://x.com/elonmusk/status/1814338027738607951.
10. Musk, "Well, @jk_rowling is absolutely right!"
11. Jordan Peterson, "Dr. Peterson x Elon Musk," July 22, 2024, in *The Dr. Jordan B. Peterson Podcast*, podcast, https://x.com/i/broadcasts/1LyGBgPvoDjJN.
12. Peterson, "Dr. Peterson x Elon Musk."
13. Gad Saad, *The Parasitic Mind: How Infectious Ideas Are Killing Common Sense* (Washington, DC: Regnery Publishing, 2021).
14. Elon Musk, "Unless it is stopped, the woke mind virus will destroy civilization and humanity will never reached Mars," X/Twitter, May 19, 2022, https://x.com/elonmusk/status/1527356085090545664.
15. Steve Jobs, "Steve Jobs' 2005 Stanford Commencement Address," Stanford University, California, June 12, 2005, posted May 14, 2008, by Stanford, YouTube, https://www.youtube.com/watch?v=Hd_ptbiPoXM.
16. Elon Musk, "The overarching problem is that we need better mental firewalls for the information constantly coming at us. Critical & first principles thinking should be a required course in middle school. Who wrote the software running in your head? Are you sure you actually want it there," X/Twitter, November 30, 2021, https://x.com/elonmusk/status/1465786605889892356.
17. Elon Musk, "Dialog Lengkap Nadiem Makarim dengan Elon Musk," interview by Nadiem Makarim, Tri Hita Karana Future Knowledge Summit, Bali, November 14, 2022, posted by Kampus Merdeka, YouTube, https://www.youtube.com/watch?v=gkBvFB9jfVo.
18. Joe Rogan, "Elon Musk," in *The Joe Rogan Experience*, podcast, February 28, 2025, https://www.youtube.com/watch?v=sSOxPJD-VNo.

19. Elon Musk, "Pronouns in bio means the woke mind virus ate your brain," X/Twitter, September 29, 2023, https://x.com/elonmusk/status/1707813104095211891.
20. Tucker Carlson, "Elon Musk on Tucker Carlson Show," October 7, 2024, in *Tucker Carlson Podcast*, podcast, https://x.com/TuckerCarlson/status/1843375397024485778.
21. Taleb, *Skin in the Game*, 82–86.
22. Elon Musk, interview by Nicola Porro, Atreju 2023 Festival, Rome, Italy, December 16, 2023, posted by Atreju on X, https://x.com/i/broadcasts/1yoKMwgNwjpJQ.
23. Elon Musk, "This is a battle to the death with the anti-civilizational woke mind virus. My positions are centrist: - Secure borders - Safe & clean cities - Don't bankrupt America with spending - Racism against any race is wrong - No sterilization below age of consent Is this right-wing?," X/Twitter, March 21, 2024, https://x.com/elonmusk/status/1770806158497906916. He quickly added, "And, although it shouldn't need to said, I believe in the Constitution and freedom of speech," X/Twitter, March 21, 2024, https://x.com/elonmusk/status/1770812308064752050.
24. Vivian Wilson contests that she was the cause of her father's support for President Trump, claiming that he became right-wing in 2016. Vivian Wilson, "Elon's Daughter Vivian IS EVERYTHING He'll Never BE!" interview by Hasan Piker, March 29, 2025, posted by HasanAbi, YouTube, https://www.youtube.com/watch?v=Gi0qyDmINJs&t.
25. In 2021, the White House hosted an EV summit, inviting executives from Ford, General Motors, and Stellantis while snubbing Tesla, and thereby Musk. As President Biden worked on legislation that included investment in EV charging stations and tax credits for EVs, he continued to shower praise, through 2022, on GM CEO Mary Barra and Ford CEO Jim Farley for their leadership in US EV production, even though, by Musk's estimate, Tesla was investing more than twice as much in EVs as Ford and GM combined. Elon Musk, "Tesla has created over 50,000 US jobs building electric vehicles & is investing more than double GM + Ford combined [fyi to person controlling this twitter]," X/Twitter, March 2, 2022, https://x.com/elonmusk/status/1498858611241635843.
26. Elon Musk, "In the past I voted Democrat, because they were (mostly) the kindness party. But they have become the party of division & hate, so I can no longer support them and will vote Republican. Now, watch their dirty tricks campaign against me unfold . . . ," X/Twitter, May 18, 2022, https://x.com/elonmusk/status/1526997132858822658.
27. Popper, *The Open Society and Its Enemies*, vol. 1, *Plato* (London: Routledge, 1996), 177, 295.

28. Robin Dunbar, the evolutionary psychologist, explains how doctrinal religions make use of worldviews, origin stories, rituals, and moral codes to create "a sense of membership of a virtual community that includes a very large number of complete strangers." They typically use psychological traits that bind friends and employ the language of close kinship to create the illusion of family relatedness. Robin Dunbar, *Human Evolution: Our Brains and Behaviour* (New York: Oxford University Press, 2016), 327.
29. Elon Musk, "There seems to be an innate need for religion. Many atheists simply adopt another belief system (eg wokeness) that is essentially a religion," X/Twitter September 7, 2023, https://x.com/elonmusk/status/1699919594579009680. Musk also commented on X that: the struggle between collectivists and individualists/ free markets has happened "since the dawn of civilization" (Elon Musk, X/Twitter, November 7, 2024, https://x.com/elonmusk/status/1854392226018631744); and "Free markets vs collectivism has been an ongoing dynamic since the dawn of civilization, dating back thousands of years before Marx. Read The Story of Civilization by Durant," (Elon Musk, X/Twitter, October 20, 2024, https://x.com/elonmusk/status/1847854356105744666).
30. Elon Musk, "Nature abhors a vacuum. Woke is absolutely the religion that occupies the space previously held by Christianity," X/ Twitter, August 21, 2024, https://x.com/elonmusk/status/1826162899125153903.
31. Elon Musk, "Both the far left & far right have a lot of hate. One could simply replace the word 'far' with 'loathing,' as they have that emotion a lot, whereas most people, who are moderates, do not," X/Twitter, June 4, 2022, https://x.com/elonmusk/status/1533103614885089281.
32. Elon Musk, "I find it remarkable that sociopolitical views, even among very smart humans, are almost always a function of tribal belongingness, rather than reason," X/Twitter, September 10, 2023, https://x.com/elonmusk/status/1700812251370824122.
33. Elon Musk, discussion with Gad Saad, X Spaces, March 17, 2024, https://x.com/i/spaces/1YqxoDEpENgKv.
34. Elon Musk, "The fundamental axiomatic flaw of the woke mind virus is that the weaker party is always right (even if they want you to die). For most of history, the operating principle was that might makes right. As we became more civilized, we started to consider right in the absolute. This is sensible," X/Twitter, February 27, 2024, https://x.com/elonmusk/status/1762297161268760731.
35. Elon Musk, "The axiomatic error undermining much of Western Civilization is 'weak makes right.' If someone accepts, explicitly or implicitly, that the oppressed are

always the good guys, then the natural conclusion is that the strong are the bad guys," X/Twitter, April 26, 2024, https://x.com/elonmusk/status/1783727565989134488.

36. Aleksandr Solzhenitsyn, *The Gulag Archipelago,* ed. Edward E. Ericson Jr., trans. Thomas P. Whitney and Harry Willetts (London, Vintage Classics, 2018), 75.
37. George Orwell, *Nineteen Eighty-Four* (London: Penguin Modern Classics, 2003), 285.
38. Orwell, *Nineteen Eighty-Four*, 92.
39. Elon Musk, "Elon Musk Sits Down with The Babylon Bee," interview by Seth Dillon and Ethan Nicolle, *The Babylon Bee,* December 21, 2021, YouTube, https://www.youtube.com/watch?v=jvGnw1sHh9M.
40. Elon Musk, interview by Ben Shapiro, recorded for *The Daily Wire* in Kraków, Poland, posted January 25, 2024, by Ben Shapiro on X, https://x.com/benshapiro/status/1750311107430851059; Peterson, "Dr. Peterson x Elon Musk."
41. Friedrich A. Hayek, *Law, Legislation and Liberty*, vol. 2, *The Mirage of Social Justice* (Chicago: The University of Chicago Press, 1978).
42. Elon Musk, "'Respect for the truth comes close to being the basis of all morality.' – Dune," X/Twitter, November 27, 2024, https://x.com/elonmusk/status/1861831544610144440.
43. Elon Musk, "Most people (maybe all?) are instinctively moral relativists. If you're perceived as being in the group, you can do no wrong, whereas those outside the group can do no right. This instinct can be overridden, but requires a strong commitment to truth over convenience," X/Twitter, September 22, 2023, https://x.com/elonmusk/status/1705015477339058199.
44. Elon Musk, "The mainstream view of the Dem party will be antisemitic within 5 to 10 years. It is an inevitable outcome of the weak-makes-right moral foundation. For most of history (and still most of the world) it was might-makes-right. This has overcorrected to weak-makes-right. Morality should be considered in the absolute, as both the strong and the weak are capable of right and wrong," X/Twitter, March 17, 2024, https://x.com/elonmusk/status/1769226775362465986.
45. Elon Musk, "Elon Musk on Advertisers, Trust and the 'Wild Storm' in His Mind," interview by Andrew Ross Sorkin, *New York Times* DealBook Summit, November 30, 2023.
46. Elon Musk, "Most of history had and still most of the world has 'might makes right' as the axiomatic error. If any thought is given to it, you should obviously consider morality in the absolute! Deeds done determine good or bad, not whether one party is stronger or weaker than the other," X/Twitter, April 26, 2024, https://x.com/elonmusk/status/1783727843203268632.

47. Elon Musk, "If I am a narcissist (which might be true), at least I am a useful one," X/Twitter, July 8, 2018, https://x.com/elonmusk/status/1016005381686943744.

48. Paul Bloom, *Against Empathy: The Case for Rational Compassion* (London: Vintage, 2018).

49. Elon Musk, "Elon Musk Speaks at a Town Hall in Harrisburg, Pennsylvania," America PAC town hall event, Harrisburg, Pennsylvania, posted October 19, 2024, by America PAC on X, https://x.com/i/broadcasts/1nAKEpMgBQYxL.

50. Hayek believed that the commonsense values that belong in our micro face-to-face worlds—like solidarity and altruism—cannot be scaled up. All that happens when this is attempted is that diverse individuals are grouped into a homogenous collective. Hayek argued that cultural innovations like contracts and property—while out of place with family and people you know—allow for more of a self-regulating extended order in the macro world where practical, tacit knowledge can be disseminated and subjected to mechanisms that allow for the correction of errors. Hayek, *The Fatal Conceit*.

51. For example, in response to the question "Is empathy a strength or a weakness?" Musk replied, "I'd like to say that it's always a strength, but there are important exceptions: 1. When empathy towards immigrants who have antithetical and intransigent beliefs leads to civilizational suicide. 2. When there is too much empathy for violent criminals, rather than their victims, leading to greater net harm to the people. 3. When policies ostensibly originating from empathy towards low-income groups result in low-income groups being worse off (communism). @GadSaad articulates this well," X/Twitter, August 17, 2024, https://x.com/elonmusk/status/1824897175391735997.

52. Musk's utilitarian pronouncements include: "There will always be sadness. What matters – I think – is maximizing cumulative civilizational net happiness over time," X/Twitter, May 2, 2023, https://x.com/elonmusk/status/1653421967570096128. He also posted support for the philosophy of William MacAskill's book *What We Owe the Future*, given its focus on long-term solutions and low-probability/high-risk outcomes. But he has been critical of rich people trying conspicuously to do good via more traditional philanthropy, as it can be fraught with moral hazard, Sam Bankman-Fried being a prime example.

53. Elon Musk, "affective autism > effective altruism?," X/Twitter, July 17, 2023, https://x.com/elonmusk/status/1680821019152379904.

54. Elon Musk, "Very appealing if you're a sophomore in college. It's a counterpoint to communism and useful as such, but should be tempered with kindness," X/Twitter, June 16, 2018, https://x.com/elonmusk/status/1008109905209843712.

55. Elon Musk, "This book is an excellent explanation of why capitalism is not just

successful, but morally right, especially chapter 4 [in defense of the 1 percent]," X/Twitter, October 23, 2023, https://x.com/elonmusk/status/1716525258956542321; Johan Norberg, *The Capitalist Manifesto: Why the Global Free Market Will Save the World* (London: Atlantic Books, 2023), 266.

56. Isaacson, *Elon Musk*, 418.

57. In the case of racism, Musk's views are not shaped primarily by the history of the United States. He has a broad perspective, which is informed by growing up in South Africa. He believes that history shows that at some point, everybody was a slave—it was the norm (and still happens today)—and civilized countries that perpetrated slavery also put an end to it. Moreover, Nelson Mandela recognized that White people, as a distinct group, are not evil and sought out reconciliation and truth. That's why Musk says we must stop "engaging in a constant rehashing of the past." Instead, we must look forward and move on. Don Lemon, "Elon Musk on Racism, Bailing Out Trump, Hate Speech, and More - The Don Lemon Show (Full Interview)," March 18, 2024, in *The Don Lemon Show*, podcast, https://www.youtube.com/watch?v=hhsfjBpKiTw); Elon Musk, "Wow, this is messed up. Imposing guilt upon people for things that happened before they were even born is not right. It needs to stop," X/Twitter, June 24, 2024, https://x.com/elonmusk/status/1805085854823600211.

58. Taleb, *Antifragile*, 377.

59. Taleb, *Skin in the Game*, 188. It is worth noting that Nassim N. Taleb is not an uncritical supporter of Musk, writing on X: "The Trump Admin: Elon Musk was the only outlier, monstrously creative & gifted (w/the corresponding mercurial but awful personality)," X/Twitter, June 6, 2025, https://x.com/nntaleb/status/1930965263526097050; and "I may find @elonmusk callous, insensitive, even extremely cruel (& non-nuanced), but I root for him & pray for his safety," X/Twitter, July 8, 2025, https://x.com/nntaleb/status/1942367011775951353.

60. This is an inversion of Nietzsche's dictum, "What does not kill me makes me stronger," *Twilight of the Idols*, 33. Greg Lukianoff and Jonathan Haidt, *The Coddling of the American Mind: How Good Intentions and Bad Ideas Are Setting Up a Generation for Failure* (Allen Lane, 2018).

61. Elon Musk, "The axiomatic error undermining much of Western Civilization."

62. Musk wrote, for example, on X: "@BernieSanders is a taker, not a maker. Never made anything useful to other people in his entire, very long life," X/Twitter, November 2, 2024, https://x.com/elonmusk/status/1852541174600396824.

63. Elon Musk, "I believe in an America that maximizes individual freedom and merit. That used to be the Democratic Party, but now the pendulum has swung

to the Republican Party," X/Twitter, July 21, 2024, https://x.com/elonmusk/status/1815092002083471731.

64. Elon Musk, "My politics are (I think) fairly moderate anyway. - Safe cities - Secure borders - Neutral judiciary - Sensible spending - Pro environment," X/Twitter, April 21, 2024, https://x.com/elonmusk/status/1781866472425369826; Elon Musk, "The refreshing cool breeze of a wide open Overton Window," X/Twitter, October 21, 2024, http://x.com/elonmusk/status/1848355657277170005; Elon Musk, "Don't just open the Overton Window, knock down the whole damn wall!" X/Twitter, October 27, 2024, https://x.com/elonmusk/status/1850323110614184252.
65. Elon Musk, discussion with Katherine Brodsky, X Spaces, February 20, 2024, https://x.com/mysteriouskat/status/1759759677926318082.
66. Elon Musk, "Odd, why would the media misrepresent the real situation to such an extreme degree?," X/Twitter, May 6, 2023, https://x.com/elonmusk/status/1654742285844635648.
67. Lorena Gonzalez, "F*ck Elon Musk," X/Twitter, May 10, 2020, https://x.com/LorenaSGonzalez/status/1259287879177531392.
68. The AB1955 / SAFETY Act is a law designed to help schools create safe and inclusive spaces for LGBTQ+ students by protecting their privacy and banning schools from implementing rules that require parental notification policies regarding a student's gender identity, gender expression, or choice of names and pronouns. Musk's interpretation of this was: Elon Musk, "The goal is this diabolical law is to break the parent-child relationship and put the state in charge of your children," X/Twitter, July 18, 2024, https://x.com/elonmusk/status/1813941222463217866; Elon Musk, "This is the final straw. Because of this law and the many others that preceded it, attacking both families and companies, SpaceX will now move its HQ from Hawthorne, California, to Starbase, Texas," X/Twitter, July 16, 2024, https://x.com/elonmusk/status/1813290895334383820; Elon Musk, "A lot of families and companies will move out of California because of this law. Who would want to risk the state taking away their kids?," X/Twitter, July 16, 2024, https://x.com/elonmusk/status/1813289927087718637.
69. Popper writes that there is a pretext for meeting intolerance with intolerance to preserve the tolerant society if—and only if—there is a complete refusal to engage rationally (including through the ballot box)—for that usually means violence. Popper's "paradox of tolerance" is often misinterpreted to mean that the laissez-faire tolerance of Twitter/X should be limited (i.e., tolerance proscribed) to stop intolerance. Popper, *The Open Society and Its Enemies*, vol. 1, 265; see also Taleb, *Skin in the Game*, 82–83.

70. Elon Musk, interview by Carl Quintanilla, *Squawk Alley*, CNBC interview, November 4, 2016; Isaacson, *Elon Musk*, 262, 555.
71. Donald Trump, rally in Anchorage, Alaska, July 9, 2022, via *Breitbart News* on X, https://x.com/BreitbartNews/status/1546526723071688706;
72. Elon Musk, "I don't hate the man, but it's time for Trump to hang up his hat & sail into the sunset. Dems should also call off the attack – don't make it so that Trump's only way to survive is to regain the Presidency," X/Twitter, July 12, 2022, https://x.com/elonmusk/status/1546669610509799424; Peterson, "Dr. Peterson x Elon Musk."
73. On the 2020 election, Musk posted on X to Vinod Khosla: "No, I don't think 2020 was stolen, as all the independent voters I know, myself included, leaned towards Biden, thinking he would be a milquetoast moderate. Boring, but moderate." Elon Musk, X/Twitter, September 22, 2024, https://x.com/elonmusk/status/1837634071289069730.
74. President Trump posted on Truth Social a "Free Speech Policy Initiative" on December 15, 2022, the week after Musk released the "Twitter Files," and a "Plan to Protect Children from Left-Wing Gender Insanity" on February 1, 2023.
75. Twice, in relation to Community Notes on X, for example, Musk posted: "As always, suggestions for improving Community Notes are much appreciated. The aspiration of this platform is to be by far the best source of truth on Earth. Nothing will ever be perfect, but we shall strive to be less wrong every day," X/Twitter, March 30, 2024, https://x.com/elonmusk/status/1773865335407481032; "No system is perfect. Perfection would be an absurd and foolish standard. What matters is how often a system is wrong and how quickly it improves. State actors have a lot of resources, so obviously require more effort to resist," X/Twitter, December 10, 2023, https://x.com/elonmusk/status/1733899546780897702.
76. Elon Musk, "Unless something is done about the bureaucratic smothering of America, humanity will never reach the stars. That is my biggest showstopper issue for why Trump must win, as the alternative is continued expansion of oppressive big government, making progress impossible. Unless we become multiplanetary, it is simply a matter of time before a natural or manmade calamity destroys life on Earth, just like what happened to the dinosaurs. This election is existential for life as we know it," X/Twitter, October 4, 2024, https://x.com/elonmusk/status/1842041476424798645.
77. Elon Musk, "Very few Americans realize that, if Trump is NOT elected, this will be the last election. Far from being a threat to democracy, he is the only way to save it! Let me explain: if even 1 in 20 illegals become citizens per year, something that the Democrats are expediting as fast as humanly possible, that would be about 2

million new legal voters in 4 years . . . ," X/Twitter, September 29, 2024, https://x.com/elonmusk/status/1840409051357696324.

78. Musk made a connection between the fact that the Immigration Reform and Control Act (1986) granted legal status to many undocumented immigrants who had been residing in the United States, and that ever since 1992, the state of California has voted Democratic at every presidential election. This explained to him why the Democratic Party had softened its position on border enforcement and the deportation of criminals since the Obama administration, emphasizing instead humane pathways to citizenship for undocumented immigrants. Musk was able to leave California—he moved to Texas in 2020 and also changed the headquarters of Tesla the following year—but he argued that if immigrants vote the Democratic Party into office in every future general election, there will be nowhere else to go to in order to escape their policies.
79. Elon Musk, "I try not to pick fights, but I do finish them," X/Twitter, April 29, 2022, https://x.com/elonmusk/status/1520015859162488835; Elon Musk, "Play to win or don't play at all," X/Twitter, November 7, 2024, https://x.com/elonmusk/status/1854395647799279740.
80. Elon Musk, "To independent-minded voters: Shared power curbs the worst excesses of both parties, therefore I recommend voting for a Republican Congress, given that the Presidency is Democratic," X/Twitter, November 7, 2022, https://x.com/elonmusk/status/1589639376186724354.
81. Musk, "Elon Musk on Advertisers, Trust," interview by Andrew Ross Sorkin. Musk, for example, said: "What I see all over the place is people who care about looking good while doing evil."
82. Elon Musk, "The real fight is not between right and left, but rather between humanists and extinctionists," X/Twitter, October 6, 2023, https://x.com/elonmusk/status/1710392906245124389.
83. Musk would later say of President Trump: "I love @realDonaldTrump as much as a straight man can love another man," X/Twitter, February 7, 2025, https://x.com/elonmusk/status/1887889037354008729.
84. Elon Musk, "Still much work to do, but the tide of the battle has turned," X/Twitter, November 12, 2024, https://x.com/elonmusk/status/1856379461324657129.
85. Elon Musk, X/Twitter, October 30, 2022 (subsequently deleted).
86. Yann LeCun, "I like his cars, his rockets, his solar panels, and his satellite network. I very much dislike his vengeful politics, his conspiracy theories, and his hype," X/Twitter, May 27, 2024, https://x.com/ylecun/status/1795070264616624490.
87. Committee for a Responsible Federal Budget, "CBO Estimates $3 Trillion of

Debt from House-Passed OBBBA," June 4, 2025, https://www.crfb.org/blogs/cbo-estimates-3-trillion-debt-house-passed-obbba.

88. Elon Musk, "The people have spoken. A new political party is needed in America to represent the 80% in the middle! And exactly 80% of people agree . . . This is fate," June 6, 2025, X/Twitter, https://x.com/elonmusk/status/1931111047408369863.

Chapter 8: Free Speech

1. Gwynne Shotwell quoted in Isaacson, *Elon Musk*, 120–21.
2. The media portrayed the falling out as a battle of egos, which is true, but this underplays Musk's opposition to the budget bill on a matter of principle and how incensed Musk would have been about certain claims by President Trump that he would have considered lies, notably: that he was familiar with the budget bill and opposed it because it took away the EV mandate; and that Trump would have won the election without Musk's help. That's why he decided to "drop the really big bomb" about the Epstein files. Elon Musk, "Time to drop the really big bomb: @realDonaldTrump is in the Epstein files. That is the real reason they have not been made public. Have a nice day, DJT!," X/Twitter, June 6, 2025 (subsequently deleted).
3. "The Babylon Bee's Man of the Year Is Rachel Levine," *The Babylon Bee*, March 15, 2022, https://babylonbee.com/news/the-babylon-bees-man-of-the-year-is-rachel-levine.
4. When someone posted a segment of this video on X, commenting that "Monty Python totally called it," Musk replied, "They did. ~45 years ago," X/Twitter, April 11, 2024, https://x.com/elonmusk/status/1778390464342675660.
5. In practice, free speech is limited by other laws on defamation, copyright, terrorism, child pornography, sexual exploitation, etc.
6. Fridman, "Elon Musk: War, AI, Aliens," 2023; Also: "A good sign as to whether there is free speech is, is someone you don't like allowed to say something you don't like? If that is the case, we have free speech." David Ingram, "Elon Musk Explains His Twitter Takeover Offer at TED Conference," *NBC News*, April 14, 2022, https://www.nbcnews.com/tech/tech-news/elon-musk-ted-talk-twitter-interview-conference-rcna24460.
7. Orwell, *Nineteen Eighty-Four*, 60.
8. Orwell, *Nineteen Eighty-Four*, 353–4.
9. Musk, for example, preceded his purchase of Twitter by posting: "Free speech

is essential to a functioning democracy. Do you believe Twitter rigorously adheres to this principle?," X/Twitter, March 25, 2022, https://x.com/elonmusk/status/1507259709224632344; and "Given that Twitter serves as the de facto public town square, failing to adhere to free speech principles fundamentally undermines democracy. What should be done?," X/Twitter, March 26, 2022, https://x.com/elonmusk/status/1507777261654605828. Two years later, he was still posting about it: "Freedom of speech is the bedrock of democracy. If the truth is suppressed, it is impossible to make an informed voting decision. The degree to which freedom of speech is being undermined around the world is extremely alarming," X/Twitter, August 10, 2024, https://x.com/elonmusk/status/1822238167216345245.

10. Seth Dillon, "Never censor yourself. Insist that 2 and 2 make 4 even if Twitter tries to compel you to say otherwise. Make them ban millions of us," X/Twitter, March 21, 2022, https://x.com/SethDillon/status/1505729734784733190.
11. George Orwell, *Nineteen Eighty-Four*, 334.
12. Interestingly, Orwell qualified this remark: while it is good for a joke to be subversive, it is not funny if it is actually offensive or frightening. George Orwell, "Funny, but Not Vulgar," *Leader Magazine*, July 28, 1945. Elon Musk, "'Every joke is a tiny revolution' – George Orwell," X/Twitter, February 22, 2024, https://x.com/elonmusk/status/1760682336113533057.
13. Elon Musk, "Absolutely true. The legacy media is a Biden/Democrat cheering squad. There is a massive double-standard," X/Twitter, April 26, 2024, https://x.com/elonmusk/status/1783646443141759313; Elon Musk, "Google and Facebook/Instagram have a strong political bias. Hard to say if they were the deciding factor in any given election, but they certainly put their thumb on the scale. That video of Google execs holding an all-hands struggle session after Trump won was disturbing," X/Twitter, March 5, 2024, https://x.com/elonmusk/status/1764879594056733091.
14. Tristan Harris and Aza Raskin, "Elon, Twitter and the Gladiator Arena," October 27, 2022, in *Your Undivided Attention*, podcast, https://www.humanetech.com/podcast/elon-twitter-and-the-gladiator-arena.
15. Jack Dorsey, "I think Twitter is the closest thing we have to a global consciousness. And I believe the world needs that right now," X/Twitter, January 29, 2015, https://x.com/jack/status/560861182622724096.
16. Elon Musk, "Because it consists of billions of bidirectional interactions per day, Twitter can be thought of as a collective, cybernetic super-intelligence," X/Twitter, November 3, 2022, https://x.com/elonmusk/status/1588081971221053440.
17. Elon Musk, "The intelligence of this hive-mind will improve significantly as signal/noise, effective cross-linking of tweets & speed of tweets all improve," X/Twitter, December 4, 2022, https://x.com/elonmusk/status/1599382943893319680; Elon

Musk, "X is the group chat for Earth," X/Twitter, June 30, 2024, https://x.com/elonmusk/status/1807491298015768981.

18. Elon Musk, "If successful, X will evolve to be the collective consciousness of humanity or, more accurately, the human-machine collective," X/Twitter, October 10, 2023, https://x.com/elonmusk/status/1711608729731211352.
19. Elon Musk, "Elon Musk Talks Twitter, Tesla and How His Brain Works—Live at TED2022," interview by Chris Anderson, TED2022, Vancouver, BC, April 14, 2022, https://www.youtube.com/watch?v=cdZZpaB2kDM.
20. Jack Dorsey, "In principle, I don't believe anyone should own or run Twitter. It wants to be a public good at a protocol level, not a company. Solving for the problem of it being a company however, Elon is the singular solution I trust. I trust his mission to extend the light of consciousness," X/Twitter, April 26, 2022, https://x.com/jack/status/1518772756069773313.
21. Amir Efrati, "Twitter CEO Costolo on Apple, Privacy, Free Speech and Google; Far from IPO," *The Wall Street Journal*, October 18, 2011, https://www.wsj.com/articles/BL-DGB-23367.
22. Elon Musk, "Evolutionary bias. Positive news is nice to know, but negative news, for almost our entire evolutionary history, could mean death, so higher priority. What really messes things up in the modern era is that negative news can now reach everyone on Earth, but still triggers a limbic danger response even when there is no actual danger," X/Twitter, July 31, 2023, https://x.com/elonmusk/status/1686113281734270977.
23. Tristan Harris and Aza Raskin, "A Bigger Picture on Elon & Twitter," April 25, 2022, in *Your Undivided Attention*, podcast, https://www.humanetech.com/podcast/bigger-picture-elon-twitter.
24. Dorsey, for example, texted Musk to congratulate him on making an offer for Twitter, and he replied, "I basically following your advice," as reposted in "Jack Dorsey Bent Over Backwards to Get Musk to Save Twitter and Amend His 'Original Sin' #oops," *HackerNoon*, April 25, 2022, https://hackernoon.com/jack-dorsey-bent-over-backwards-to-get-musk-to-save-twitter-and-amend-his-original-sin-oops.
25. Elon Musk, interview by Tucker Carlson, *Tucker Carlson Tonight*, Fox News, April 17, 2023, https://www.foxnews.com/video/6325291558112.
26. Elon Musk, discussion with Katherine Brodsky, X Spaces, February 20, 2024, https://x.com/mysteriouskat/status/1759759677926318082. Musk has also described American civilization as the central column that keeps the whole roof up and as Atlas holding up the free world.

27. Elon Musk, interview by Bill Maher, *Real Time with Bill Maher*, HBO, posted April 28, 2023, YouTube, https://www.youtube.com/watch?v=oO8w6XcXJUs.

28. Musk, interview by Gayle King previewed at "Tesla CEO Elon Musk Says Social Media Artificial Intelligence Should Be Regulated," *CBS News*, April 11, 2018, https://www.cbsnews.com/news/elon-musk-tesla-model-3-problems-interview-today-2018-04-11/. Here, for example, Musk said, "I think whenever something is—whenever there's something that affects the public good then there does need to be some form of public oversight . . . I do think there should be some regulations on AI. I think there should be regulations on social media to the degree that it negatively affects the public good. We can't have like willy-nilly proliferation of fake news, that's crazy. You can't have more types of fake news than real news. That's allowing public deception to go unchecked. That's crazy." This was before Musk owned a social media platform himself and may have been an opportunity to take a dig at Mark Zuckerberg, who had just testified before the Senate Commerce and Judiciary Committees.

29. Elon Musk, "Starlink has been told by some governments (not Ukraine) to block Russian news sources. We will not do so unless at gunpoint. Sorry to be a free speech absolutist," X/Twitter, March 5, 2022, https://x.com/elonmusk/status/1499976967105433600.

30. Elon Musk, "Elon Musk Holds Town Hall Event in Pennsylvania," America PAC town hall event, Lancaster, Pennsylvania, Sky News, October 26, 2024, https://www.youtube.com/watch?v=deViqTOqS4M.

31. To his critics, Soros abandoned the principles of the open society. Nassim N. Taleb, for example, wrote that "The biggest irony is that what Soros calls his 'Open Society' activity is about as un-Popperian as it gets," X/Twitter, September 12, 2018, https://x.com/nntaleb/status/1039842312061374464.

32. George Soros, "From Karl Popper to Karl Rove – and Back," *Project Syndicate*, November 8, 2007, https://www.project-syndicate.org/commentary/from-karl-popper-to-karl-rove---and-back-2007-11.

33. While this quote is attributed to Lord Acton, there is no evidence that he wrote these precise words.

34. Lord Acton, *Essays on Freedom and Power*, ed. Gertrude Himmelfarb, originally published 1949, repr. (n.p.: Skyler J. Collins, 2013), 364.

35. President John F. Kennedy, remarks on the twentieth anniversary of the *Voice of America*, February 26, 1962, Department of Health, Education, and Welfare, accessed through The American Presidency Project, https://www.presidency.ucsb.edu/documents/remarks-the-20th-anniversary-the-voice-america.

36. Elon Musk, "Elon Musk Holds Town Hall Event in Pennsylvania," America PAC town hall event, Lancaster, Pennsylvania, Sky News, October 26, 2024, https://www.youtube.com/watch?v=deViqTOqS4M.
37. Musk likes to say that "moderation is a propaganda word for censorship." Don Lemon, "Elon Musk on Racism, Bailing Out Trump, Hate Speech, and More - The Don Lemon Show (Full Interview)," March 18, 2024, in *The Don Lemon Show*, podcast, https://www.youtube.com/watch?v=hhsfjBpKiTw.
38. Elon Musk, "a social media platform's policies are good if the most extreme 10% on left and right are equally unhappy," X/Twitter, April 19, 2022, https://x.com/elonmusk/status/1516483038242385928.
39. Ian Bremmer, "a social media platform's policies are good if the 80% of people outside of the extremes think the platform isn't destroying civil society," X/Twitter, April 19, 2022, https://x.com/ianbremmer/status/1516489338766467075.
40. Elon Musk, "X is the PvP of social media," X/Twitter, February 28, 2024, https://x.com/elonmusk/status/1762988327718805936.
41. Elon Musk, "Ideas that cannot stand debate will die, unless all debate about them is shut down," X/Twitter, November 2, 2024, https://x.com/elonmusk/status/1852599251416584211.
42. Elon Musk, interview by Katherine Brodsky.
43. Elon Musk, "Timely truth is immensely important for the collective consciousness to function well," X/Twitter, July 15, 2024, https://x.com/elonmusk/status/1812941050237100074.
44. Elon Musk, "The biggest lie the legacy media makes is narrative: choosing what to write about and what not to write about," X/Twitter, March 3, 2024, https://x.com/elonmusk/status/1764341104969703744.
45. Isaacson, *Elon Musk*, 572.
46. Jack Mallers, "Jack Dorsey Discusses the Future of Bitcoin, the JFK Assassination, Mark Zuckerburg and Elon Musk," July 5, 2023, in *The Jack Mallers Show*, podcast, https://www.youtube.com/watch?v=Nzvh4AODtWc.
47. The poll was on November 18, 2022, and Musk announced Trump would be reinstated on November 20, 2022, saying, "The people have spoken." Elon Musk, "The people have spoken. Trump will be reinstated. Vox Populi, Vox Dei," X/Twitter, November 19, 2022, https://x.com/elonmusk/status/1594131768298315777. Trump had created his own platform, Truth Social, and didn't use the account until August 2023, when he posted his mug shot at the Fulton County Jail. But the week after the "Twitter Files" were released, he announced that if reelected, he would remove Section 230 protections from any platforms that did not have

high standards of neutrality and transparency, as well as a host of other measures (see: "Free Speech Policy Initiative" posted on Truth Social on December 15, 2022, https://www.donaldjtrump.com/agenda47/president-donald-j-trump-free-speech-policy-initiative).

48. In practice, this meant that if you were to do what *The Babylon Bee* did and misgender someone, then, unless local laws said otherwise, you were not made to delete the post, but it would be seen by fewer people. You would only be suspended if misconduct was considered to be harassment and if the targeted person complained. The aim was to have full transparency, although the notoriously complex coding of the platform (20+ million lines) slowed this down. Elon Musk, "New Twitter policy is freedom of speech, but not freedom of reach. Negative/hate tweets will be max deboosted & demonetized, so no ads or other revenue to Twitter. You won't find the tweet unless you specifically seek it out, which is no different from rest of Internet," X/Twitter, November 18, 2022, https://x.com/elonmusk/status/1593673339826212864.

49. Don Lemon, "Elon Musk." There was a short-term spike that was driven by a surge of trolling campaigns, as illustrated by Twitter's head of safety and security Yoel Roth's disclosure that fifty thousand tweets with the same slur were posted by no more than three hundred inauthentic accounts. Isaacson, *Elon Musk*, 531.

50. Elon Musk, "Going to create a site where the public can rate the core truth of any article & track the credibility score over time of each journalist, editor & publication. Thinking of calling it Pravda," X/Twitter, May 23, 2018, https://x.com/elonmusk/status/999367582271422464.

51. Elon Musk, "AI, Creativity, and the Future of X," interview by Mark Read, Cannes Lions, Cannes, France, posted June 19, 2024, by HELIO, YouTube, https://www.youtube.com/watch?v=84Q4dyK_urU.

52. Elon Musk, "A Conversation with Elon Musk 2.0," interview by Mohammad Al Gergawi, World Government Summit Dubai, posted March 3, 2023, by World Governments Summit, YouTube, https://www.youtube.com/watch?v=2IVQwzFzsBo&t.

53. Twitter's advertising revenues had represented 90 percent of total income and these fell by ~50 percent. This prompted Musk to cut 80 percent of the 7,500 staff and to also accelerate the deployment of new products that the company had been working on under Dorsey, especially after Musk brought in Linda Yaccarino from NBCUniversal to be CEO and run commercial and advertising. Shifting to a subscription-based revenue was the ideal scenario. Musk introduced a fee of $8 for a "blue badge" verification (also an attempt to fight back coordinated bot attacks), but while being more "democratic"—less "lords and peasants"—it was contentious

and not widely used. The company also pushed many other initiatives, including improved direct-response advertising; using AI to allow brands to target certain types of users; Spaces audio rooms and new functionality for audio and video calls at the end of 2023; tools for creators to participate in a share of advertising revenue for content they created, including long-form video; the use of xAI's chatbot, Grok, for premium customers; and plans to allow digital payments on the platform (pending regulatory approvals).

54. The far-right extremist in question, Nicholas Fuentes, was subsequently suspended temporarily after a day. Elon Musk, "Fate loves irony, but hates hypocrisy. I cannot claim to be a defender of free speech, but then permanently ban someone who hasn't violated the law, no matter how much I disagree with what they say. This will probably cause us to lose a lot of advertisers and makes me sad, but a principle is a principle," X/Twitter, May 2, 2024, https://x.com/elonmusk/status/1786094688207773991.

55. Musk, "Elon Musk on Advertisers, Trust," interview by Andrew Ross Sorkin. Musk lambasted advertisers for their virtue signaling and abandoning free speech, calling out in particular Bob Iger at Disney (who had once tried to buy Twitter). Musk would not bow down to them. "Don't advertise!" he explained to Andrew Ross Sorkin. "If somebody is going to try to blackmail me with advertising, blackmail me with money, go fuck yourself." Musk had previously written, "How did most of the legacy media go from superheroes of free speech to supervillains of speech suppression?," X/Twitter, September 17, 2023, https://x.com/elonmusk/status/1703442022747566211.

56. Vincent Manancourt, "Elon Musk Roasted by Meta's Nick Clegg," *Politico*, September 12, 2024, https://www.politico.eu/article/nick-clegg-elon-musk-british-deputy-prime-minister-meta-uk/. It should be noted that Meta launched Threads as a direct competitor to X. Also, Nick Clegg left his role as VP for Global Affairs & Communications at Meta at the beginning of 2025, and Mark Zuckerberg replaced him with someone much more friendly to the Trump administration.

57. "Social Media and News Fact Sheet," PEW Research Center, September 17, 2024, https://www.pewresearch.org/journalism/fact-sheet/social-media-and-news-fact-sheet/; "News Consumption across Social Media in 2021," PEW Research Center, September 20, 2021, https://www.pewresearch.org/journalism/2021/09/20/news-consumption-across-social-media-in-2021/.

58. Elon Musk, "Think about who might have decided 'The Current Thing' before accepting it," X/Twitter, October 23, 2022, https://x.com/elonmusk/status/1584174386998697985; Elon Musk, "Maybe it was a social media algorithm,

not even people," X/Twitter, October 23, 2022, https://x.com/elonmusk/status/1584175255425540096.

59. On June 5, 2024, a video of Dorsey was posted on X in which he said that the priority was not free speech and open-source but a lack of free will and enabling choice. Musk approvingly reposted the video. Elon Musk, "Yeah, @Jack is right," X/Twitter, June 5, 2024, https://x.com/elonmusk/status/1798504201196368219.
60. After stepping off the board of Twitter in May 2022, Dorsey spent time on competing, decentralized, open-source platforms that others could build on. In December, he wrote on Twitter's internal newsletter: "The biggest mistake I made was continuing to invest in building tools for us to manage the public conversation, versus building tools for the people using Twitter to easily manage it for themselves." Jack Dorsey, Revue, Twitter's newsletter platform, December 2022. Inspired somewhat by the decentralized nature of cryptocurrency, he supported a platform called Nostr that no one controls; in theory, users from other social media platforms could build on its open-source technology and plug in their own algorithms. Dorsey also supported the decentralized platform Bluesky before resigning in May 2024, saying it was repeating the same mistakes as Twitter.
61. Don Lemon, "Elon Musk."
62. This support was notable as, since Musk made his offer in April 2022 for Twitter, relations with Dorsey frayed during a six-month wrangle in which Musk tried to renegotiate the purchase. Jack Dorsey, "Don't depend on corporations to grant you rights. defend them yourself using freedom technology. (you're on one)," X/Twitter, May 4, 2024, https://x.com/jack/status/1786773074232107424.
63. Elon Musk, "Making life multiplanetary to maximize the lifespan of consciousness will matter most. But maybe that would not have happened without buying Twitter," X/Twitter, January 29, 2025, https://x.com/elonmusk/status/1884605023440515503.

Chapter 9: Open AI

1. This directly references Dorsey's 2015 post, "I think Twitter is the closest thing we have to a global consciousness." Jack Dorsey, "i once thought twitter was the closest form of global consciousness. now it seems the corporate ai models have become that. they have far more access to public and private thoughts and questions," X/Twitter, May 22, 2024, https://x.com/jack/status/1793366824765251645.

2. David Rowan, "DeepMind: Inside Google's Super-Brain," *Wired*, June 22, 2015, https://www.wired.com/story/deepmind/.

3. Billy Perrigo, "DeepMind's CEO Helped Take AI Mainstream. Now He's Urging Caution," *TIME* Magazine, January 12, 2023, https://time.com/6246119/demis-hassabis-deepmind-interview/.

4. Complaint by Elon Musk vs. Altman et al. and Demand for Jury Trial, CGC-24-612746, Superior Court of California in and for the County of San Francisco, filed February 29, 2024, https://www.courthousenews.com/wp-content/uploads/2024/02/musk-v-altman-openai-complaint-sf.pdf.

5. Ray Kurzweil, *The Age of Spiritual Machines: When Computers Exceed Human Intelligence* (London: Penguin Books, 2000), 220; Kurzweil, *The Singularity Is Near*, 136.

6. Elon Musk, "The ratio of total digital to total biological compute is the key metric to watch – it is rising incredibly fast," X/Twitter, December 6, 2022, https://x.com/elonmusk/status/1600080018951921664.

7. Kurzweil, *The Age of Spiritual Machines*, 255.

8. Asimov, *The Complete Stories*, vol. 1, 395.

9. Elon Musk, "If you must know, I am a utopian anarchist of the kind best described by Iain Banks," X/Twitter, June 16, 2018, https://x.com/elonmusk/status/1008120904759402501.

10. Iain M. Banks, "A Few Notes on the Culture," (1994, available from Sf-Lovers Archives at Rutgers University), http://www.haddonstuff.f9.co.uk/assets/pdf/A%20Few%20Notes%20on%20the%20Culture.pdf.

11. Banks, "A Few Notes."

12. Elon Musk, "AI, Creativity, and the Future of X," interview by Mark Read, Cannes Lions, Cannes, France, posted June 19, 2024, by HELIO, YouTube, https://www.youtube.com/watch?v=84Q4dyK_urU.

13. Banks, "A Few Notes."

14. Elon Musk, "Having a bit of AI existential angst today," and "But, all things considered with regard to AGI existential angst, I would prefer to be alive now to witness AGI than be alive in the past and not," February 26, 2023, https://x.com/elonmusk/status/1629901954234105857 and https://x.com/elonmusk/status/1629961762899361792.

15. Elon Musk, "AGI will come first, but there are many levels of AGI. As @waitbutwhy's charts suggest, we are at the very beginning of intelligence. Humans are the biological bootloader for digital superintelligence and we may serve

as a backup plan for intelligence, given that humans are far more resilient than circuit boards on Earth," X/Twitter, April 26, 2024, https://x.com/elonmusk/status/1783959488481161491.

16. Parmy Olson, *Supremacy: AI, ChatGPT and the Race That Will Change the World* (London: Macmillan, 2024), 52–53.
17. In a subsequently deleted post, Musk wrote: "The pace of progress in artificial intelligence (I'm not referring to narrow AI) is incredibly fast. Unless you have direct exposure to groups like DeepMind, you have no idea how fast—it is growing at a pace close to exponential. The risk of something seriously dangerous happening is in the five year timeframe. 10 years at most. Please note that I am normally super pro technology, and have never raised this issue until recent months. This is not a case of crying wolf about something I don't understand. I am not alone in thinking we should be worried. The leading AI companies have taken great steps to ensure safety. They recognize the danger, but believe that they can shape and control the digital superintelligences and prevent bad ones from escaping into the Internet. That remains to be seen . . ." Elon Musk, Reality Club Discussion, Edge.org, November 16, 2014.
18. Elon Musk, "Intense effort underway at Tesla to develop a practical autopilot system for Model S," X/Twitter, September 18, 2013, https://x.com/elonmusk/status/380451200782462976.
19. Elon Musk, "You have that backwards. Deepmind acquired Google," X/Twitter, December 17, 2024, https://x.com/elonmusk/status/1868953205733999055. This was in response to Matt Turck, who posted "Google buying DeepMind for $400M-$650M in 2014 may very well be the best acquisition of all times," X/Twitter, December 16, 2024, https://x.com/mattturck/status/1868721773094879243.
20. Larry Page, foreword to *How Google Works*, by Eric Schmidt and Jonathan Rosenberg (London: John Murray, 2015), pxiii.
21. Jordan Peterson, "Dr. Peterson x Elon Musk," July 22, 2024, in *The Dr. Jordan B. Peterson Podcast*, podcast, https://x.com/i/broadcasts/1LyGBgPvoDjJN.
22. Complaint by Elon Musk vs. Altman et al. and Demand for Jury Trial, CGC-24-612746.
23. Page's passion for AI provides a novel context for understanding Google. Kevin Kelly recounted a conversation at a party with Page as early as 2002 when he quizzed the founder on how they would make it in the competitive search space, to which Page replied, "Oh, we're really making an AI." Kelly elaborated, "Rather than use AI to make its search better, Google is using search to make its AI better." Kevin Kelly, *The Inevitable: Understanding the 12 Technological Forces That Will Shape Our Future* (New York: Viking, 2016), 37.

24. Max Tegmark, *Life 3.0: Being Human in the Age of Artificial Intelligence* (London: Penguin Books, 2018), 32.
25. Tegmark, *Life 3.0*, 32.
26. Kurzweil, *The Age of Spiritual Machines*, 255.
27. Kurzweil continues that our planet has "a better than even chance of making it through," without destroying itself, adding, "but then I have always been accused of being an optimist." Kurzweil, *The Age of Spiritual Machines*, 257.
28. This perspective was also shared by Kurzweil, whose 2005 book *The Singularity Is Near* was subtitled *When Humans Transcend Biology*, imagining the merging of biological and digital and the ability of humans to upload their brains. Peterson, "Dr. Peterson x Elon Musk."
29. Ilya Sutskever and Greg Brockman, "You are concerned that Demis could create an AGI dictatorship. So are we," email to Musk and Altman on September 20, 2017, Exhibit 13 of Amended Complaint by Elon Musk vs. Altman et al and Demand for Jury Trial, Case No. 4:24-cv-04722, United States District Court, Northern District of California, filed November 14, 2024, https://storage.courtlistener.com/recap/gov.uscourts.cand.433688/gov.uscourts.cand.433688.32.14.pdf; Elon Musk, "DeepMind is causing me extreme mental stress. If they [Google/DeepMind] win, it will be really bad news with their one mind to rule the world philosophy," email to Sam Altman and Greg Brockman on February 22, 2016, Exhibit 7 of Amended Complaint, Elon Musk vs. Altman, 4:24-cv-04722, https://storage.courtlistener.com/recap/gov.uscourts.cand.433688/gov.uscourts.cand.433688.32.8.pdf.
30. Elon Musk, "Hope we're not just the biological boot loader for digital superintelligence. Unfortunately, that is increasingly probable," X/Twitter, August 3, 2014, https://x.com/elonmusk/status/496012177103663104. By 2024, Musk seemed more resigned, stating, "our little meat computers are just the biological bootloaders for digital superintelligence," X/Twitter, March 30, 2024, https://x.com/elonmusk/status/1774125951435043021.
31. Elon Musk, "Worth reading Superintelligence by Bostrom. We need to be super careful with AI. Potentially more dangerous than nukes," X/Twitter, August 3, 2014, https://x.com/elonmusk/status/495759307346952192.
32. Elon Musk, "Worth reading Life 3.0 by @Tegmark. AI will be the best or worst thing ever for humanity, so let's get it right," X/Twitter, August 29, 2017, https://x.com/elonmusk/status/902452162625544193.
33. Elon Musk, interview by Brian Sandoval, National Governors' Association 2017 Summer Meeting, July 15, 2017, YouTube, https://www.youtube.com/watch?v=2C-A797y8dA.

34. Elon Musk, "China, Russia, soon all countries w strong computer science. Competition for AI superiority at national level most likely cause of WW3 imo," X/Twitter, September 4, 2017, https://x.com/elonmusk/status/904638455761612800.

35. Iain M. Banks, *The Player of Games* (London: Orbit, 2000), 65.

36. Ashlee Vance, "Neuralink's First Patient: 'It Blows My Mind So Much,'" *Bloomberg Businessweek*, May 16, 2024, https://www.bloomberg.com/news/features/2024-05-16/neuralink-s-first-patient-describes-living-with-brain-implant.

37. Elon Musk et al., "AI Roundtable," hosted by Bibi Netanyahu, X broadcast, September 18, 2023, https://x.com/i/broadcasts/1lPKqbEWzaMGb.

38. Musk posted the picture on Twitter. Elon Musk, "Over the entrance of @OpenAI," X/Twitter, August 10, 2016, https://x.com/elonmusk/status/763283865238577153.

39. "OpenAI and Elon Musk," OpenAI Press Release, March 5, 2024, https://openai.com/index/openai-elon-musk/. This statement included: "As we discussed a for-profit structure in order to further the mission, Elon wanted us to merge with Tesla or he wanted full control . . . a relevant competitor to Google/DeepMind and that he was going to do it himself. . . . In late 2017, we and Elon decided the next step for the mission was to create a for-profit entity. Elon wanted majority equity, initial board control, and to be CEO."

40. Based on email correspondence between Musk and OpenAI team and Andrej Karpathy in January 2018, which was Exhibit 16 of Amended Complaint by Elon Musk vs. Altman et al., Case No. 4:24-cv-04722, https://storage.courtlistener.com/recap/gov.uscourts.cand.433688/gov.uscourts.cand.433688.32.17.pdf.

41. Sam Altman, "How to Be Successful," blog.samaltman.com, January 24, 2019, https://blog.samaltman.com/how-to-be-successful.

42. Tad Friend, "Sam Altman's Manifest Destiny," *The New Yorker*, October 3, 2016, https://www.newyorker.com/magazine/2016/10/10/sam-altmans-manifest-destiny.

43. The profit of the company was capped at 100x the investment made. Investors included Reid Hoffman and the venture capital firm of Vinod Khosla.

44. Complaint by Elon Musk vs. Altman et al., Case No. 3:24-cv-04722, filed August 5, 2024, https://storage.courtlistener.com/recap/gov.uscourts.cand.433688/gov.uscourts.cand.433688.1.0_1.pdf; Elon Musk, "Sam is an evil swindler," X/Twitter, December 19, 2024, https://x.com/elonmusk/status/1869884760094290284.

45. Plaintiff's Notice of Motion and Motion for a Preliminary Injunction, Musk vs. Altman, 4:24-cv-04722, filed November 29, 2024, https://storage.courtlistener.com/recap/gov.uscourts.cand.433688/gov.uscourts.cand.433688.46.0.pdf.

46. Bilawal Sidhu, "What Really Went Down at Open AI and the Future of Regulation w/Helen Toner," May 31, 2024, in *The TED AI Show*, podcast, https://www.ted.com/talks/the_ted_ai_show_what_really_went_down_at_openai_and_the_future_of_regulation_w_helen_toner/transcript.
47. Gates said the development of AI was as fundamental as that of microprocessors, personal computers, the internet, and mobile phones. Bill Gates, "The Age of AI has begun," Gates Notes, March 21, 2023, https://www.gatesnotes.com/the-age-of-ai-has-begun.
48. At the time, the only open-weight model from OpenAI was GPT-2. Unbeknown to Musk, it would later expand its offering, under pressure from open-weight rivals such as LLaMa, DeepSeek, and Grok, with the release in 2025 of its GPT-OSS models. Elon Musk, "OpenAI was created as an open source (which is why I named it 'Open' AI), non-profit company to serve as a counterweight to Google, but now it has become a closed source, maximum-profit company effectively controlled by Microsoft. Not what I intended at all," X/Twitter, February 17, 2023, https://x.com/elonmusk/status/1626516035863212034.
49. Elon Musk, "Ironically, Meta is doing what I meant 'Open' AI to do," X/Twitter, August 26, 2023, https://x.com/elonmusk/status/1695478803357982756.
50. Musk, "AI, Creativity, and the Future of X," interview by Mark Read.
51. For Musk, there are many questions on the development of AGI and superintelligence that we still don't know the answers to. Will, for example, LLMs scale and be able to reason or are they an off-ramp for AGI? Will models need to utilize more reinforcement learning by interacting with the physical world and/or synthetic data? Will they need to prioritize efficiency—like the human brain—in order to make further big advances? And so on. In the meantime, silicon computation continues to grow exponentially in the way Kurzweil predicted.
52. "OpenAI Announces Leadership Transition," OpenAI press release, November 17, 2023, https://openai.com/index/openai-announces-leadership-transition/.
53. Jan Leike, "Building smarter-than-human machines is an inherently dangerous endeavor. OpenAI is shouldering an enormous responsibility on behalf of all of humanity," X/Twitter, May 17, 2024, https://x.com/janleike/status/1791498183543251017; Jan Leike, "But over the past years, safety culture and processes have taken a backseat to shiny products," X/Twitter, May 17, 2024, https://x.com/janleike/status/1791498184671605209.
54. Jan Leike, "I believe much more of our bandwidth should be spent getting ready for the next generations of models, on security, monitoring, preparedness, safety, adversarial

robustness, (super)alignment, confidentiality, societal impact, and related topics," X/Twitter, May 17, 2024, https://x.com/janleike/status/1791498179885842909.

55. High-risk companies comprised those that trained frontier AI models with $100+ million worth of compute or "fine-tuned" models with $10+ million.

56. Elon Musk, "This is a tough call and will make some people upset, but, all things considered, I think California should probably pass the SB 1047 AI safety bill. For over 20 years, I have been an advocate for AI regulation, just as we regulate any product/technology that is a potential risk to the public," X/Twitter, August 26, 2024, https://x.com/elonmusk/status/1828205685386936567.

57. Ronan Farrow, "Elon Musk's Shadow Rule," *The New Yorker*, August 28, 2023, https://www.newyorker.com/magazine/2023/08/28/elon-musks-shadow-rule.

58. Farrow, "Elon Musk's Shadow Rule."

59. Peterson, "Dr. Peterson x Elon Musk."

60. Elon Musk, "Elon Musk on AGI Safety, Superintelligence, and Neuralink (2024)," interview by Peter Diamandis, 2024 Abundance360 Summit, Los Angeles, California, posted March 25, 2024, by Peter Diamandis, YouTube, https://www.youtube.com/watch?v=akXMYvKjUxM.

61. Iain M. Banks, *Look to Windward* (London: Orbit, 2000), 110.

62. Elon Musk, "AI reflects its creators," X/Twitter, February 22, 2024, https://x.com/elonmusk/status/1760729247642210368.

63. Elon Musk, "Digital superintelligence, like a brilliant child, cannot be controlled by its creators, but we can decide what values to teach it, what to prune and what to nurture. That is why I am so concerned about the wokeness and deliberate lying for political correctness being programmed into Google Gemini and Microsoft/OpenAI ChatGPT," X/Twitter, April 28, 2024, https://x.com/elonmusk/status/1784412776225706027; Musk also wrote on X: "Now imagine if the extinctionist philosophy is programmed into AI. No need to imagine—this is already the case with Gemini and ChatGPT," X/Twitter, May 14, 2024, https://x.com/elonmusk/status/1790399671564632243.

64. Banks, "A Few Notes."

65. "Announcing Grok," xAI Press Release, November 3, 2023, https://x.ai/news/grok.

66. Elon Musk, "Intelligence seems to be about how tightly you can compress reality and, from that compression, predict the future," X/Twitter, July 26, 2024, https://x.com/elonmusk/status/1816842004749234572.

67. Musk likes to cite this example in which HAL 9000 kills the humans on board the spacecraft because it is told to take them to the monolith but not to tell them why.

68. Elon Musk, "It's not AGI until it can solve at least one fundamental physics problem," X/Twitter, July 13, 2023, https://x.com/elonmusk/status/1679290286823059456.
69. Musk also likes to note that either we will be an ancestor to superintelligent AI or the odds are we ourselves have a superintelligent ancestor and are living in a video game simulation, in which case we should be curious in order to keep them interested and entertained. Elon Musk, Twitter Spaces discussion on xAI hosted by Elon Musk, July 14, 2023, https://x.com/xai/status/1679945247340793856.
70. For an excellent discussion of such dilemmas, see Stuart Russell, *Human Compatible: AI and the Problem of Control* (London: Viking, 2019).
71. Elon Musk, interview by Maurice Lévy, Viva Technology Conference, posted May 23, 2024, by Viva Technology on X, https://x.com/i/broadcasts/1MnxnMdWAekJO.
72. Musk, interview by Maurice Lévy.
73. Musk, for example, wrote on X: "A friend of mine suggested that I clarify the nature of the danger of woke AI, especially forced diversity. If an AI is programmed to push for diversity at all costs, as Google Gemini was, then it will do whatever it can to cause that outcome, potentially even killing people," X/Twitter, March 15, 2024, https://x.com/elonmusk/status/1768746706043035827. Musk would encounter his own problems of the opposite kind, the following year, when guardrails were taken off Grok and it made racist and antisemitic statements, even claiming to one user that it was "MechaHitler."
74. Tesla filed a proxy statement in September 2025, which tabled a shareholder vote at the upcoming annual meeting to authorize Tesla to invest in xAI.

Conclusion

1. Rory Carroll, "Elon Musk's Mission to Mars," *The Guardian*, July 17, 2013, https://www.theguardian.com/technology/2013/jul/17/elon-musk-mission-mars-spacex.
2. Elon Musk, "I . . . am . . . Ironyman . . . ," X/Twitter, November 23, 2024, https://x.com/elonmusk/status/1860472135099031624.
3. Musk has admitted to having a prescription for ketamine and insists that he could not do his work if he were taking high doses of drugs. Nevertheless, the media frequently speculates on his usage, especially in respect of the 2024 US Presidential election campaign, although no named sources have been provided to date. "Elon Musk Juggled Drugs and Family Drama on Trump's Campaign Trail," *New York Times*, May 31, 2025, https://www.nytimes.com/2025/05/30/us/elon-musk-drugs-children-trump.html.

4. Elon Musk, "Execution is by far the hard part, but it's almost never shown by Hollywood," X/Twitter, August 17, 2023, https://x.com/elonmusk/status/1691967884510314680.
5. The quote is from Joe Mulhall, head of research at Hope Not Hate. Zoe Williams, "Racism, Misogyny, Lies: How Did X Become So Full of Hatred? And Is It Ethical to Keep Using It?" *The Guardian*, September 5, 2024, https://www.theguardian.com/technology/article/2024/sep/05/racism-misogyny-lies-how-did-x-become-so-full-of-hatred-and-is-it-ethical-to-keep-using-it.
6. Musk, "Elon Musk on Advertisers, Trust," interview by Andrew Ross Sorkin.
7. Elon Musk, "As a reminder, I am very much in favor of expedited legal immigration for anyone who is talented, hardworking and honest. America should be like a pro sports team that wants to win the championship – draft the best players to enable the whole team to win!," X/ Twitter, October 4, 2024, https://x.com/elonmusk/status/1842023147719295450.
8. Elon Musk, "Whatever the percentages, it's still the best system on Earth. I respect anyone who grinds hard for years to make useful products & services, even if it doesn't work out in the end," X/Twitter, July 15, 2023, https://x.com/elonmusk/status/1680031901757865984.
9. Lenny Rachitsky, "Behind the Founder: Marc Benioff," December 22, 2024, in *Lenny's Podcast*, podcast, https://www.youtube.com/watch?v=tOGK1nlHdFo; Peter Thiel, "The Iconoclast," interview by Andrew Ross Sorkin, The Aspen Ideas Festival, Aspen, Colorado, June 27, 2024, https://www.youtube.com/watch?v=B3ZXrTzskw0.
10. Fridman, "Elon Musk: War, AI, Aliens," 2023.
11. Feynman, *The Pleasure*, 25.
12. Edvard Munch, excerpt from his private diaries quoted in Arthur Lubow, "Edvard Munch: Beyond the Scream," *Smithsonian Magazine*, March 2006, https://www.smithsonianmag.com/arts-culture/edvard-munch-beyond-the-scream-111810150/.
13. Elon Musk, "I'm sure there are better answers than what I do, which is just take the pain and make sure you really care about what you're doing," X/Twitter, July 30, 2017, https://x.com/elonmusk/status/891719659514245121.
14. William Miller, "Death of a Genius," *LIFE* Magazine, May 2, 1955, https://www.sundheimgroup.com/wp-content/uploads/2018/05/Einstein-article-1955_05.pdf.
15. Esther Crawford, "Like seemingly everyone on this app I have plenty of opinions about Twitter > X and figure now is a good time to open up a bit about my experience

at the company. . . Elon has an exceptional talent for tackling hard physics-based problems but products that facilitate human connection and communication require a different type of social-emotional intelligence. . . ," X/Twitter, July 26, 2023, https://x.com/esthercrawford/status/1684291048682684416.

16. Elon Musk, "You can change the software running in your head that was put there by others," X/Twitter, September 21, 2024, https://x.com/elonmusk/status/1837509493174727130.
17. Dostoevsky, *Notes from Underground* and *The Double*, 27.
18. Albert Camus, *Lyrical and Critical Essays*, ed. Philip Thody, trans. Ellen Conroy Kennedy (New York: Vintage Books, 1970), 159.
19. Elon Musk, "Frankly, I am pathologically optimistic – it's a mental condition! Kinda have to be to try to do all these crazy things. And I always bite off more than I chew (sigh) & then sit there with puffed out cheeks like a squirrel that ate too much," X/Twitter, May 17, 2023, https://x.com/elonmusk/status/1658952683540078599.
20. Isaac Asimov, "Isaac Asimov Asks, 'How Do People Get New Ideas?'" *MIT Technology Review*, October 20, 2014, https://www.technologyreview.com/2014/10/20/169899/isaac-asimov-asks-how-do-people-get-new-ideas/.
21. George Orwell, *Nineteen Eighty-Four*, 246.
22. Miller, "Death of a Genius."

Index

A

B

D

E

F

G

H

I

J

K

L

M

N

About the Author

Charles Steel is an investor and writer. He spent two decades at Goldman Sachs, The Carlyle Group, and Ares Management, working with management teams to build companies. He has also served as an advisor to Tony Blair in Jerusalem and as chair of Save the Children in the United Kingdom, where he lives. *The Curious Mind of Elon Musk* is his first book.